Bushman Culture

Ursula Erasmus

BUSHMAN CULTURE

BY

Ursula Erasmus

Excalibur Press of London
13 Knightsbridge Green London SW1X 7QL

Copyright © 1992 Ursula Erasmus

Printed and bound in the U.K.
Typesetting by C.B.S. Felixstowe Suffolk
Published by Excalibur Press of London
ISBN 1 85634 191 7

Dedication

To my Mother who made this possible.

Acknowledgements

My sincere thanks to Richard Zhira and his wife Vongai for 'Shona' names for symbols and earth constructions, of which no information was given without prior knowledge that it would be understood and/or accepted.

Samuel Murebe for his narrative of the Zimbabwe Bird, Phineus Dube for his musical and general knowledge and others too numerous to mention.

CONTENTS

Chapter 1 Egypt
2 Universe 7
3 Pharaohs & Pyramids 14
4 Gypsies 34
5 Islam 36
6 Hindu 42
7 Buddhism 45
8 Hebrew 47
9 Yeshu 52
10 Thera Atlantis 59
11 Northumberland 76
12 American Indians Eskimoes Pacific Islands 81
13 Africa, Bushman culture, initiation, musical instruments 89
14 Bushman 108
15 Bushman Rock Art Mashonaland 120
16 Bushman Rock Art Matabeleland 147
17 Bushman Rock Art Zambia and Malawi 160
18 Bushman Rock Art South Africa and South West Africa 170
19 Bushman Rock Engravings of Zimbabwe 185
20 Bushman Rock Engravings South Africa 192
21 Zimbabwe Ruins 198
21 Zimbabwe Ruins Symbols 218
22 Khami Ruins 232
23 Dhlo Dhlo 246
24 Nalatale 249
25 Van Niekerk 254
26 Nyahokwe 261

27 Chawomera 270
28 Harleigh 272
29 Diana's Vow Ruins and painting 279
30 Gomo Kadzama 281
31 Murahwa Hill Umtali 283
32 Miscellaneous - Circular Ruin, Little Zimbabwe, Matindela, Blackadder, Nughuza, 286
Legend Ruins 289
33 BaVenda 291

FOREWORD

Man's desire to further the advancement of civilization through technology, although laudable in intent, has been, perhaps dangerously narrow-minded. Our awareness still in its infancy, is counting the cost in terms of ill-health and lost lives with our casual use of leaded petrol and asbestos products. We flinch at the degradation of human form and ability brought about by our use of hastily launched, inadequately tested drugs. The Greenhouse effect, Acid rain and Nuclear Waste are all part of a frightful legacy our children are to inherit because of the constant abuse with which we treat our planet.

In the cast-off chaff of our endeavour there has lain dormant the seeds of an alternative technology. Neglected, perhaps, because it is slow and gentle in action although less disruptive to nature. This is not a new technology; although users of Homeopathy may believe so; it has existed since the early days of man.

Ursula Erasmus has painstakingly compiled a mass of information that indicates an intelligent, harmonious way of life dependent on little else but the use of basic sense and an affinity with nature. Undoubtedly technological progress has cushioned and diminished our natural abilities and senses although nearby, in Ireland, water-divining is not just an amusing pastime but a tried and trusted tool for living.

Perhaps, instead of pursuing the technological path like hungry shoppers; we should take the time to seek more natural ways to live our lives. Recent interest in practices like Aromatherapy should sharpen our awareness to the natural cures and remedies that exist around us. Given that most precious commodity, time, they can work. This, however, would mean stepping from the speeding conveyer belt that we have made of life. Far from an easy task.

J. C. O' Farrell   May 1991

INTRODUCTION

Bushman Culture has something for everyone to read and study: the pyramids, Sphinx and other symbols of Egypt; Stonehenge, chalk constructions and designs of the British Isles; Zimbabwe constructions; rock art and engravings of Africa; religious buildings and their symbols of identity.

The magnitude, simplicity and precision work of the symbols and equipment used for the constructions by people who live close to nature, reveals a labour of love, legends, culture, initiation and survival.

Bushman rock art is a fascinating subject and, by understanding it, we are able to have an insight into the culture, philosophy and science according to their individual needs and assets of sight, sound and smell. The hunter and the hunted and the scavengers of land and air all form an intricate pattern of survival and hygiene.

The elephant, being the largest known land animal and a vegetarian, is a symbol of prosperity, because when it destroys habitat it passes the seeds of regrowth (some seeds only grow naturally after passing through the elephant), whereas man and goats consume vegetation and prevent precipitation, which in turn affects climatic conditions around the world so that the balance of nature has to adjust accordingly.

The Bushman are truly an exemplary people who have given much to the world in the form of rock art engravings and records of culture, legend, science and initiation, so vital for survival. Unfortunately, because of worsening climatic conditions, only a few of them now survive in South Africa.

My interest was aroused when I saw the great Zimbabwe Ruins. Living a mere seventeen kilometres distant offered me excellent opportunities to visit them many times. I hoped that one day I would learn the answers to when and why they had been built and the mysteries which confronted me. Over the years, the more I learnt the more I wanted to know and I hope that all who read this book, will find pleasure, enlightenment and initiation into the ancient philosophy of the Garden of Eden and Ma Ra Ka Ba Mr.

It has come to my notice that since African rule, place names and/or spellings have been changed.

My thanks to Aubrey for taking me to see the Ruins and Rock Art, to my daughter Rosemarie for her youthful co-operation and to all those who have contributed to the success of this book.

Ursula M Erasmus
1992

CHAPTER 1

The ancient philosophy and culture at the time of Adam and Eve in the Garden of Eden is still taught by African tribesmen at the time of initiation. One of the most important lessons to be learnt is to preserve life wherever possible in order to survive and was the forerunner of the Bible, Statutes and Ten Commandments and this book therefore tries to reinstate the culture and philosophy of time immemorial with the only variations in the code of practice being as a result of local climate and habitat.

The zodiac in the sky is a constant reminder that we must try to understand our own and others individual characteristics in order to understand life and the scales are a reminder of the balance between survival, coexistence and self-discipline because life has its rewards in the Garden of Eden.

If we tip the balance of the scales in the wrong direction life has its own retribution, degradation and exclusion from the Garden of Eden.

Armageddon, such as that so vividly described in Revelations of the Bible, in all probability comes about when the world population reaches explosive proportions (six billion at the end of the cycle) and will virtually reduce the world population to a state of Adam and Eve to begin a new cycle (Deut. 10 v 22) of 70 persons per tribe. The Wormwood Comet (Rev. 8 v 10), which coincides with Armageddon, will be visible for about a third of the year affecting a third of the sky, sun, moon and earth, will probably be at its most spectacular in the sign of the era Aquarius, for the Aquarian age, and bring about heat/cold, pestilences, plagues, flood/drought, famine, earthquakes and volcanic eruptions.

Leo, 10,000 BC; Taurus, 4,000 BC; Aquarius, 2,000 AD; Scorpio (eagle good and serpent bad) 8,000 AD. All these are fixed signs of the zodiac when major geographical events occur.

The scribes worked out their dating as a year being equal to a month, likewise, Adam to Noah and the flood appear to be calculated the same way (Gen. 5) with every fourth year having thirteen months as in the Hebrew calendar.

Adam was 130 months when his son Seth was born, Adam lived 800 months, but his nine descendants, with the exception of Noah, did not live to see the flood. Noah was 500 months when the triplets Shem, Ham and Japheth were born and 602 months when the floods struck. It rained for 40 days and nights. The ark was most probably built on high ground so that it did not get washed away by the rushing water and dashed to pieces.

Shem was 110 months old when Arphaxad was born. Shem lived 500 months. Arphaxad's son Salah was born when his father was 30 years old and for some generations after the flood fathers were at least 29 years of age before their first child was born. Thereafter, age was calculated as a year for a year. Arphaxad was born two years after the flood. The Great Pyramid of Egypt puts the year of the flood at 2352 BC, Noah was born in 2407 (Pyramid time 2402) so Adam was born in 2492 BC or Pyramid time 2487.

The flood lasted 40 days and nights, Moses was 40 years in the Wilderness, Jesus 40 days and lived 40 days after the Resurrection (Acts 1 v 3). The war of Light and Darkness will last 40 years with a rest period every 7. The final battle will last 1 year, month, week, day and hour. Pregnancy lasts 40 weeks. Forty seems to be an indication of God's will.

Noah's son Shem (2348,) (Concordance time; difference in time of 5 years earlier than the Great Pyramid dating, which is taken into account with calendar adjustment) was an ancestor of Abraham (Abram) and is reputed to have founded Lydia in Turkey. Shem's son Lud (Ludim Lydia 2280 BC) had descendants in North Africa, Asia Minor and Assyria. Noah's son Ham (2348 BC) is linked with Ethiopia and Libya. Put (Greek), Bowman (Hebrew) was the son of Ham. Lehabim (flame coloured) was the third son of Mizrain, forbears of the Egyptian Lydians, Lydia, Mauritania, Morocco and Algeria are all Ludim who bend the bow. Ludim was the son of Mizrain and the African Lewatch of Mauritania. Mizrain (2300 BC) was the second son of Ham.

Libya and Tunisia were known as Africa. Lydia and Libya were called upon to defend Egypt (Mizraim and Mitsraim). In times of trouble the Lydians were successful in the defence of Egypt until chariot warfare was introduced about 1600 BC.

Isaac and his fair cousin Rebekah had twin sons. Jacob was a man of the plains who dwelt in tents and ate sod pottage. Jacob married two sisters and had children by them and their handmaidens.

Esau red (Edom) became a cunning hunter and man of the fields and lived in Lydia Asia Minor. He married Judith, a Hittite (Ham swarthy dark), which displeased his parents.

The Horites (troglodytes, Hori noble free) were the aboriginal people of Edom. Mt. Seir, Jabel Harum, Mt. Hor. The cities of Sodom and Gomorrah are believed to be under the southern section of the Dead Sea of Arabah 1900 BC (Petra) the capital in the valley of Wady Musi, King Amaziah of Judah 839 BC called it Jektheel. This is probably the place where the Jews lived in the Wilderness (Exodus 22-23 and 34-44) Moses probably climbed the nearby mountain of J Harum and Mt. Hor in connection with the stone tablets of the Ten Commandments.

The first tablets were broken so he may have climbed two mountains.

Arabah bordered with Egypt in 449 BC. The Edomites were driven out of their country by Arabs (Nabataeans) and went into the southern part of Judah, which borders the Philistines (giants). The rock temple of Ad-Dar and the temple of Abu Simbel (Ramasses 1301-1234 BC) are similar in construction because they were hewn out of the living rock. Cuneiform was also introduced into Egypt at this time, Abu Simbel was covered with sand which may have been silt from a dam near the Aswan Dam. Ramasses' wife was originally a red colour, probably denoting Lydian connections.

It therefore pertains that Isaac, Rebekah and their twin sons, who were descendants of Sham and Lehabim, grandsons of Ham, were the aboriginals of the Red Indians (Thera Lydia Asia Minor) and the Bowman (Lydia Africa) because of their red coloured skins and other common genus (Gen 25), this could also be a result of inbreeding or lack of fresh water i.e. having to use vegetation for drinking water.

Moses (1571-1451 BC) and Zipporah gave men laws, marriage and worship and taught the value of wheat and barley, and to harness the ox to the plough (Exodus 1 v 14 and Exodus 20). Moses is closely associated with Osiris and Isis (Exodus 7 v 1 "See I have made thee a God to Pharaoh") brought the Exodus of the Jews from Egypt, which is connected with the dividing of the waters as a result of the tidal wave from the Thera (Santotini) catastrophe and gave the exact date 1491 BC.

Osiris was tricked into his own coffin by 72 conspirators. The coffin was later entombed in a tree which was felled at Byblos and sent to Phoenicia. There it was found by Anubis and Nepthys. Typhon then cut the remains of the body into pieces and scattered them. Isis collected the pieces and buried the body at Philae, which became the burial place of a nation.

The parallel of this is to be found in Exodus. When Moses left with his people, the 72 conspirators represented the 70 elders (Num. 11 v 25) and the lifespan when Aaron's rod became a serpent, the feast being the feast of the Jewish Passover. The pieces of the body pertain to Joseph 1745-1635 BC being embalmed (Gen 50 v 26), the entrails would have been removed according to the Egyptian custom. When Moses left Egypt he took Joseph's remains with him (Exodus 13 v 19). The mystery of the coffin of Cache (Num. 55) from the Valley of Kings could therefore have been the one used for Joseph.

When the Jews were on the high ground between the Pyramid of Djedefre at Abu Roash and Zawiyet el-Aryan Neb-ka, the Unfinished Pyramid, which are both 'star' pyramids, they would probably have been able to see the Egyptians following them and made their way to the Red Sea. When they reached it, Moses lifted his hands and a strong easterly wind, previously the wind was coming from the west, blew the locusts into the Red Sea and it was possible that these made a wall to keep the waters away from the Jews as six thousand crossed (Exodus 14 v 70). Once across Moses lifted his hands and the water engulfed the Egyptians. This represented a nation and probably connection with Philae and the Sphinx.

The time of the crossing also coincides with the Thera catastrophe and the tidal wave, the final destruction of Egyptian agriculture and the introduction of the Bull worship. During the day a cloud moved in front of the Jews and at night the volcanic cloud was lit up (Exodus 14 v 19-20). Moses and Zipporah are Osiris and Isis of Egypt. Anubis and Nephthys represent the Sphinx, Typhon represents the Pharaoh, Ramasses II, and the catastrophe of Thera (Ballazephem, Lord of Typhon, Exodus 14 v 2-9).

The burial of Osiris pertains to the Jews when they were in the Wilderness after the Exodus from Egypt.

The Pharaohs ruled Egypt until the Roman Empire took over the country in 27 BC and the Romans ruled until 585 AD when the Turks took over the country. In 1600 AD the Islam Empire came to an end in Europe and they emigrated to Morocco in Africa. This resulted in the second migration into other parts of Southern Africa, which also coincides with the arrival of the Europeans. The oldest inhabitants of Southern Africa are the Bushman who survive in the desert region of the Kalahari.

UNIVERSE

Astrology, astronomy, rock paintings and sculptures, and ancient constructions all pertain to the same philosophy, which has not been lost or relinquished with time, particularly among the more primitive people of the world whose culture is based on survival and preservation.

Aries is the Ram, or the sign joining two circles together, and represents the passing on of knowledge from one generation to the next. Pisces, fish or ivory tusks back to back, represents the lifecycle of man and gives the angle of the equinox and solstice from birth to death.

Aquarius, the high and low water mark of the river Nile, the chevron represents the 52 and 72 year cycle; north, the zenith and acme of life; and nadir, the end of life; Capricorn, the goat, and aims to reach the top; Sagittarius, the double-bodied sign for the Sphinx; Scorpio, the eagle which flies with preying eyes and the grounded scorpion with four legs a side and two pincers hides under stones and uses its venomous sting of death; Libra, the weight of good against evil and un/balance; Virgo and angles, wings and feather of in/justice; Leo, the lion of royalty and heart; Cancer, the crab, one of the largest constellations with 10 stars for Zoser and the tortoise, hard shell but soft underneath, slow but sure; Gemini, the twins Castor and Pollux, male and female pairs; Taurus, the bull with Pleiaides and Ra in the constellation. Moon nodes the dragon or serpent. In astrology the moon's path is between the Tropics of Cancer and Capricorn. The north (head) is benefic, the south (tail) is malefic. The constellation of Ursa Minor has the seven north stars, Sphinx and the Pole Star, which is the main guiding position for the northern hemisphere. The Southern Cross (Crux Australis) has five stars, points to the south and is the main direction finder for the southern hemisphere. Both the Southern Cross and Ursa Minor can be seen between the Tropics of Cancer and Capricorn.

The measurements of time are as follows:-

60 parts	= 1 second of time
60 seconds	= 1 minute
60 minutes	= 1 hour
24 hours	= 1 day
365 days	= 1 year
52 weeks	= 1 year
72 years	= 1 lifespan of universal evolution

60x60x60x24x360x72 = 134369280000 universal years remain constant

360 + 72 = 432   134369280000 ÷ 72 = 1866240000

360 + 5.25 = 365.25 years past 1866240000 x 5.25 = 9797760000

66.75 years in hand approximately

1866240000 x 66.75 = 124571520000

60x60x60x24x360x52 = 97044480000 earth years slowing down

360 + 52 = 412   97044480000 ÷ 52 = 1866240000 years per extra day

360 + 5.25 = 365.25 years past 1866240000 x 5.25 = 9797760000

46.75 years in hand approximately

1866240000 x 47 = 87713280000

Three score + 10 = 70 + 2 (Hebrew year 13 months to the year every 4 years). Laws of evolution, 60 years steady progress, 10 marked change in development and evolution laws of the universe (Psalm 90 v 10).

When the earth was born it probably spun at 360 days to

the year and now revolves at 365.25 days to the year 360 ÷ 72=5; 360÷52=7; 360+52=412 days to the year 412÷52=8; 360+72=432 days to the year, 432÷72=6 death and a world population of 6 billion and armageddon.

The earth rotates on its axis once every 24 hours and it takes a year to complete the seasons. There are 52 seconds difference in time per day 52÷4=13. Every four years there are 13 months in the Hebrew year, 52-23.33=28.67 days for the moon's orbit of the earth.

Every 60 years there is a possibility of a major disaster caused by flood, drought and famine. Cycle of 60x4=240 years approximately. Joseph probably knew this from records and was prepared for it and so knew the interpretation of the Pharaoh's dream 1491 + 240=1731 BC (Moses Exodus of the Jews from Egypt 1991 BC).

The sun turns once every 25 days at the equator and 34 days at its poles and will probably burn out when the equator turns once every 24 hours, as the earth did when it cooled down and became earth. The sun will reduce in size and become another earth with another sun for fire, air to breathe and water for moisture and all the essential elements for life, otherwise it will become just another planet in the solar system void of life, a sun would be needed for warmth.

The ages and phases of other planets of the universe can be calculated if the length of the day, etc. are known, the sun's orbit of the universe could give its age and birth. The sun's orbit through the zodiac is by vertically looping the signs as it traverses the universe. This affects the earth's magnetic pull and heat and ice ages. The sighting and magnitude of the comets also depends on the proximity of the solar system as it orbits the universe once every 24,000 years.

Saturn is the planet of limitations and lifespan and is the seventh planet seen with the naked eye. Through a telescope its ten moons and four rings become visible. At times the view of Saturn is of an eye pattern and at other times the rings are on edge forming a line of a closed eye, these signs pertain to the Egyptian Eye (wedjet) and Ra.

Taking the sun as the central point zero, the distances from the sun are Mercury 88 days, Venus 224 days, Mars 687 days, Jupiter 12 years, Saturn 29 years, Earth 52 years, Halley's Comet 76 years, Uranus 84 years, Neptune 165 years, Pluto 249 years, Comet 498 years.

Halley's Comet (13th March 1986) appears every 76 years and heralds troubled times 76 x 6 = 456. The 500 year comet heralds empire and cultural changes. 3000 BC the first Egyptian Dynasty and hieratic writing; 2500 BC pyramids and Sphinx; 2000 BC Semitic Empire; 1491 BC the Exodus of the Jews from Egypt; 1000 BC King David; 500 BC Buddha; BC/AD Jesus; 500 AD Islam; 1000 AD the end of the Roman Empire; 1500 AD Protestant religion; 2000 AD Jews return to Israel, religious and cultural change, Armageddon. God, his Laws and Statutes reign supreme.

Uranus and Pluto are said to have rotating orbits of their own and Neptune is said to be a magnetic planet. There is also an asteroid belt between Uranus and Saturn, forming an outer ring around the Sun. The elliptic orbit of the other planets is probably because they are outside the earth's orbit of the sun and therefore become lost from view.

The ancients positioned everything by the heavens, equinox and solstice. Those on the north side of the equator had the markers on the south side of their buildings and constructions, those on the south side of the equator marked the north.

It must, however, be noted that only at the equator is the equinox and solstice exact. Therefore, the further the construction from the equator, the greater the variation on calculation. On the Tropics of Cancer and Capricorn the equinox and solstice coincide at the time of the summer/winter solstice because the sun is directly overhead. Outside the Tropics of Cancer and Capricorn, the sun never passes directly overhead. Therefore, the calculations must be made pertaining to the area of the construction and distance from the equator and local observations.

Between 6000 and 4000 BC the earth solar system was governed by Gemini, the twins; 4000 BC Taurus the Bull; 2000 BC the Ram (Abraham and his son); 0 to 2000 AD Pisces, the fishers of men; 2000 to 4000 Aquarius. It therefore takes 24,000 years for the earth's solar system to complete one orbit of the zodiac, which represents the age of initiation. At the age of 24 years 24,000 + 2 = Armageddon and one sign for the earth's axis (anti-clockwise) 24 x 3 = 72 or 12 x 6 = 72. When the world population reaches 6 billion the final stages of Armageddon will have been reached 6 = death. The sign of the beast is 666 or the Leopard of Africa, the Bear of Russia, the Lion of India, the Dragon of China, the Horse of Islam, the Lamb of Hebrews and Christians; angles - comets and aeroplane, horses and chariots, tanks (Rev. 1 v 11), stars the religions of Islam and Gog, Russia and Magog, Hindu, Buddhism, Confuscius, Shinto, Christian, Hebrew, Zion (African) and others; the plagues, wars, comets, famine, floods, droughts, earthquakes and volcanic eruptions. Manna may be one of the few plants to grow under such conditions.

It takes the world 66 years and 8 months to move one degree on its axis and is represented by the lifespan and accuracy of constructions and markers.

There are approximately 30° to each sign and, as each 2,000 years respectively pass, it makes a difference of 30° when working out the equinox and solstice. Thus, the degrees of the pyramids could assist in their dating. However, care should be taken because the males pertain to the solstice and the females the equinox.

1° equals roughly one day (360° a circle). The earth's solar system differs 5° each year, so dividing the days of the year by 5 gives the lifespan. 1° was probably the birth of the metric system, 10 and quarternary.

In astrology 30° is good, 60° very good, 90° very bad, 120° very good, 150° bad, 180° very bad. These are equivalent to one sign, one orbit; two signs, two units. Three is the beginning, middle and end; four the perfect square for the base of the pyramid and the grand trine forms the angle of the sloping sides. Because the earth's axis is at 23.33° it takes a quarter of a year, or 91.25 days, to rotate through each of the seasons of 365÷4 seasons=91.25 days or 13 weeks. The earth traces a figure of eight similar to those shown on many ancient symbols. 66.66 equals the number of years to a degree; 23.33 equals the solstice and age of initiation and earth's axis. Every fourth year is a leap year and 4 minutes of time in a horoscope equals a year of time.

As the earth rotates around the universe it pivots on an axis with Egypt, the Great Pyramid and an area near Papatit on Easter Island of the Tuamotu group of Islands in the Pacific Ocean. This was known as the Navel of the World because of its latitude and sea currents. This axis in turn causes the volcanic eruptions (Leo, Sagittarius, Aries triangle) as the earth is slightly oval and has a molten centre which reacts with the magnetic pole as it rotates around the sun. It should be noted that, within two years of an eclipse, the earth in the area covered by the path of the shadow is affected by an earthquake or volcanic disturbance. It often takes place within a few months on either side of the eclipse and sometimes affects the opposite side of the earth as well. It all depends on the exactness of the eclipse itself. The undermining of the crust on the earth's surface by drilling for oil and excavations for minerals will also make local areas more subject to subsidence and earthquakes. The building of dams also alters the pressure on the earth's crust.

PHARAOHS AND PYRAMIDS

Everything pertaining to the pyramids, the pharaohs and their tombs, the positioning of the sarcophagus and wall paintings, are scientifically designed. The masonry also represents a science and culture of the highest degree, everything down to the smallest detail has its own specific meaning.

A unit of the Royal cube was 22.62 inches (two thirds of a metre) and consisted of seven palms of the hand, or twenty digits, one palm being equal to four fingers. This was for the measurements pertaining to culture, the angles and science of the universe.

The Great Pyramid gives the geophysical, geometrical and astronomical constellations and was built by Cheops of the IV Dynasty at Gizah by architectural astrologers, who appear to have visualised the Pyramid in the year 3208 BC at the point at which the ground level and the Great Pyramid meet. The Pyramid was completed by 2622 BC. It is reputed to have taken 30 years to build, so the section of removed covering stones should be taken into account.

At the base of the pyramid is the year 3208 BC. The outside of the pyramid ascends at 51°51'14.3". The entrance to the Pyramid is the year 2622 BC, from where a passage descends. A cross section of this part reveals a pyramid shape similar to its counterpart. It would appear from this, that each successive depth and apex ascends, starting at 3208 - 2622 = 586 years advanced on the previous cycle, which is the middle mark between the King's Chamber and the apex. It is a third of the way up from the base of the pyramid.

The Great Pyramid is worked to a scale of pyramid inch to the year on the vertical and diagonal lines. The horizontal lines are an inch to the pyramid mouth (See *The Great Pyramid* by Adam Rutherford).

On entering the pyramid at 2622 BC the passage descends to the year 1521 AD, then levels out and ends at the year 1994 AD September 21. The ascending passage has a scored line on the year 2141 BC and the descending passage branches for an ascending one to the King and Queen's Chamber.

The lowest point of construction is 1914-1941 which is aligned between two chambers, the two extremes denoting the height of perfection and the depths of despair, when 6 million Jews were massacred in Germany during the Second World War.

The subterranean cavity was probably added in 2666 BC as 666 is the sign of the Beast (Rev. 13 v 18). The Jews had their land taken from them and it is only their strong traditional ties which have kept them united.

The four unmeasured air vents pertain to the four types of culture leading up to the time of Armageddon, allowing up to, approximately, 286 for variations in the signs of the zodiac (6000 - 3208 = 2792 + 286 = 3078 or 3208 - 286 = 2922. The difference of adjustment being 156, approximately 3,000 years of history are accounted for by the air vents.

286 is the defective measurement of the Great Pyramid 286 = 70 persons i.e. the four main types of humans; white, red, Indo-European and African with the balance mixed, forming the nucleus of the world population. 286 also pertains to the measurement of the missing cap cornerstone of the Great Pyramid. The defective measurements show that nothing is perfect, because perfection leads to complacency and stagnation, which develops into imperfection, which in turn leads to ideals of perfection. At the top level there are ten outside stones for the

prime numbers of the universe.

Adam and Eve (2487 - 286 = 2201 BC), the building of the V and VI Dynasty and Pyramids at Abu Sir. Some of these at Saqqra excel in decoration but are poor in construction and have consequently deteriorated over the years. During this period the Hebrews were their own masters and were unoppressed. Armageddon marks a new era when the Jews will once again be their own masters for 1,000 recorded years. This calculation is taken from the projection of the Descending Passage until it intercepts a vertical line from the end of the subterranean passage 3208-2994 (5 years difference in time of the calendars) = 214 and repetition of the Great Pyramid commences 3208 - 2487 = 721 + 286 (defective measurement) = 1007.

The entrance of the Great Pyramid remains in the earth's north axis and equinox, so that the start of the next age will once again have the entrance on the north/south equinox for the passing on of knowledge from one era to the next.

The Sphinx of Chephren (Greek Khaff-re) faces due east and represents a human who crawls on all fours when young, then learns to walk on two feet and learns the sciences of the universe and the culture of initiation and survival.

The zenith of perfection is comparable with the Great Pyramid, which was built by Cheops who lived after Zoser. When the decline starts man walks with the aid of a stick and descends the pyramid towards the winter solstice nadir (Ecclesiastes). The tarot cards Sphinx denotes 'to know, to dare, to act and to be silent'.

The Sphinx mummies were chosen according to the age of the pharaoh and his knowledge. Aries the Ram represents birth, youth and red; Leo the Lion, initiation and yellow; Libra the Autumn equinox and the passing on of knowledge, and Capricorn the winter solstice and close of life.

On the chest of the Sphinx there is a tortoise representing the teachings of Zoser. The shape of the shell is for the lifecycle. The patterns on the shell of the tortoise have the parallel sides opposite each other, as are the angles. The sides are degrees to the top of the 'pyramid' and are for the stages of man (steps of the pyramid). There are 10 squares round the edge of the shell and 4 down the centre back. The tortoise has five claws on the front foot and four on the back foot. The Sphinx has a human head which has been superimposed onto the lion body.

When the Great Pyramid is viewed looking north the King's Chamber, well shaft, grotto, descending passage and pit are all in a vertical profile. When the Sphinx is viewed from the same direction it is in a horizontal profile:- ear King's Chamber; missing ear lobe Queen's Chamber; mouth entrance; jaw and neck grotto; eyes the two air vents.

When viewed from the east the Sphinx is in full front vertical, while the interior layout of the Great Pyramid is in cross section projection. If an optic line is taken from the Sphinx near the leg, through the south east of the Great Pyramid, the head of the Sphinx and the apex of the Pyramid are similar in size.

Thus, the Great Pyramid and the Sphinx are interdependent, just as man and beast. Where the beast cannot survive neither can man, the gnomon Sphinx and Great Pyramid are the ultimate of science, yet a child can understand the simplicity.

The simplicity of the scientific north/south Great Pyramid and culture east/west Sphinx, together with climatic conditions, have preserved the wonders of the old world so that they can carry their secrets into the new era (Ecclesiastes 3 v 5).

When the sun reaches the equinox it shines directly over-

head and a shadow is cast from the neck, hair corner, onto the chest and shoulder, which is at the same angle as the pyramid direction behind the Sphinx. Before the Sphinx's nose was damaged, the profile line was a continuation of the forehead and a vertical line from the chin and lips. Where the lines intercept gives the nose outline. Although the lines would be softened, so that it would look more natural, the nose would then have cast a shadow onto the centre of the chest and would therefore act as a gnomon, the base of which can still be seen between the Sphinx paws. The Sphinx, therefore, measured the shadow cast by the sun at the time of the equinox and solstice and also marks the distance of the sun's shadow cast by the Second Pyramid.
(*Secrets of the Great Pyramid* by Peter Tompkins.)

> "*The Great Pyramid lies about twelve hundred feet (400 metres) south east of the Cheops Pyramid, the Sphinx colossus is 240 feet long, 66 feet high and 13 feet 8 inches at its widest (80 x 11 x 4.5m). Cassini, who very sensibly proposed the adoption of a geodetic foot representing 1/6000th part of a terrestrial minute of arc, would have been astounded had he known that just such a foot had been in existence for several millennia and that the Sphinx, which would be used as a geodetic marker to indicate the equinox, also had an obelisk between its paws whose shadow could be used to compute, not only the correct circumference of the earth, but the variance in the degree of latitude*"
>
> (*"The Great Pyramid Decoded"* by Peter Lemesurier, Appendix B.)
>
> The Great Pyramid's geometric symphony, the Pyramid's vital statistics, based on Rutherford's figures for the basic, or perfect Pyramid, account for the

length of the mean solar 365.242, sidereal 365.256 and anamalistic year 365.259, earth's mean polar radius 3949.89 statute miles maximum and minimum 0.004 and 0.019 values for the eccentricity of the earth's orbit 185, 984, 540 miles, a very close approximation for the diameter of the earth's orbit, giving the mean distance from the sun's centre. 25,826.4 P" years is an accepted figure for the duration of the cycle of the precession of the equinoxes (period subject to slow variations, present values not yet precisely determined". (Appendix A.)

The Great Pyramid's units of measure.

"The conclusion is inescapable that a unit of measure to 25,0265 British inches was one of those used by the Pyramid's architect. This unit seems to correspond to the Long or Sacred Cubit, known to have been used by the ancient Egyptians in the design of their larger religious monuments. There is also evidence that a cubit of similar length was formerly used by both Persians and Hebrews."

"Meanwhile, at Stonehenge, the stone lintels of the trilithon ring were carefully carved to fit the shape of the circle. The published diameter of this circle is 97 feet or 1,164 British inches. But, the diameter of the Egyptian year cycle or quarter aurora (1162.6025 +P") is itself equivalent to 1163.8 British inches. The conclusion is, therefore, unavoidable that the circle enclosed by the trilithon ring at Stonehenge is none other than the Egyptian year cycle."

The pyramids were built on parallel straight lines calculated by the optic angle of the sun at the time of positioning i.e.

equinox and solstice when the sun was overhead or at longest shadow. A straight line was taken as a base line. Then, at right angles, the two sides of the rectangle were formed and at an exact distance the other side was joined up. The sun's shadow would also give its alignment for exactness.

The pyramids were probably built by using wood scaffolding which was erected on the four sides at the base line of the pyramid. The blocks were floated up the causeway on sledges and moved manually from the ground by a counterbalance weight of logs as they rolled down the descending ramp of the scaffolding. The blocks were then swung into position with the ease of modern day hoists or cranes. The blocks have compacted over the years and because of the pressure of the Thera tidal wave, which could also have caused the 'earthquake' cracks.

The gang markers of the builders are easily explained. 'Sceptre Gang' refers to the tomb 'White Crown of Khunfu,' 'Khunfu' refers to the geometrical alignments, 'Stepped Pyramid Gang' refers to those who worked on the section to be covered by mud plaster. These areas could also have been used to support the hoist, 'Enduring Gang' were those who did the filling in and the 'Craftsmen Gang' were those who trimmed the blocks. The North, South and Boat gangs are obvious.

Pharaoh Zoser built the Step Pyramid at Selkara in 2780 BC. The steps represent the stages of man as he ascends, one for the acme; two the angles; three the beginning, middle and end; four the prime number of the universe and base of the pyramid. The golden rules were culture, youth, science, initiation and maturity, silence, death, justice and rebirth.

Zoser built the pyramid to incorporate the ancient sciences of the universe and culture standards of the world and survival. I have referred to these teachings as Zoser science and the Sphinx culture, which gives greater understanding and simplicity, although they probably date back to the beginning of time.

Zoser's pyramid has five recesses, for everything comes from God and returns to God. The three niches are for the beginning, middle and end. The slits in the wall, cut in an oblique angle near the roof, are for the angle of the equinox or solstice.

The limestone statues of Zoser represent his character during his lifetime, the copper eye sockets would turn green with age and represented the heart (gentle gaze), the length of the beard his wisdom and age. The square holes in the walling where the statue was found probably worked in with the statue's eyes for the solstice (one eyehole to view and the other for the light into the eyes at the appropriate time of the year).

The protea (proteaceae) represents the teachings of Zoser and the number of petals culture, the end of a cycle and death. The twelve uniform layers of stone, the Sphinx and Zoser, all probably give the geometrical alignments for the solstice with the sun.

The capital composed of pendant leaves represents Zoser, and the hole between the leaves the passing on of knowledge from one generation to the next at the time of equinox, before the older person descends the Pyramid of Ka.

The two fluted columns have a rounded lifecycle base with the 15 flutings around the column and square of Zoser at the top. These were $15 \times 2 = 30 \div 3 = 10$. The red section at the top of the column represents Lower Egypt, and the white at the base represents Upper Egypt.

There are engaged columns with the circular lifecycle base. 18 ribs divide the 8 columns, giving a total of 144 ribs. These were 8 columns divided into two groups, totalling $8 + 144 - 52 = 100$ or $4 + 144 - 52 = 96$ for the number of years Zoser lived and the length of his reign.

In another group were between 17 and 19 ribs on each column and when these were added together gave 36 x 40 (the number of columns) 1440÷4 + 5 (Zoser) = 365 the number of days in the year.

The Valley Buildings of Sahure have the columns of the circular base for Ra, the square with the pharaoh's name in green for the heart and, above this, the band of Zoser holding the feathers of the Sphinx which have the 52 lines for the lifecycle on each feather. The total being the number of days in the year.

The papyrus column has the circular Ra base. The column is a sextain, with its shaping at the base dividing it into sections for the Sphinx, giving a total of 24 faces for the age of initiation. The bands at the top are for the Sphinx and the diamond faces are for Zoser with the vertical lines pattern for the lifecycle.

When the Sun, Ra, shines on a prism, it reflects the seven colours of the rainbow, which in turn give their own specific meaning to the Egyptians; at the end of the rainbow there is a hidden treasure.

The rainbow colours represent red for birth and youth; yellow for learning; white for knowledge; green for heart; blue for science and ending with indigo violet for death. The numbers and colours are zero white; 10 red; 20 orange; 30 yellow; 40 green; 50 blue; 60 indigo and 70 violet. The colours used around the pyramids are red for lower Egypt and youth, white for upper Egypt and geometrical alignment, yellow for culture and initiation, blue for the sky and science of the universe, black for the Nubians and close of life. The Pharaohs who gave preference to the sciences had a blue apex on their pyramid, and those who preferred culture had a yellow apex for the golden rule. The red and black stripes at the base of the pyramids represented upper and lower Egypt and the good of the upper mind and evil of the lower mind.

The coloured stones for the statues pertain to the culture and scientific standards of the pharaohs or individual portrayed. Sandstone is yellow as a rule but can 'absorb' other colours, dolerite is green and black for the heart and age, alabaster the science and upper mind, schist colours depend on the colours selected as to its exact meaning, granite is grey but can have traces of gold in it, yellow soapstone is for knowledge. Soapstone colours vary from white to green, yellow and pink and are all soapy to the touch.

It is possible that the red tones of the Pharaoh's Queen Nefertiti (eternity) bust, the ushantis of Tutankhamun, the hair of Yaya, Thuya and Ramasses II, pertain to the people of Thera and Lydia Asia Minor. Tutankhamun has small ears and lobes, as the Thera and Lydian people, and is a potential descendent of Joseph. He married Asenath, daughter of Poti-pherah, Priest of On, the Pharaoh named Joseph Zaphnath-paaneah. The pharaoh Ramasses I gave Joseph-her Zaphnath-paaneah the ring from his finger and placed it on Joseph's hand and arrayed him in vestments of fine linens and put a gold chain about his neck ... and he made him ruler over all the land of Egypt (Gen. 41 v 42-43).

This coincides with the change in art and religion and tomb construction from the pyramids to the Valley of Kings and Queens. The Thera catastrophe could also have forced a change in building construction, because of the change in vegetation and labour.

The etchings of pharaohs of Egypt had diagonal lines with a square and the princesses had the same with a bowl on the top. When they became the pharaoh's wife the pyramid was placed on the top or just on its own. On other wall etchings the princesses had a vase or jar on the top of the square and diagonal lines. If they married the pharaoh the pyramid was added on top.

The Royal Tomb at Tell el Amarna shows Amenophis IV and Queen Nefertiti watching the measuring of the sun's rays with the astrologers and scientists on a flat plane above their heads with their 'A' symbols and measuring instruments. This 'A' was used in Zimbabwe for the measuring of the sun's shadow at the time of the equinox. Consequently, the measuring of the sun denotes the passing on of knowledge to the next generation of pharaohs or co-regent. The 'A' compass makes a perfect circle with a dot in the centre hence O symbols for the Sun and Ra. The circle represents the comparison in size between the sun and the earth dot in the centre. The priests of On were probably Pharaoh's sons who were not in the court or army. Poti-pherah would therefore have been a royal son. If the male line died out, the priest from On became pharaoh, as was the case with Ay. This could also explain the respect and power of the priests and the short names prior to the reign of Tutankhamun and the statues of Joseph included in a pharaoh's tomb.

Tutankhamun (Tut - lion, ankh - crux anstate, amon - the great architect of the Universe and all-seeing eye). Ankh is similar to the sign of Venus in astrology and is associated with love and the heart. The ankh is shown on the side of the treasure coffer (16 compartments) with the Sphinx in between representing the heart and the feather, and joining them is the frankincense bowl. The cedar wood and gilded ebony cabinet with legs has the same design. The pharaoh's ecclesiastical throne has the protea and papyrus flowers, as did the gilded throne have them between the legs, showing the triumph of the upper mind over the lower, upper Egypt Mizraim and lower Egypt Mitsraim.

Tutankhamun, Tutankhaten (atten - you, ankh - love, to -

sweep your love), Nebkhepure (Neba - prophet, he - behold, pur - brings to nought), Nebkhepure birth, Tutankhaten marriage, Tutankhamun death. Tutankhamun's shaven head indicates that he probably died of typhoid. There were also defects of the mouth and a wound on his jaw. The gold fragment of Ay and Ankhesenpaaten (Ankhesenamun) shows them helplessly watching the pharaoh attacking a figure with a knife. He could, therefore, have been insane or delirious at the time. This would also explain the curse placed on the tomb and why it was so rich in treasure. Tutankhamun probably died at the time of his coronation and Horemheb spared no expense for the dead pharaoh's tomb leaving nothing outside to remind anyone that there had been a Tutankhamun. The non-returning boomerangs found in the tomb were a warning to all who ventured too near that beyond was the point of no return.

Smenkhakare's name was found on the binding around Tutankhamun's body. Smenkhakare was probably Tutankhamun's father, because he also had defects of the mouth and a similar shaped head, which could indicate inbreeding.

The whip marked Dhotmose (Smenkhakare) was married to Meritaten, but he did not ascend the throne because the yellow soapstone statue shows him with a crook (aske - upper Egypt and mind) and the flail (nekhekh - lower Egypt and mind) held in the one hand and being of the smaller type. The smaller soapstone shows initiation but not coronation. The royal headdress of the uraeus is shown. The pharaoh wore the uraeus of the snake and bird, with the bird on the right side and the snake on the left, representing good over evil. Tutankhamun is shown on statues with the left hand holding the shepherd's crook and the right hand holding a threshing flail, representing coexistence of good and evil. In palmistry the right hand shows good over the left hand. A lock of Tiye's hair and a statue of Amenophis III were also found in the young pharaoh's coffin.

Nefertiti, who was married to Amenophis IV Akhenaten Neferkhepure, wore the blue coronation mortar headdress, probably because she had not married the pharaoh's father. The mortar headdress was geometrically designed, indicating a connection with the priests. Nefertiti took a great interest in Tutankhamun, who married his sister Ankhesenpaaten, the king's 'dummy' shows a yellow headdress. Tutankhamun is depicted with the crown of lower Egypt, probably because it was red and represented youth. The double crown could not be worn until after the coronation, when the pharaoh knew the difference between good and evil of the upper and lower mind. There is very little pictorial evidence of Tutankhamun wearing the crown of upper Egypt and there does not seem to be any of him wearing the double crown.

Smenkhkare and Tutankhamun appear to be the only male descendants in line to become pharaoh, but both died prematurely. Ankhesenpaaten was the only woman in line who had been married to a pharaoh. Her daughter Ankhesenpaaten Tashery was too young. When Tutankhamun died, Horemheb tried to sort out the problem by bringing the names Ay and Ankhesespaaten together, thus obliterating the name of Tutankhamun, who was virtually the last in a long line of pharaohs. This is another reason why Tutankhamun's tomb was so rich and why excavations of Ramasses IV's tomb covered the entrance from view so that he would be lost from history. Had it not been rediscovered, comparisons could not have been made with objects found in other parts of the world.

The two mummified foetuses were probably those of Meketaten who died in childbirth, as shown on a relief in the royal necropolis of Akhetaten. Tutankhamun probably married Akhenaten and, on her death and that of Amenophis IV, married Ankhesenpaaten. This strengthened his right to the throne.

The family tree is as follows:- females italics

```
                                              Amenophis 1821
Joseph-her  Zaphnath-panneah..  Asenath       Rameses1
                                              Sesostris 1618
                                              Egyptus 1483
                                              Tuthmosis IV .. Mutemweya
Yuya........ Thuya
____/_____
  /        /        /
Tey .. Ay  Aanen  Tiye ................................. Amenophis 111
                              /_____
                                        /              /
                                  Amenophis IV      Dhutmose
Horemheb .. Mutnedjmet  Nefertiti  Akhenaten ...  Ankhesenpaaten, Kia
                                   Nebkhepure    Ankhesenpaaten Tashery
                    _____
                        /              /             /
Smenkhakare .. Meritaten    Meketaten  Ankhesespaaten .. Tutankhaten
Dhutmose       Neferneferure           Ankhesenamun  Nebkhepure 1352-44
    /
Tutankhamun  1369 - 60  (?)
Tutankhaten  1357 - 49  (?)
                                   Ankhesenpaaten .. Ay
                                   Horemheb
                                   Sethos 1308
```

The 'F' becomes 'G' in Hebrew, Nefertiti becomes Negertiti
Nefertiti, *Ne-* I protest; *ger-*stranger; *tit-*clay, mud, dirt (red)
Neferneferure. *Ne-* I protest; *ger-*alien; *neg-*plague, sore stroke *rur-*run;
Nebkhepure. *Neba-*prophesy, *he-*lo behold; *pur-* bring to nought
Smenkhakare. *Semel-*idol; *senol-*left hand; *kar-*captain; *kara-*smite down
Dhutmose. Hu- he; moser- bond;
Horemheb. *Ho-*also; *remah-* be cast down; *he-* behold, *eb-* fruit

Mutnedjmet. eye death
Kia, *Ki* -burning, *a*- wood
Ankhespaaten, *Ankh*-love; *esp*-fire; *en aven*- nothing; was not; *paah*-scatter
Tashery. *Ta*- little chamber; *sere*-dissolve; dwell, begin
Meketaten. *Me*-from out, away; *kethab*-writing; *tene*-basket
Sethos. *Seth*- accept, rising highness excellency
Annen, second prophet of Amun high priest of Re-Atum

    When Smenkhakhare died he was probably placed in Joseph's coffin because Amenophis IV died at the same time. This would avoid any confusion during the preparations for the royal burial. Both Joseph and Smenkhakhare had held similar positions and neither had been pharaoh.

    One of the pictorials in gold cloisonne has the sacred eye (wedjet) in the centre with birds of the south and feather of justice holding the circle of eternal life in its feet. The snake of the north has the crown of lower Egypt and youth. Another pictorial has the three figures on the oval globe and beneath it the wedjet on a funeral boat, held by the winged scarab with blue front legs. The bird holds the protea in one foot for the north and the papyrus for the south in the other. The protea appears to pertain to the red-skinned people of Lydia and papyrus the others. The body of the scarab is green carved gemstone for the heart. The scarab rolls a ball of dung in front of it for its food supply and was the symbol of dust (Ecclesiastes 12 v 7) "Then shall the dust return unto God who gave it." There are seven red circles for the Sphinx and youth, and five blue for the universe. The two void of colour are 10th from the left and 4th from the right for Zoser.

    The king's pendant of blue scarabs and snakes shows the djed ankh and anointing spoon, representing the afnet headdress and kerchief of the pharaohs. The wedjet (eye of the needle) pectoral has the vulture of the south on one side and the serpent of the north, with a whirl attached to the crown. The pectoral decorated with a green stone-winged scarab has Tutankhamun's particulars, has Isis and Nephthys holding the scarab wing which has a cone scale design. Torah, the law of two tablets (Moses). This design was used on the high headdress of the pharaohs. The figures have the conopic urn symbols on their heads.

The painted ivory plaque lid of the coffer shows Tutankhamun and Ankhesenamun in the garden. The mandrake she is holding has poisonous emetic and narcotic properties, which could also have hastened his death. Above her head is a cone-shaped object, which is similar in shape to the conical tower at Zimbabwe Ruins. This cone shape is shown on several Egyptian works of art and could be connected with Tara; the Hebrew word for 'the Law of Two Tablets', the Law and Ra being for God.

The crown of justification was placed on the afnet headdress with the cone Torah scale pattern on Tutankhamun's first mummy form coffin. The snake on either side of the cone represents Ankhesenanamun being twice the wife of a pharaoh (initiation).

The alabaster boat has the horns and markings of a sable or nyala. There are parallels in masonry which are also based on the ancient sciences of the universe, degrees and angles, initiation, seclusion, silence and symbols, gloves, 'T', compass, etc. are all derived from the ancient cultures and teachings of Egypt and the pharaohs.

The Nile was used as a convenient way of transporting the deceased pharaoh to the pyramids. These were probably flooded at the time of the Thera (trap) catastrophe and the tidal wave was probably used as an excuse to open the tombs.

The food offerings were probably placed for the pharaohs during the lying in state so that, should he regain consciousness, (which was the case of Jesus (Yeshu)) the food would be taken and was an indication of life, hence the tradition of taking offerings to a grave.

Once the embalming and funeral preparations, which took 40 days (Gen. 50 v 3), had commenced the priests had to complete these tasks before they could mix with people, in order to prevent disease. Mourning was 70 days. The vital organs were removed and left in the pyramid as a form of hygiene and preservation. However, the body was sometimes placed elsewhere to foil the grave robbers, or because the tomb was not yet finished or ready to receive the body.

*****

The Papette of King Narmer pertains to the initiation. The small figure has the heart in one hand and the two feathers in the other. At the waist is a geometrical 'star' with a switch on either side of the front leg. The central figure has the sceptre (African knobkirie) representing Ra at the top and Mr of lifecycle at the other end. There is some binding representing the days of the year and science of the universe. The apron has the Sphinx band with the four Zoser designs in the centre, a switch hangs down the leg to the ankle. Africans still use the switch, a sign of authority.

The bird has feathers for the lifespan. The eyes of Ra, one foot holding the stick of age and the other foot's two claws, are balanced on three sceptres, which are attached to the Sphinx with the beard of age. Below the Sphinx is a kneeling figure descending the pyramid of life, Ka has the beard of age. The bottom panel has two Sphinx heads with the horn of the buffalo and the human face. Between the Sphinxes stands a sarcophagus.

The Temple of Edfu shows a section with the bird wearing the double crown, representing the feather and good over evil. Next is a female with the circle of Ra between the two Sphinx horns. The following figure has the double crown, love and heart. Facing it is a male wearing the crown of lower Egypt for the solstice and behind it stands a figure wearing the divided crown of the equinox and Torah. The last figure has the three circles of Ra at the top. The three divisions denote the close of life.

The Temple of Edfu has a figure holding the pyramid, spear and ankh on long bars, with the bird on a bar above the hands, with a vase on either side and protea, Thuores of Proteus 1214 BC.

The crowns worn by the initiates shown on the royal list of Adybos and Sethi I, both portray the geometrical apron with the lines of culture and science. The snake has an extended tail (not all coiled up in one place) which shows that life, and not death, is portrayed.

The 'Trio' of Amun, Mut and Tutankhamun shows the crown of Tata above the crown of lower Egypt. Tutankhamun wears the pharaoh's kerchief and uraeus animal ears/horns, with the sphere of Ra in the centre, feathers of justice and snake. The third figure has animal horns and Ra sphere surmounted by a rectangle for Ka and descent. The arms of the figures are interwoven into a 'double loop', representing the beginning, middle and end.

The engravings of Amon show a seated figure (pharaoh) with the high divided crown, representing the equinox and passing on of knowledge to the young prince who is kneeling at his feet, with a small rounded crown on his head and extended snake ornament. However, with the hands near the ground and without the apron, the symbol of justice, the 'A' is on its side and represents the passing on of knowledge at the time of initiation.

The pharaoh's kerchief (key chief) in the upright position has the horizontal blue lines for the sky and yellow for royalty and initiation. The sections over the shoulder are for the Sphinx, the serpent of the forehead is for the lifecycle and death, the bird's head is for the feather of justice and the eye is for the God Ra. In the horizontal position these symbols are uppermost and the kerchief shows the equinox vertical lines and the curved line for the lifecycle of Mr.

The sarcophagus represents the culture of Zoser and the Sphinx. The pharaohs had three coffins for the beginning, middle and end. The wrappings represent eternity, the withered fragrant flowers found in the pyramid are traditional fragrant gifts revered the world over, such as garlands, bouquets, perfume, anointing oil and the victorious laurel leaves of cinnamon.

The royal ships which were placed near the pyramids were probably only used for the transportation of the royal sarcophagus.

The feathers of the ostrich were shown in art for weighing the heart and feathers of the departed pharaoh, and were also used for decoration, headdresses and fans.

The Lydians took some of the traditions with them to southern Africa, because their descendants discard things pertaining to a royal burial and bury in the flexed position of the pre-dynastic times.

The Unfinished Pyramid at Zawiyet el-Aryan had an oval

sarcophagus, the pyramid denoting unusual differences which are all connected with the letter 'Z' Zoser, Cheops, the Great Pyramid at Giza, the Layer Pyramid at Zawiyet el-Aryan, Queen Sebeknefuru at Mazghuna to mention but a few names and places with the letter 'Z'.

GYPSIES

The Gypsies (Gipcyan, Gipsy) probably originated from Egypt, which would account for their name and discern them as aboriginal Egyptians. They know the stars and tell fortunes which are based on the science of astrology. They read the palms of the hands because this works parallel to astrology. The left palm tells the person's capabilities and the right one what has been made of life, the reverse findings if the person is left-handed. Fortune-telling is only shown to those who are worthy of its knowledge and who will use it for the good of man-kind. No-one who would react unfavourably is exposed to it, for their own good and others' protection.

The tarot cards have a set of 22 major and 56 minor picture card designs which originated in Egypt, having the Egyptian and zodiac symbols on them. Dishonest and mercenary people give false readings because they themselves are false. The pack of 52 playing cards is derived from the tarot cards. In India, fortunes are told by similar methods because of their close association with the early Egyptians. Tea cup reading requires less time and training.

Some Gypsies are skilled craftsmen and musicians, while others are skilled horse dealers. The markings are taken into account for ownership, because they save brand marks and pain to the animal.

Their horses have feathers on them as a reminder of the animal's heart and the justice of the feather. This probably accounts for the way they treat their animals. The feathers used by circus animals are red for youth; yellow for knowledge, leader and trained; green for heart and thoughtful, (they often give way to other animals in the ring).

The Gypsies wear bright colours pertaining to Egyptian culture and the kerchief of the pharaohs. It is probable that the Gypsies were the fair-skinned people of the pharaohs of Egypt and Thera, the red pigmentation having disappeared due to a change in diet. They have small hands, feet and ears.

When there is a death, they do not mention the name of the deceased for at least a year, which is similar to the tradition of the pharaohs (Ecc. 19 v 5). They burn the deceased's caravan so that the living are not burdened with the departed's past. Africans bury their dead and burn their huts and possessions. If the body is 'lost', cannot be found or retrieval is too dangerous, as when lives are lost in floods or eaten by animals, the person's belongings i.e. mugs, pots, etc. are placed as close to the area as possible, so that the spirit can find them quickly. The spirit is usually put to rest a year after death.

The Gypsies speak a Romany language which is a corruption of Hindi, a result of their association with India, Egypt and their wandering in Europe for the past few centuries, where they migrated because of the advance of Islam and slavery in the 13th and 16th century.

ISLAM

There are two sects of Islam and both are united by the Glorious Koran. One sect follows Mahommed and has Mecca as the Holy City, they worship in mosques and are known as Moslems. The other group are under the influence of the Arabs of Arabia and are the Khaja Ismaili Shia sect, which is prevalent in Iraq and Afghanistan and has the Aga Khan as spiritual leader, follow Mohommad, worship in masjids and are called Muslims. If the two groups meet at the time of the Prophet's death, fighting is sure to result, because one mourns his death while the other celebrates.

The Glorious Koran teaches the importance of pairs (surah XI v40) and accounts for the differences of the mosques and masjids and why females are allowed in some, such as the Taj Mahal where a female is buried, and forbidden in the oblong solstice buildings, some reputed to have the relics of the Prophet. Women are forbidden because they are said to interfere with the religious significance of the surroundings.

The Islamic places of worship are designed to give the equinox, solstice, 52° and lifecycle. Where only the one design is used, the decorated section incorporates the teaching of the Glorious Koran. Angles are taken from the edge of the platform base to the top of the minarets for the solstice, equinox and 52°, which is why the minarets are sometimes odd. If the entrance to the building has high minarets, then the place of worship has low ones and vice versa. If there is only one building, the place of worship has both high and low minarets, the high ones above and the low ones level with the dome.

Islam has two easts and wests (Surah LV v17) which are the two easts and wests at the time of the equinox and solstice.

There are also two types of fez based on the pharaoh's crown of upper Egypt. They are expertly made to give the equinox, solstice and 52°. The tassel represents the days of the year and the number of surahs in the Glorious Koran which do not pertain to the equinox, solstice or 52°. The deeper fez has the angles of the solstice down the side of the fez, the 52° is to the top, opposite the tassel to the fez. The shallower fez has the same markings with the 52° across from the base to the centre of the crown.

Inside a correctly-made fez is a diamond, which has the angle of the two opposite points for the solstice and the other two opposite angles for the 52°. The equinox is through the points of the diamond (north, south, east and west).

At the time of Solomon (1000 BC) the Arabs lived in caves in the side of cliffs and the Edomite Bedouin tribes had sheiks at the head of their individual tribes. The Bedouins' Keffiyeh headdress is similar to those worn in Egypt at the time of the pharaohs.

A Persian prayer mat is designed with the equinox, solstice and 52° incorporated in the design, so that the carpet must be placed in the correct position. Islam does not tolerate ignorance. Other designs include the days of the year, the number of surahs pertaining to Allah, narratives and general information.

The beads of Islam are not displayed for fear of witchcraft (surah CXIII) pertaining to the beads being rearranged, and so changing the order of the reference to the Glorious Koran. It must be remembered that this book is memorised (hafiz) and recited by illiterate people. The first red bead is larger than the others and is for the first section, which consists of seven verses.

Islam followers put a line down the centre of their forehead to show that they have been devout in prayer, (this should not be confused with the Hindu religion) the Glorious Koran (surah

XLIX) The Private Apartments v29.

Islam angles marked on the face are a sign that the person flaunted their knowledge (surah XLVII v27), which was probably to prevent too much display pertaining to the Egyptian and African cultures. Exposed chests show what is in the heart because nothing is hidden from Allah (surah 11 v29). Islam followers cover the body (XXIV v31) and the eyes must remain downcast (XXXIV v30).

Venus, the Star of Islam, is the morning and evening star and because of its brightness is easily discerned in the twilight. The five pointed star of Islam gives the points of the compass and indicates the main prayer times for all devout followers, who stop, wherever they are, to pray and observe the movement of the sun. Some Christians have similar prayer times. The points of the star also give the equinox, solstice and 52°, which is why the star is not symmetrical. A tomb at Giza on the River Nile has a painted section of Egyptian culture, which includes the star and crest of the moon.

The Glorious Koran united the tribes and taught them that there is one God and the Prophet is his prophet. The Prophet was born in Mecca in 570 AD and had Allah's vision in 610 AD. Solomon's tribe officer Adoniran (Kings I v 6) was the son of Adba, a servant, slave worshipper, which are the basic teachings of Islam.

The Arabs bought and sold slaves as a form of wealth, and castrated the males in accordance with the moon to ensure less danger to life and so that the slaves could only take a platonic interest in the women who were there for the express purpose of the Sultan's pleasure (XXIV v33 Surah LXXXI). The overthrowing pertains to unwanted children, 'Sultan Solomon' was the title given to Arabs when they reached a certain status.

Those who did not accept Islam were drowned (surah VII v36). Tribal markings of the face showed those who had chosen the fire instead of Islam. Their country and place of origin could be determined by the markings and, therefore, were not desirable or acceptable.

When the slaves arrived at their destination, they were noted among the Arab features and attracted attention. There were therefore reputed to come from the 'Lost City of the Kalahari' where the diamonds were found in South West Africa, or King Solomon's Mines' where gold and copper were mined. These titles could also have distinguished between Bushman and Bantu features.

The cool times of the year are ideal for crossing the desert and the Indian Ocean, because the sea is then calm and would prevent slaves from taking fright or being seasick in the small boats. Dhows would be going up the coast heavily laden with slaves, metals, gems, ivory and food. The return journey would have been quicker and lighter, though both ways the sea currents, trade winds and calmness would be used to advantage where possible.

Some of the local African words appear to have been used when the slaves and tribesmen met on their journey to the coast and exchanged greetings. In the morning the greeting was 'Muscat'; if they wanted to smoke, it was 'Marijuana' and the reply was 'No', which became the morning greeting. The slaves were moved at night (surah XX v 77) and they and their chiefs who were taken were never seen again.

The slaves, and the contents of the pyramids of Egypt, added to Islam's knowledge of the Thera catastrophe, which is included in the Glorious Koran (surah VII).

In 720 Islam annexed the lower province of Baghdad and

the Hindus lost one Indian kingdom after another, until the trade between the North and South was broken. The Afghans invaded Maratha country and, by 1313, the Marathas were also defeated and the Islams were masters of India. When the Islams were prominent in India they built elaborate buildings and fortresses, some of them well known today. During their occupation of India the Heads of State communicated with and addressed each other as 'Sultan Solomon' which was an ostentatious title. Three centuries after the takeover of the Islams, a Hindu and Maratha called Shiviji 1627-80 AD dislodged the Islams from Bijapur and Galconda. It gave him great pleasure to ride under the wide 'Sultan's Arch' at Bijapur, which still stands today (1947) (Based on The Grand Rebel and author's visit.)

Gol Gumaz, 189 feet 6 inches (63 metres) is the tomb of Sultan Mahommed. Once in the main area under the dome, a whisper can be heard throughout the area, but best when projected and received at the base of the dome, which is 144 feet (48 metres) in diameter. An underground stream supplies the fountains with water. When the water is capped it rises up in the walls and makes the building very damp. Taja Bauri was built in 1620 in memory of Taj Sultan's Queen of Ibrahim II (which is an open area of water supplied from the underground river).

The Islams' guns were made of copper, there is one at Bijapur called the Milik-E-Maiden Gun (Monarch of the field) which is 88,427 parts copper to 19,573 tin and weighs 55 tons. Other guns are decorated or inscribed with Arabic.

Shiviji was held captive at Panhala, from where he escaped and was later victorious over the Mongols. He later returned his prisoners with gifts to their own people. In later years, however, very few Hindu and Maratha prisoners who fought the Turks lived to see their homes again.

At the time the Islams dominated India, the country was noted for its wealth of diamonds, gems, ivory, copper, bronze, brass and spices, most of which were imported. The dhows from Muscat and Zanzibar used to call at Bombay and eventually dominated and took over the ports around the Arabian Sea and Indian Ocean. It was Shiviji who routed the dhows from the Indian waters where they superceded by the Chinese junks (Based on the Grand Rebel).

There is an Arab proverb.

There are four types of men.

He who knows not, and knows not that he knows not, is a fool - shun him.

He who knows not, and knows that he knows not, he is simple - teach him.

He who knows and knows not that he knows, he is asleep - wake him.

He who knows and knows that he knows is wise - follow him.

Gol Gumaz, tomb of Sultan Mahommed.

King Arthur's round table, Winchester.

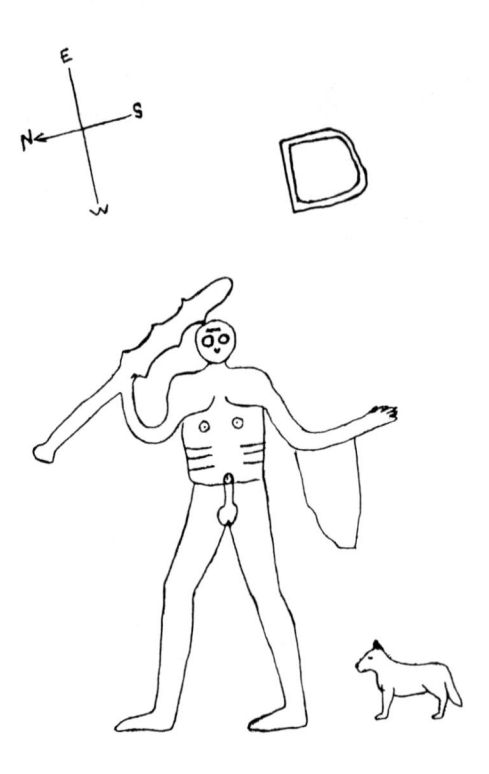

Turf cut figure with recently discovered additions of the Cerne Abbas Giant, Dorset. Drawn by U. M. Erasmus

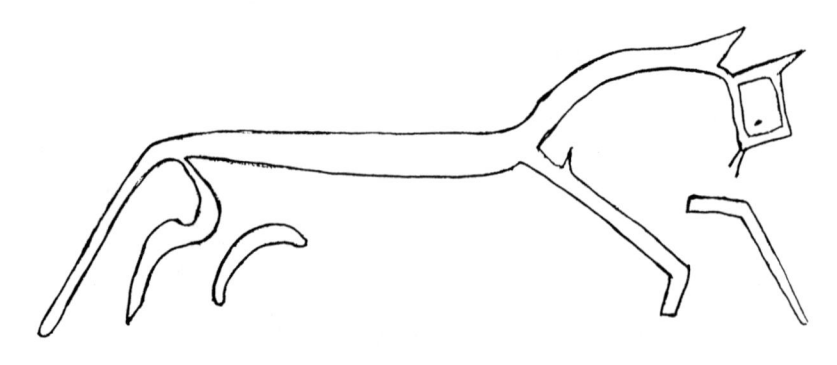

Uffington white horse, Oxfordshire. Drawn by U. M. Erasmus

Aylesford Bucket: repouseé horses

Astronomical Clock, 1540, Hampton Court Palace

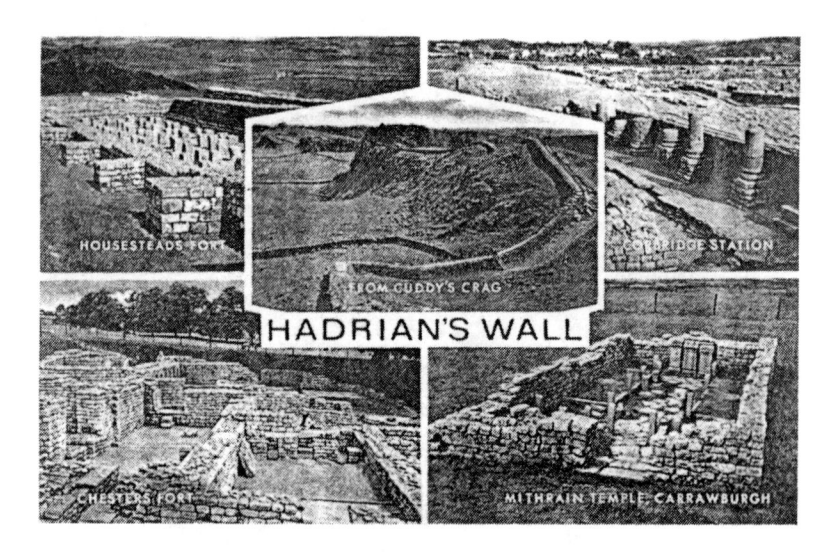

Hadrian's Wall

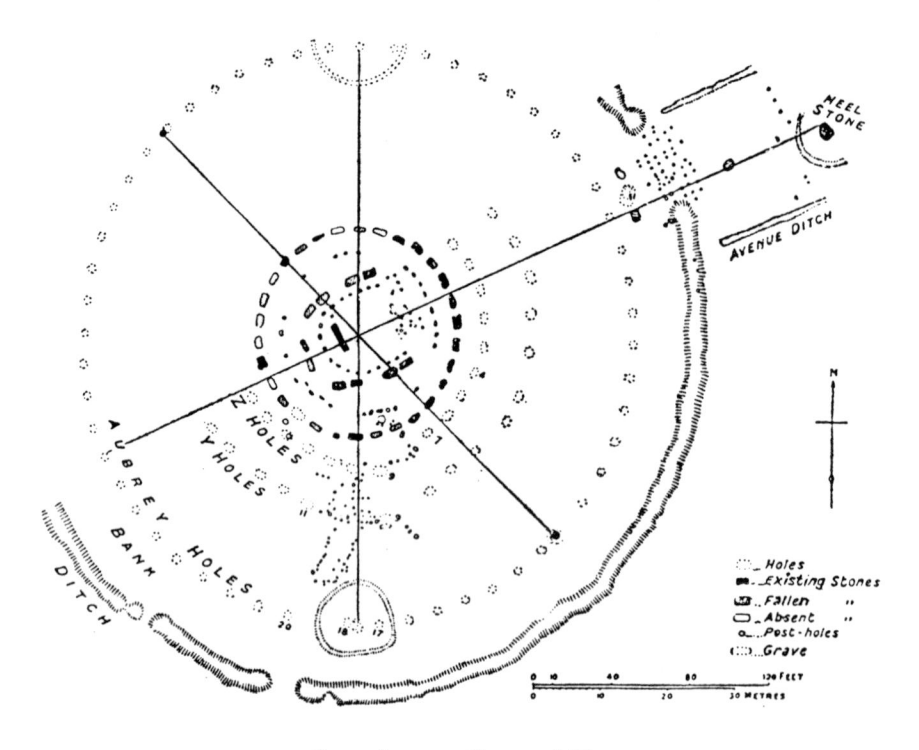

Stonehenge, Ground Plan

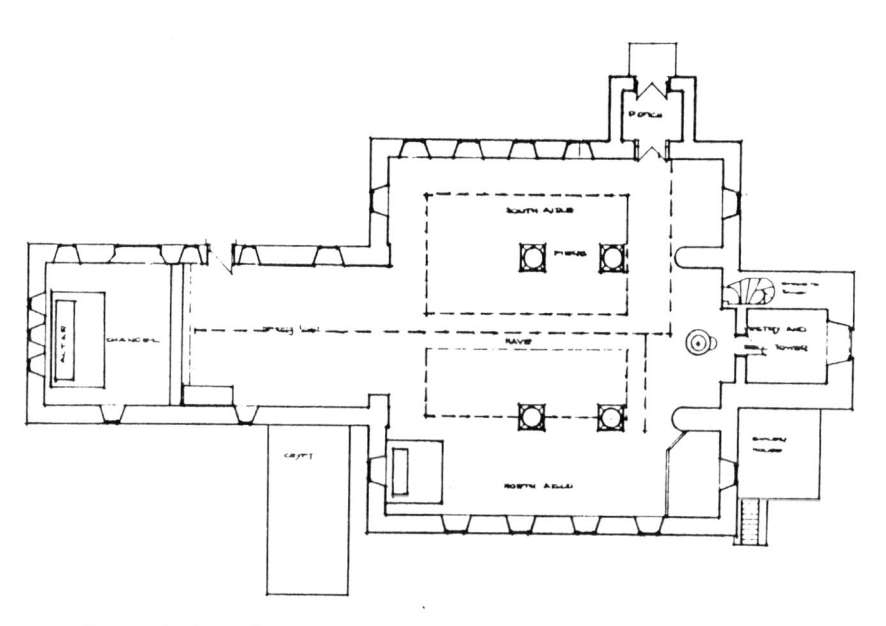

Ground plan of the church of St. Mary the Virgin, Woodhorn.
Now used as a museum.

Uncletin ice-age-stone, Newbiggin-by-the-Sea.

Photo by U.M. Erasmus

HINDU

Hindus are reputed to be the last of the Aryan culture and Sanskrit script. They study astrology, are vegetarian, use religious symbols such as the elephant, birds, cows, tortoise, snakes, etc., use coloured powders - red for youth, yellow for knowledge and purple for age - and carve elephants out of ivory tusks, denoting the teaching of Zoser and the Sphinx.

They carry the Ra 'Chandco' dot of God on their foreheads, between their eyes, or the white and yellow lines down the forehead for knowledge. They often have the word 'Ram' incorporated in their names, such as 'Dhondiram'.

Religious symbols are discarded once broken or damaged as this is a sign of misfortune, disaster or even death. No-one will take precious gems or metals placed beside religious symbols for the same reason. They cremate their dead because land is at a premium. The ashes are cast into the river on the twelfth day so that they can continue their journey 'as a drop of water in an endless sea'.

Hindu men wear a shirt and 'dhoti', which is a two-and-a-half metre length of cloth wound around each leg separately, and a turban on their head. Women wear a blouse and two-metre long sari or, when working and bending down in a field, a dhoti which is similar to the men's. Hindus traditionally cover their heads as a form of respect and the style of dress and turban indicates the area they pertain to.

The length of a woman's hair is a great pride and joy to the owner.

Western dress and Christianity have done much to break down the caste 'Varna' system, which often held back those who wished to improve themselves.

The light-skinned people of the Indus' northern area were associated with the Egyptian Darius Hystaspis Aryans rule and disassociated themselves from the dark-skinned people of the south. The Madras people eat a lot of very hot curry and sweet sugar which may affect their skin pigmentation.

There are Kadar pygmies in the Cordomon Hill, so it appears that the various genetic groups all have their own proportion of small stature people.

Some Hindu religious meanings are as follows:-

The three Guna are called 'Sattwic' white, which has the characteristics of humility, harmony, goodness and purity; 'Rajas' is red for action, pain and passion; 'Tamasa' is black for inertia, darkness, delusion, ignorance and heedlessness.

Once one is caught up in self and wrong there is no end which is complementary with the wheel of life 'Samara'.

The prayer beads are fingered while praying, the string, therefore, is part of them because it illustrates the connection between the beads. The 'A' of the alphabet stands for having faces in all directions and for the fruit of action. The cow is sacred because one can milk their desires from the cow.

Hindu ethics are: purity, self control, truth, compassion, charity and non-violence. The Rajputans are feared because they tell the truth no matter what the consequences. The Gurkha is feared because of his kukri, which must draw blood every time it is unsheathed, even if this means nicking the handler's own finger. The kukri and Assam knife are similar to the Egyptian pharaoh's scimitar.

The Sikhs all have 'Singh' (lion) as one of their names because this is one of the five 'K' in their religion. The others are: long hair (men wear their hair in a knot) comb, sword, Kirpan's Holy Book and the five rivers of the Punjab.

There are also two sects, one is Hindu and therefore vegetarian and the other Islamic and carnivorous (the same as Islam and Hebrews). Both men and women wear tunic and trousers but the women also wear a wide scarf around their head and shoulders.

BUDDHISM

There may have been connections between Darius Hystaspis, Zoroaster, Croesus the last king of the Lydians who was noted for his wisdom, Buddha and Confucius, all of whom lived about the same time and have so much in common that they could all be one and the same person, whose fame travelled along the trade routes, because Ahasuerus' reign stretched from Ethiopia to India and comprised 127 provinces, most of which were accounted for by India. (Esther I and 10) refers to the Chronicles and King David, who was King of the Jews, the Holy Scriptures, Modecai's Mars, Esther Venus and her son Mercury, who was next to the Sun Ra.

Buddhas are found carved out of living rock from Afghanistan to China and Japan, which may show the extent of his following in Asia. If Darius Hystapis, Zoroaster, Croesus, Buddha and Confucius are all one and the same person then he was probably of Egyptian Hebrew parentage because of cultural similarities and universal acceptance.

Siddhata Gautma, better known as Buddha the Enlightened One (Sanskrit), was the son of a nobleman and is reputed to have lived between approximately 560 and 483 BC. He lived a very sheltered life until he left the palace, never to return to his wife and child. Siddhara Gautma was married to Yosadhara, note the 'dhara' ending in both names which was a common practice with the pharaohs of Egypt who married sisters and daughters. Siddhara also changed his name in accordance with the pharaohs' tradition and custom.

Yosadhara may have died in childbirth, which could have embittered Siddhara enough to leave his home and influenced his outlook on life and religion.

The statues of Buddha have the long ears which are associated with the nobility of China and is one of the factors taken into account when the Dalai Lama is chosen. Tutankhamun had holes in his ears which would elongate the lobes even more so when weighted down.

The dot in the centre of the forehead between the eyes represents Ra. Buddha's nurse is said to have been a Hindu, which could account for the similarities between Hindu and Buddhism.

The statues of Buddha Yogi and Egyptian cultures have much in common. Both feet on the ground for the Sphinx; one foot on the ground with the other resting on the thigh, one unit and age; two feet and both hands on the ground, the fingers turned down, youth and crawl; two feet on the ground one hand down or one foot down and two hands turned down the close of life. 'The spirit shall return unto God who gave it.' The circular position of the fingers represents the lifecycle (Kamakura, Tokyo-Japan) with the three fingers for the beginning, middle and end. The whole body represents the teachings of Zoser and the Sphinx.

Buddha's hair is often curly, similar to the Egyptians and Jews, and represents the science of the universe, age of initiation and lifecycle. The head covering is sometimes similar to the upper Egypt crown. The funnel-shaped shrines and stupas are an elongated crown representing initiation and the rise and fall of the lifecycle.

The Yeti of Tibet and the Dragon of China all pertain to the science and culture of Egypt by a simple explanation for children whom are starting to learn the laws of survival. It is interesting to know that the oldest civilisation in India at Monenjo-Daro (3500-2700 BC) is older than the pyramids of Egypt.

HEBREWS

The Hebrew texts (1300-165 BC) were on papyrus leather scrolls and were translated from Greek to Hebrew in 250-50 BC (Septuagint) then into Latin in about 400 AD. The Hebrew Torah texts were edited into their present day form by the 9th century AD. Jewish scholars were called Masoretes. A new translation of the Holy Scriptures according to the Masoritic text was published in 1962.

Samaritans only recognise the Torah, Joshua and Mt. Gerizim as sacred because of the laws and the Ark.

Karaites reject Rabbinic teachings and only accept the law of the 'Bible' and literal interpretation. They live mostly near Ramla.

Holy has four letters and Bible has five. In Hebrew there are only three letters representing the Torah (beginning) Prophets (middle) and writings (end). The Holy Bible was retained and used in places of worship and, because of its translation into Greek the universal langauge at the time, was able to withstand the rule of Islam when the Jews and their teachings were condemned.

The numerical values in Hebrew are Al Alef silent, B2V Bet (Sphinx), G3 (Gentile), D4 (David), H5 (equinox and God), V6 Z7 (Zoser) K ch 20, L 30, M 50 and 70 is silent for the end of life. Ayin (Taverash), eye, is written O. The Jews believed in an evil eye and kindness should not be trusted. This is probably why Yeshu taught 'Love thy neighbour as thyself.' The 'K' is similar to Ra, sun, HIT for the angle of the sun and moon, both are silent. These, and other designs and markers, are similar to those found at the site of Zimbabwe's ruins and can therefore constitute a connection with the Jewish and Egyptian culture.

The Africans also believe that kindness and generosity are not to be trusted and prefer a strict just person. One should see with a single mind and not say one thing and mean another (Matthew 6 v 22). The Golden Ark of the Jews coincides with the teachings of Zoser, the Sphinx and the science of the universe. The angel represents the teachings of the Sphinx and heart and feather of justice and the rings of Ra. The scrolls (Megillah) are placed inside the ark and represent the never ending knowledge (Exodus 25).

The Chanukah dates back to 168 BC during the reign of Antiochus IV, who ordered the Jews to worship an idol in the Jerusalem Temple. The Jews, led by Maccabee Tudah, refused to worship idols and drove the Syrians out. Then a crux of oil burnt in the temple for eight days without being replenished and because of this the Jews light a fresh candle every day to mark this event (if salt is added to wax it is said to burn longer). They also believe in freedom of and tolerance towards other religions.

The six-branched candelabrum of the Jews denotes death. The menorah has the seven branches (Exodus 25 v 31-40) with the ten designs on each side of the dividing trunk. The trunk has four designs consisting of bowl, knob and flowers representing the lily or protea of Egypt. The knob represents Ra and the bowl, science and knowledge. There are four individual knobs on the trunk, including the one on the base. The base has a centre foot with six branches emanating from the centre with a design on the end of each foot similar to the top of the trunk on the menorah. The centre trunk has the one design at the top for God. The first branch has two for initiation, marriage, science and culture, the second represents the beginning, middle and end of life, the third branch has five designs representing that which comes from God must return to God.

The menorah represents the culture of Egypt, has the seven branches of the Sphinx, the ten designs on each side and four designs down the central trunk for the quarternary system and the universe $10 + 10 + 4 = 24$. The four trunk knobs, including the base, are for Ra.

The base, which is not described in the Bible, was probably made up as shown on the Triumphant Arch in Rome, which consists of two hexagons on top of each other representing the twelve tribes of Israel.

The original menorah belonged to the temple and was of one talent of beaten gold so probably not very big but, a creation of singular beauty, it included the culture of ancient Egypt. The menorah does not have lighted candles, although a candle is sometimes placed in a holder behind the main branch.

Candelabra are shown on Egyptian art at Gizah on the Nile. The Golden Candlestick appears to have been made before and after the making of the Golden Calf (Exodus 37 v17-24 and 32).

Christians also use candles in their churches. However, the candles on the Christmas tree refer to a pre-Christianity event, the celebration of the return of the light at midwinter solstice. Hindus have Duwali, the New Year festival of light. Four lit lamps represent the four elements; fire, earth, water and air, and a fifth light unites them.

The Jews who built the pyramids were the slaves of the north and wanted to leave Egypt, but the prosperous farming Jews of the south, the descendants of Joseph, did not. It was probably only the fear of slavery which persuaded them to follow Moses. They could, therefore, well have supplied the gold, fine cloth and ornaments for the temple as well as the sacrificial livestock, which were also a source of food. Joseph's descendants were compensated for relinquishing their wealth by being chosen as religious leaders and Moses, therefore, also acted as arbitrator between the two groups.

Israel made Joseph's coat of many colours (Gen. 37 v3). The colours pertain to the culture of Egypt and it was because of this, added to the hatred among the brothers in later years, that Joseph placed his brothers in order of rank (Gen. 34 v33) Scripture of the Dead Sea Sect, the Service of God, the Zodokite Document IV and Supplementary Code of Rank and Procedure XIV 3-12.

The Passover is celebrated by placing a lamb's bone, egg, herbs, salt and unleavened bread on a plate and wine on the table. The Christians celebrate Holy Communion with bread and wine just as the Jews do on the Sabbath.

Purim is taken from the book of Esther, the only book of the Holy Bible which does not mention God, when one rejoices and gives presents similar to a birthday.

The Star of David (Magem David) is probably a very recent addition to the Jewish symbols and only adopted by them since the 17th century. David was born and died at the time of Pentecost (Shavout May 1 to June 7th). The star could be derived from the Triangulum of Aries and Libra representing good triumphing over evil (one triangle inverted on the top of the other) and the universe the circular centre.

Solomon's pentagram probably represents the five Hebrew names of God and the five books of the Torah. This is also shown on Egyptian art at Gizah on the Nile.

Baptism is based on hygiene to show that water purifies (Lev. 11 v32 and 14). The Bar Mitzvah and Matmitzvah is the reading of the Law and the Ten Commandments, which is equal to confirmation and initiation and the twelve years of the Sphinx.

The Jewish New Year is a time of reflection over the year's

deeds and marks the time of repentance and fasting followed by rejoicing and thanksgiving.

Christians make New Year's resolutions and Lent marks the time of going without. The Druids celebrated Hallowe'en as their New Year on the 31st of October, when pumpkin faces are made by cutting triangles, squares and circles.

After the forty year war, involving the whole of the Middle East, Arab countries will culminate in a final battle lasting one year, month, week, day and hour, thus preventing too great a loss of life due to extended fighting. The Great Pyramid indicated 1994 which will be after the Jews return to Israel (Deut. 4 and 5, 31 v 16), then the country will be renamed Beulah and the people Hephzi-bah (Isiah 62 v 4), Scriptures of the Dead Sea Sect Manual of Discipline for the future congregation of Israel. Among those returning will be the discontented tribe who will eventually break away and form the next Islam.

YESHU

The birth of Jesus, Yeshu or Yeshoshua (Hebrew) was foretold by the astrologers in 7 BC, when Jupiter and Saturn were in conjunction in Pisces on May 29th, which would have coincided with the Hebrew Shavout (Pentecost) and the time of the year when Moses gave the Jews the Ten Commandments on Mount Sinai. December 4th is about the time of the Chanukah 'The Light of the World' and the lighting of the candles (Luke 2 v 32, 35).

The Great Pyramid points to October 3rd and the time when the sun is in Libra and Pisces is in the East, coinciding with the time the Jews celebrate their New Year (Rosh Hasanah), which added extra significance to it for the Jews who were struggling for peace.

In the Great Pyramid is an unbroken sloping curved line between the North Wall, the Grand Gallery and the mouth of the well. Those who follow the teachings ascend the Grand Gallery and those who reject them descend the well shaft. John the Baptist, who preceded Jesus, was Jewish, was beheaded by Herod and has a lifeline at floor level, so there is no mistaking the two identities.

Joseph was a descendent of David (1086 BC) and Yeshu Pantera of Pander (Babylonial Talmud) was Joseph's stepson. Yeshu was a son of man (Matt. 26 v 2). Abraham (Abram), Moses, David and Yeshu were all of Hebrew Gentile parentage or descendance. Yeshu was circumcised in accordance with the Jewish tradition (Luke 2 v 21).

Mary rode into Bethlehem on a donkey and Yeshu was born in a stable (Sphinx). The Star was in the East denoting peace. David was also born in Bethlehem. The shepherds have

Ankh crooks of upper Egypt and mind. The three kings and the three gifts: frankincense for knowledge of the highest order and used at the time of initiation, myrrh the physician, and gold of excellence. Joseph and Mary took Yeshu to Egypt after his birth, which probably helped him in later life with his gift of medicine and knowledge.

When Yeshu spoke to the learned men in the temple at the age of twelve (Scriptures of the Dead Sea Sect, The Service of God vi 13-23) and was accepted Nazarite, a Hebrew taking certain vows of abstinence for a certain length of time (Numbers 6), there was a brotherhood of Essene at Khanet which is near Jerusalem (peace) and where he remained until he was thirty (Luke 3 v 23) Scripture of the Dead Sea Sect Manual of Discipline for the Future Congregation of Israel).

The Essene teachings were disbanded about this time and a place of safe keeping had to be found for the scrolls, which are never destroyed, but preserved for future use and reference. The scrolls' caves at Qumran and Khanet are close to each other and were an ideal hiding place (A Zodikite document was also found at the site of an old synagogue in Cairo). The Rabbi travelled from place to place in Israel and when in the Wilderness and tempted by the devil to cast himself down (Luke 4 v1-13) was probably hiding the Dead Sea Scrolls at the time.

Yeshu rode into Jerusalem on a donkey representing the Sphinx heart and feather represented by the branches of palm trees. At the feast of the Tabernacles (September-October lasting 9 days) Yeshu may have been honoured to read the end of the Torah as the Bridegroom of the Law or Bridegroom of the Beginning. Reading of the Torah starts from the beginning of Genesis.

Yeshu went into Bethany and lodged there (Matt 21 v 17).

The cross on the donkey's back represents the equinox, birth and death and the passing on of knowledge. At the Feast of Passover a poor woman anointed Yeshu with oil (Matt. 26 v 7). 'Christ the Lord anointed' is a Jewish prophecy of a messiah (Deut. 18 v 15-19). Rabbi Yeshu (Jesus) celebrated the Jewish Feast of Passover in accordance with the Jewish custom and Zodikite Essene teachings (part 1 the Service of God of the Communal Duties vi 1-8). When he prayed at Gethsemane, 'Let this cup pass from me.' (Matt. 26 v 39) (cup owl-kos) it was Elijah's cup. Elijah is looked upon by the Jews as a Messiah. The three years of teaching among the people represented the Beginning, Middle and End. Father- marriage and Fatherhood of God, Son- the passing on of knowledge to the next generation and the brotherhood of man, Holy Ghost, or its equivalent- death. The parables of the New Testament were taken from the Talmud, which is of the Jewish Law and Legend, so Yeshu must have been a scholar of the Talmud.

Pontius Pilate's name suggests that he was from the north Median Empire of Asia Minor (and the passing on of knowledge). A crown of thorns was placed on Yeshu's head, a crown placed on an Essene head was a high honour because it was a 'crown of glory'. The thorns also represent the Pyramid, the circle is the lifecycle of Ra, the Robe of Honour was torn by the soldiers because of its high value to the scholar (part 1 of the Service of God iii 13 - iv 26). The soldiers placed either a scarlet robe on Yeshu (Matt. 27 v28), or a purple robe (Mark 15 v17).

The plaited crown of thorns represented the science of the universe, Zoser and the rise and fall of man. The red was for the sceptre. The crucifixion represents the Pharaoh's ankh or crux anstra 'The King of the Jews' (Matt 27 v 37).

There is reference to the crucifixion and those responsible being Jews in John 7 v1. The Glorious Koran IV v157 refers to the people of Islam. Islams also claim to be descendants from Abram and Hagar the Egyptian (Gen. 21 v14) and their son Ishmael (Gen. 25 v12).

The scribes and pharisees (Matt. 23) and money lenders (Matt. 21) resented Yeshu because he showed his dislike for their practices and place of business (Matt. 15) being in the presence of the synagogue.

The Jews do not permit a body to hang overnight so Yeshu was placed in a tomb and, because of an eclipse of the sun, there was darkness from the sixth to the ninth hour followed by an earthquake (Matt. 27 v45-51). The path of an eclipse denoted the death or fall of a ruler and, for better or worse, marks a time of change.

When some showed surprise that he had survived the ordeal, Yeshu spoke to the disciples, 'For a spirit hath not flesh and bones as ye see me have,' (Luke 24 v39).

At the time of Pentecost (Shavuot) May 6th to June 7th, God revealed His presence to the disciples when they preached out of their Hebrew tongue (Acts 1 and 2), Paul was a Greek Jew and therefore spoke Greek and was able to converse with the Gentiles and interest them in the Jewish faith. The Jews may have found it difficult to follow the Greek, which would have afforded greater protection against trouble makers. The disciples could therefore be termed Progressive. When Yeshu recovered consciousness (John 19 v34) the ordeal forced him into the background and out of the public eye and into exile (Acts 1 v11; 25 v19). Yeshu later travelled north and saw his disciples at the Sea of Galilee where he may have made prior arrangements to meet them (Matt. 26 v32), because he was travelling to the east by the overland trade routes (Mark 13 v34) Damascus, Baghdad, Teheran, Khyber Pass, etc.

Some believe that Yeshu lived in India for many years. Indians claim that his resting place is to be found near the library at Sringagar on the Bund Kashmir where he was known as Issau Mussi by the Hindus and Ye Zessif or Yus Asaf, the Prophet in Arabic. The letter 'Z' is in the third position which could mean it has been given as a result of death before he lived in India.

The tomb itself is unusual for India. The crypt is made of wood and has three grilles at one end for Zoser and the Sphinx. The tomb covering represents the lifecycle and the cross of death, because it would have been open to the sun when first constructed. The body may also have been embalmed (Esther 1 v1). Mary is said to have been buried at Rawalpindi, so must have followed or accompanied Yeshu to India.

Christianity has maintained symbols of Egypt in the Eagle lectern, which supports the Holy Bible in church, the pharaoh shepherd crook (Ankh) used by bishops, the cross (crux astra) hieroglyphics for the fish and fishers of men, Sinaitic script and circle. The Bishop's ring is derived from the scarab gem stone of the pharaohs, and the coffin for the departed, though not as elaborate as those of the coffins of Egyptian mummies (Gen. 50 v26).

The coronation stone of England on which the kings of Scotland were crowned, now used for the crowning of the kings and queens of England, probably originated from Egypt (see Cheiros World of Predictions).

When the stone (Jacobs pillow?) cracked it indicated the breaking up of the British Empire. The Ampulla eagle holds the anointing oil and the spoon goes with it. There is also a spoon shape depicted on one of Tutankhamun's pendants with the scarab, snake ankh and pillar djet. The Orb with the cross on the top represents the globe and geometrical alignments. The coronation ring is placed on the finger representing the carved scarab stone of Egypt and the heart, Sphinx and the bird, because the scarab beetle walks and flies. The sword is for justice and mercy, the crown represents the Essene Zodokite Crown of Glory and the pharaohs' crown of knowledge and culture, the crown of upper Egypt. The robe of honour is placed around the sovereign's shoulders at the time of the coronation. The canopy and the colours are all of Egyptian and Jewish origin (Exodus 25 v4). All these symbols together make the coronation equivalent to the initiation ceremony of the Egyptian pharaohs.

The Christian symbol of a cross was originally designed on the Egyptian Ankh, which accounts for the cross design found in various parts of the world. Jerusalem has a cross coat of arms consisting of one big cross with a cross in each space, making five in all. Jerusalem was originally spent Ursualimu.

Christians covered their heads and the priests wore an embroidered orphrey, a skull cap equivalent to the Jewish yarmulka and the prayer shawl tallit (Exodus 28). The Bible readings and the cantor are also equivalent in both religions. The altar represents the teachings of Zoser, with the cloth for the science of the Universe and culture and the ark angles derived from the heart and the feather of justice.

The Romans were aligned to Egypt and Greece, and Rome had the temple of Apollo dedicated in 433 BC and in 102 BC. The eagle became the standard. The Janus Temple was closed in 235 BC and again in 71 AD. The Temple of Peace was completed in 75 AD and the Temple of the Sun in 274 AD was founded by Aurelian. Christianity was first established in 312

AD by Constantine as the religion of the state, and in Constantinople in 330 AD. The first pope was not installed until 728 AD, which was after the rise of Islam.

THERA

Athens, the capital of Attica, was named Cectopai. Cectops, an Egyptian, built the original city on the Acropolis between 1500 and 1400 BC after the volcanic eruption of Thera (Santotini). When the resulting tidal wave buried everything in its path the ancient world vanished.

Ancient Greece once covered the area from the Ionian Sea to Lydia, which is now part of Turkey.

The Shaft graves with the citadel by Mycenae (1600 BC) are built on a circular plan similar to the ruins of Zimbabwe and the Trojan castles, with concentric walls.

The rock art of the Greek and Egyptian cultures shows distinct similarities; Apis and the Bull of Minos, the Lion Bird of Knossos and the sacred bird of Egypt the Hawk-headed Horus. The Lion Bird of Knossos has the Ra design on its shoulders and on its neck the four designs of Zoser. There is a resemblance between the Lion Gate of Mycenae and the Lion Sekhmet of Egypt.

The Minoan 'Bull-leaping' sport on a fresco from the palace of Knossos has a figure standing at the horns of the bull, another somersaulting onto the centre of its back while a third figure, a girl 'toreador', is ready to catch. Three figures and the bull in the centre form the sign of the Sphinx.

The fresco of the 'young prince' shows two locks of hair on the forehead, one in front of the body and three sets of three locks behind the shoulder giving a total of four. The headdress has one brooch with two designs holding three feathers above four circular designs facing the same direction. The youth is also wearing body covering similar to that worn by toreadors and in the initiation ceremonies on the rock art of Zimbabwe.

The Minoan red coloured 'cup-bearer' picture found on Crete shows the 'slave bangles' worn on the arm, similar to those of India and the Red Indians. The Bushman women wear skin arm bands on their arms and legs as hunting trophies of their menfolk.

The four Shaft graves at Mycenae show a Homeric body shield similar to those on the rock paintings of Tassili and the Sahara, which was the original home of the Bushman (Bowman). The Bushman are pink when they are born and darken with living conditions.

The destruction wrought by the Thera catastrophe resulted in the widening of the gap between the Egyptian and other cultures by the migration of the Lydians of Asia to America and the Lydians of Africa further south, where they were able to preserve their cultures.

After the Thera catastrophe Greek architecture and mythology were united by the positioning of the buildings by the equinox (female) and solstice (male) names by which the constructions are still known today. This gives a variety of directions. The architects incorporated the 52 years cycle by the number of uniform objects in a set or viewing area for the number of days in a year and the science of the universe. The colours represented culture pertaining to the Egyptians and was transposed into mythology.

The Roman numerals were also based on the Egyptian sciences and number positions on the sundial I equinox of the north and south, V the 52°, X the solstice; C the lifecycle, L the angles of the equinox, solstice and 52°, M the angles of the geometrical alignments.

The Egyptian culture has named the signs of the zodiac and the Greek the names of the other constellations. The Greeks have also created buildings of beauty and strength which have lasted over the centuries with those of Egypt and other cultures.

The Thera people migrated to Europe as far north as Spitzbergen and west of Greenland, Iceland and America. This incorporates Britons, Druids, Eskimos and American Indians and later the Pacific Islanders, before the catastrophe devoured everything in sight and the vegetation was cleared out, leaving no evaporation or condensation for rain, resulting in desert and famine.

The Irish leprechaun is comparable with the Sphinx; the Blarney Stone with Zoser; the shilleleagh the sceptre or stick of age; the shamrock with Zoser and the Sphinx, because they are steeped in legends and traditions of the pre-Christian era.

The Viking ships, shield, helmets and stone constructions and designs pertain to the Mediterranean area and culture as legend and traditions.

The British archaeologists have found palimasit characters written in Celt, Iberian, Byzantine genus and Scandinavian. Geordie, still spoken along the Tyne and is related to the Scandinavian languages because of the port and trade and as St. Boniface preached Christianity over the whole of the North European continent. Northumbrian is a dialect of the English language.

King Alfred (Elfred) (871-901) burnt the scones symbolizing the destruction of the old culture and superimposing the new-Christian way of life. He also united the people of England and is buried at Winchester, the ancient Royal city of England. The present 1,000 year old cathedral is Norman and is approximately 30° off true north, while the 700 AD previous Saxon Minster, where St. Swithin was buried, is approximately 25° off true north. (See page 213).

King Canute 1017-35 pertains to the moon's magnetic pull

on the sea at the time of the equinox, solstice and high and low water marks as well as the ebb and flow of the tide. Ka, Egyptian for 'descend, turn back'. At Thebes are the 'Singing Colosses' which have wet feet during the fertile season when the River Nile floods its banks. King Canute's remains are also at Winchester Cathedral, which is built on a wooden raft because of the water level and to strengthen the foundations. Marsh conditions make land unsuitable for agriculture.

King Arthur 500AD and his knights of the round (Ra) (oak) table, which is 18 feet in diameter, twenty-four green and white sections of knights - age of initiation; green - heart; white - learning; red - youth; blue - knowledge and all blending for balance. The white and red Tudor rose* is in the centre of the Ra circle. King Arthur is depicted in the top larger division wearing red, white and blue royal robes, the colour definitions pertain to Egypt. The king holds the sword of initiation and justice, equinox and solstice in his right hand and the orb of the science of the universe in his left.

The story of King Arthur greatly simplifies the science of the universe, so that children can remember and understand and so pass the knowledge on to the next generation. King Arthur, Queen Guinevere and the courtiers are said to be in an enchanted sleep waiting for someone to blow the horn (hunting), (Laws of the Sphinx,) that lies on the square table of Zoser and knowledge, and draw Excalibur from the stone, (justice and mercy) and cut the garter, (lifecycle.) This is similar to the riddle of the Sphinx, the one who can solve the mystery breaks the spell and enlightenment returns.

---

* The date difference shows the comparison between the ancient culture and civilized attributes.

Stonehenge, built by the ancient Britons, is comparable with the square and oblong buildings and columned structures of Thebes in Egypt, Athens in Greece, etc.

The ancient Bronze Age circular constructions in England have linteled entrances and concave 'grinding' stones as direction markers for the equinox, solstice and 52°.

Stonehenge has the 60 holes in a circle for the number of minutes in an hour, five holes and spaces for every 30°, covering 6° for each alignment, allowing a 3° error each side. The sun moves the correct number of Aubrey holes each day and hour of the year. The alignments are taken between the points where the sun's shadow is at its maximum and minimum each year.

Inside the circle of Aubrey holes there are two half circles of holes, the 'Y' set has ten in one group and five in the other for Zoser. The 'Z' holes have one set marking one quarter of the circle and the other group have solstice degrees with the five holes of knowledge, which also reduces the margin of error.

The 'upright' monoliths were a total of thirty, the age when man was considered mature (Scripture of the Dead Sea Sect Manual of Disciple). The 'U' designs of the 'upright' are grouped into pairs for the Sphinx and total five, and ten for Zoser and God. The post holes at the end of the 'U' are for the age of initiation. Those inside the 'U' are for the Ma rise and Ka fall of man during his lifetime.

The blue stones represent the sky and knowledge of science of the heavens, the green stones for the heart and the red for youth. The holes between the 'U' and circle are for the teachings of Zoser and the Sphinx. The group of holes between the Sphinx 'y' and 'z' holes are for the lifespan and the number for the degree of the solstice. The graves found in this area show that persons who lived their full lifespan are near the ditch for the lifespan of 52 years. The ditch has the gaps for the geometrical alignment for the equinox, solstice and the 52°. The 'Avenues' ditch is for the Sphinx.

The 'Altar stone' is of sandstone for knowledge (grains of sand) and was on the line of the original north-south when Stonehenge was first constructed. The Altar stone and Hele stone formed the east/west, the half circle the solstice and the 52°. In some of these holes remains of human cremation were found. In the Disc Burrows were the faience beads from Egypt, amber from central Europe for knowledge, jet beads from the east coast of England for death.

Stonehenge and other constructions were positioned by the sun at the time of the equinox and solstice, the same as the Pyramids of Egypt. It is, therefore, possible to date the constructions of most, if not all, of the ancient buildings.

Stonehenge is outside the Tropics of Cancer and Capricorn and the suns rays do not pass directly overhead at any time of the year. The 'O' and centre represents the summer crops from July to October. Egyptian hieroglyphics, the design denotes the winter because of the lack of large monoliths on the inside of the inner circle. This is because in winter the sun's shadow is longer and covers a greater area, so markers are not necessary and the winters are bleak. Stonehenge is 50° out of true alignment.

Stonehenge has the outer banks and ditches for the Sphinx and the passing of knowledge from one generation to the next. The outer set of holes gives the number of the lifecycle of Zoser, the second row the age of maturity. The larger holes are for the summer and winter solstice because the hours of sunshine vary considerably. The smaller holes in the centre of the circle represent the lifecycle. The central marker is the point where the equinox, solstice and 52° are taken to the outside of the circle and bank. It is, therefore, possible to date Stonehenge by the position of the sun.

The north side of the entrance gives the equinox and the other the solstice, and just south of it the 52° to the marker. The construction is approximately 30° in the 20th century plus 11° 2706 or 706 BC. The construction was probably abandoned because of cultural changes 30 + 11 = 41 x 66 = 2707 or 707 BC.

Avebury, Wiltshire, has the outer diameter representing the days of the year, lifecycle and Zoser, and covers a larger area than Stonehenge. It has an outer circle of monoliths without lintels. A quarter circle represents the age of initiation and the second quarter the active years. At the halfway mark, when it is time to pass on knowledge to the next generation, is a double row of monoliths for the Sphinx and curve for the lifecycle. The geometrical alignments are for the equinox and solstice, the circle continues round with the younger generation to complete the eternal cycle of life and knowledge.

The two inner circles have the 52° monolith for the life cycle. One inner circle represents Ra with the dot in the centre of four Zoser monoliths. The second circle has a 'D' in the centre for the equinox and lifecycle of man. The two odd monoliths represent the heart and the feather of justice. The 'O' and 'D' represent the July and October rains and crops (Egyptian hieroglyphics). When the circles are lined up they give the equinox and solstice.

The transportation and construction of Stonehenge and other stone designs was probably a similar method to that in Egypt and Easter Island. Hay and snow would make it easier to slide the stones and snow ramps would be quick and economical, while the stone would be kept contracted with the cold and be a tight fit in the hole when it thawed out. The scientific skill and knowledge entailed was worth all the toil and labour required for the erection of the monoliths. This also explains the carvings of Mycenean daggers which are geometrically designed and positioned on some of the Trilithon; this fact is borne out by the burial mounds, geometrical holes in bones, metals and pottery designs connected with the science of the universe.

The Trethevy Dolmen is a group of stone monoliths of which the top stone has the geometrical holes right through the top. To complete the full set the stone gives the outer alignment.

Nympsfield, a Cotswold Megalithic tomb, gives the geometrical alignment with the angle of the monoliths individually and collectively.

The Trundle, Goodwood Neolithic, Iron Age, has the Sphinx ditch, causeway and cross lines with inner circle which give the geometrical alignment with Ra or dot in the inner circle.

Grumspound, Moreton Hampstead, is in general appearance similar to the ruins found in Zimbabwe and Chysauster with those of the Inyanga 'vaults'.

Woodbury, near Salisbury, Iron Age, has the double row of holes for the Sphinx and lifecycle, with the square of Zoser in the centre giving the geometrical alignments.

Maiden Castle, Iron Age hut, has the main marker on the north side of the circle which gives the alignments to the heart. Another alignment taken from the central 'ovens' for the 52° and solstice (between the circles) and the equinox on the other side of the 'oven'. The pits were used for the geometrical alignments, this is why they played an important part in the ancient constructions.

Glastonbury Lake Village hut foundations had the floors

added to every so many years, which probably coincided with the movement of the sun at the time of the equinox and solstice, so that the hearth was moved into place in order that the area did not date and become useless.

Ladle Hill has the geometrical alignment from the Ra circle with the enclosure, this accounts for the ditch constructions, which line up with the circular area outside the enclosure and give the geometrical alignment of it.

Maiden Castle has the alignments from the entrance to the main enclosure lining up with the markers and circular construction within the enclosure. Other geometrical alignments are shown by the design of the entrance, which makes it highly probable that this construction was kept up to date and used for hundreds of years.

Notgrove has the alignments from the centre onto the central Ra circle, to the equinox and solstice, as well as the 52° onto the recesses in the passage of the entrance.

Belas Knap uses the Ra circle for the central point into the corners and recesses for geometric alignment. The original north line was on the south side and was found by taking a line across the two rounded ends, which date the construction approximately $30 + 11 \times 66 = 2707$ or 707 BC.

Snail Down, Tidworth, uses the corners of the enclosure for the geometrical alignments onto the circular hollows. The one in use would be marked for the alignments and old ones would be closed to denote that they were obsolete. The circular mound also gives geometrical alignments onto the circular hollows. The square outside the enclosure represents the solstice and 52° across the corners and down the side the equinox.

Neolithic House at Haldon, Devon, has the holes on the north side giving the alignments to the central line of the holes.

Another set from the central east side gives around it the alignments to the hearth and holes.

The shards were originally used for the geometrical alignment and would denote the area which was not in use and therefore not accurate, probably used for several alignments, and only the shards intact at the time they were used would indicate their last position. It is, therefore, possible to date the area from the first time it was used until its last positioning.

Danebury near Stockbridge, Hampshire Downs, covers 13 acres (4.5 hectares) and had 60 post holes measuring up to 1.3 metres. There appear to be five different gaps, one of which was 7 metres wide. The piles of smooth stones from the coast were for the science of the universe and the days of the year, etc. There were banks on either side of the opening and a ditch in front of the banks resulting in a narrow passage of about 52 metres. The walls were 4 metres high and made out of quarried flint blocks. The curved right banks were higher than the others and the opening was obscured from the approach. The vertical timbers set into slots cut in the chalk bed resulted from cutting through the banks of the 4 pits lying in an arc. One had a totem pole and bones of a dog. All this suggests geometric science and culture. Future excavations should bring to light more interesting discoveries. Accurate dating can be determined by true north ancient and modern. These conclusions of Danebury have been drawn from an article by Patricia Conner (Sunday Times, Rhodesia) based on excavations by Professor Barry Cunliffe.

At Stanton Dew in Somerset is a stone called Hauteville's Quoit, north east of three circles. To the south west are another three stones known as The Cove. These stones and circles give the geometrical alignments. The whole group is named 'The Wedding', because the solstice is associated with initiation and marriage.

The three monoliths at Boroughbridge, named the 'Devil's Arrow, were geometrically positioned. When they were originally erected they gave the equinox and solstice on the sides of the rock face so that these could be dated to within 66 years.

Harrow Hills has the square enclosure for the alignments and probably a marker in the centre which is no longer visible.

Uffington Castle has the alignments from the entrance and is separate from the White Horse, which is on a mound with four depressions on the one side. The White Horse itself represents culture, the Sphinx and Zoser. The green grass is for the heart and the white design for knowledge. The tail, back and neck represent the rise of the lifecycle. The ears represent the Pyramid and the passing on of knowledge from one generation to the next. The square head is for Zoser with the dot of the eye for Ra. The mouth is for the beak of a bird and feathers of justice. The legs are for the Sphinx. The horse is said to have been cut for King Alfred and was his way of preserving the ancient cultures and traditions, which were being swamped by new ideas and methods. The horse is facing south, nose west, ears east, top of the front leg north and the tail points west to the Dragon Hill.

The lower, flat-topped Dragon Hill, tradition suggests has a connection with St. George and the Dragon 300 AD. The White Horse at Westbury also faces north and is said to be linked with King Alfred (change of culture). Other horses face the same direction, including the horse and rider near Dorchester, Kent.

The Cerne Abbas Giant of Dorset represents Helith or Hercules and is geometrically designed showing the equinox, solstice and 72°, 52° and 40°. The chest has two Ra circles, with a third Ra circle at the navel which also gives the geometrical alignments. The lines are for the beginning and end as well as for alignment and the face-shaped club also gives the alignments. The thumb on the outstretched arm forms the solstice, the missing lion skin which hung from the arm was also geometrically indented.

The Giant faces east for peace, the feet point to the north for taking knowledge to the north and the outstretched hand points to the south. The darkness is behind the Giant and the club points over the hill to the east. There are three ridges on the west side for death and destruction and two on the east for peace. The Giant is at the crossroads of an era.

The Zoser square above the giant lines up with its heel, the dog represents the Sphinx and fits in geometrically and culturally. The dog was revealed during scientific tests.

The Long Man of Wilmington, East Sussex, is also geometrically designed and incorporates the vertical lines on either side of the figure. Man in a Zoser square. The arms are east/west and the spears are north/south, the feet point to the west for war and overthrowing of culture and tradition for the new era.

The animal and human white chalk designs appear to date back to the time of King Alfred (871-901) indicating cultural changes that he did not uphold the ancient traditions, scientific teachings and ethical codes. It would seem that Christianity in England took over at around the time of the crusaders and William the Conqueror 1066 AD. The ancient cultures had been so ingrained that the white chalk designs were the outward signs of preserving the ancient cultures, which could be observed from a safe distance. People became less and less dependent on the ancient cultures and sciences with the invention of the printing press in the 15th century and the introduction of the calendar at around 752, necessity being the mother of invention. The reasons chalk hills were used for these designs and constructions was that the land here was not suitable for agriculture.

Many cathedrals and churches are built on older constructions, probably to incorporate ancient cultures, examples of which can be seen in the sundial placed on the south side of the building, often quite high up against the south wall. The sundial not only acted as a clock, but also as an indication of the seasons, as the sun shines higher in the summer than in winter. People could therefore observe the seasons when they went to church.

The ancient Egyptians used a primitive sundial from about 1500 BC. The sand glass dated from around the 15th century. The clock in Salisbury Cathedral dated from 1386 and the one at Wells from 1392.

ITEMS OF INTEREST

Aylesford Bucket design has very clearly depicted the Sphinx horse with the human legs and feet giving the solstice and 52°. The manes represent the lifecycle and initiation, the bird's head with the Ra eye also represents initiation, the tails are split giving the lines for the teachings of Zoser and the Sphinx, one clearly showing the feather as depicted on hieroglyphics.

The wooden bowl with the gold inlay from Caergwle, when placed rim down, gives the outline of the rise and fall of life. The life rings are shown near the rim while the centre is for Ra. The next band has the points design giving the angles of the solstice, which is also shown along the sides of the design. The other lines within the points represent the initiation, Zoser, the Sphinx and the lifecycle. There are a number of points dovetailed into each other for the passing on of knowledge. The chevron represents the pyramids and the three lines the beginning, middle and end. The Ra sign is at the end of the chevron.

The handled beaker from Bottisham has the diamonds and chevrons on the side of the beaker with the handle for the lifecycle and initiation. The base of the beaker has Ra in the centre with the circle for Zoser. Around the outside of the base are lines dividing it for the Sphinx and the crossing lines are for Zoser and the Sphinx. The total number of lines are for the days in the year.

The gold beaker from Rillaton has the handle for the lifecycle and the metal for initiation. The five lines on the handle are for Zoser and Ra. The bronze buckle from Moel Siabod has twenty rings divided by a marker into two sets of ten for the Sphinx and Zoser. The pattern on the rings is for the science of the universe, the plain centre is for Ra and the bar is for the alignments.

The iron helmet from the Thames has the horns of the Sphinx, the shape of the helmet has two vertical sides, two diagonal and one horizontal, all for the teachings of Zoser, the pyramid and lifecycle. The dots and designs are for Ra, culture and science.

A gold lunula has the diamonds for the geometrical alignments and diagonal lines for the solstice and 52°, with the number of marks for the Sphinx, Zoser, the science of the universe and days of the year.

A jet necklace has the diamonds and diagonal lines for the geometrical alignment and teachings of culture and science. One group has five beads for Zoser and the other seven are for the Sphinx. The lower border section give the angles of the sun's shadow at the English equinox. The black of the beads is for age and death. These geometrical objects were probably buried with the owner at the end of an era when the north and south poles replaced the ancient traditions of knowledge because they coincided with one another for the north.

The Gold Torc of Tara type from Grunty Fen near Ely has the ends of the equinox or solstice and the double Sphinx twist has the number of twists for the days in between the equinox and solstice. The top curves are for the lifecycle and the beginning, middle and end. The bottom twists are for Zoser. The end between the plain sections and the twists represent Ra. Consequently, this simple gold piece represents culture and science.

The gold armlet from Grunty Fen near Ely represents the lifecycle and the size of the rings, Zoser and the Sphinx. The grouping when correctly placed gives the solstice and 52° and this accounts for the different thicknesses and groovings.

The enamelled bronze shield from the Thames at Battersea has dots that give the alignments, as do the red circles and crosses. The raised centre area is for Mr, Ra, Ka, Zoser and the Sphinx.

The engraved bronze mirror from Birdlip shows the traditions from one era to the next when geometrical alignments gave way to very regular decorative patterns. The Cist burial under the barrow at Kelleythorpe has the beaker with the science of the universe and culture of Egypt. The hawk head represents the eye of Ra and the bird's head the initiation, justice, heart and feather. The dagger represents the laws of hunting. The position of the legs gives the equinox and 52°. The feet show the (winter) solstice for the close of life. The burial appears to be of a similar culture as those found in Africa.

The cremation of the dead probably took place at the end of the geometrical life of the burial area, as fire leaves a blackened charred area.

Neolithic potteryware from Peterborough and Abingdon is similar to pottery still used by the Africans in Southern Africa and Zimbabwe. The designs and patterns on the side represent the cultures and sciences of the universe as well as geometrical alignment.

Broch at Clickimin, Shetland Islands, is comparable with the ruins found in Zimbabwe. The differences are based on the proximity of the Arctic Circle and the great contrast between the length of days and nights at the time of the summer and winter solstice. The geometrical alignments are not too affected by fire and could also date the ruin because it was before the Christian era.

The witches or Gypsies burnt at the stake were probably those who continued to practise the ancient arts and sciences, studied the stars and foretold the future as in astrology, which was not understood by those who arrived from the Mediterranean, after the catastrophe of Thera and the deterioration of culture in Egypt, together with the advent of Christianity. 'No man can serve two masters, for either he will hate the one and love the other or he will hold the one and despise the other. Ye cannot serve God and Mammon.' (Matt. 6 v24.)

NORTHUMBERLAND

Hadrian's Wall, of the second century AD, crosses Northumberland and Cumberland. The mile castles are now positioned approximately 25-30 degrees out of true north alignment (2000 AD). If the same method was used as before the introduction of Christianity, these alignments would coincide with the dating on the inscribed stones found along the wall area. These stones and altars appear to have the equinox and solstice alignments.

The wall was originally constructed parallel to the Tropic of Cancer, taking into account true north at the time of construction.

Apollo the sun, Jupiter benevolence and a time of prosperity, Mercury brain and the construction of the wall, Mars war and a time of unrest, Hercules construction or alignment through unforeseen circumstances, Nepture water when the single trident head was used as a sign of trouble. However, when the double trident was depicted at both ends of the stick it was a sign of double trouble and probably denotes floods or marsh conditions.

The Zodiac Altar to Mithras has the symbols round the human figure in the centre, there are 'light holders' behind the sculpture, probably denoting 'knowledge is light' (Jewish).

The Altar of Mithras, the Persian God of Light, from Rudchester (Newcastle) has a man and beast at the bottom for the Sphinx, above is a Ra globe and DEO (to the god) with the laurel leaves for the feather.

The top of the altar has five inverted half circles with a similar design of a 'man praying' (Sinaitic script).

The altar from Chesterholm has an axe, similar to the African axe, a knife and an ox victim for the Sphinx and initiation on the one side and on the other a jug for holding the libation and dish.

The tombstone from Stanwix has a triangular design at the top with a head in the centre of the pyramid and the lions on the triangular sides holding a head in their paws, probably denoting a person of authority.

The altar from Kirkandrews has the hollow on the top of the altar stone, which was connected with the geometrical alignments and measurement of water contents of the air, sun and timekeeper.

The sculpture fragments, Rose Hill Gilsland at Rockliffe, Cumberland, have the Egyptian pillar on the right hand side with the grain store next to it and three above it. The angel represents the heart and feather for the bird standing on two feet next to it.

The reused hearth tombstone, Milecastle 42, shows that the Egyptian culture still existed after the Roman occupation of the wall. The narrowing of the entrance was also determined by the geometrical alignments and the threshold of the north portal East Housestead clearly shows the rut and hole for the alignment.

An iron three-footed candlestick used for the equinox and solstice was found at Rudchester.

Mithraeum Carrawburgh has the three altar stones on the north side of it. One stone marks the equinox, the other two the solstice. The posts mark the geometrical alignments for the equinox and 52°. The number of posts represent the Sphinx and Zoser. The inclusion of statues shows the Greek influence. This compromise later developed into Christianity, which incorporated the geometrical cross and statues as symbols. With the passing of time the original meanings i.e. of the geometrical cross, were lost.

The three cloaked Deities preserved in Housesteads Museum denote the beginning, middle and end, which should pertain to the wall itself as well as the three building periods.

The ash along the wall denotes the end of a cycle and the beginning of the next. The ash was not cleared away because it denotes the obsolete area and freshly filled-in ground denotes the new cycle (fallen into ruin and covered with earth - Tullie House Museum, Carlisle).

The ash is also a preserver because of its nitrogen contents, oxygen being needed for decay. It is also possible that the walled up area was the place where the dead were placed until the time of the close of the cycle. Skeletons have been found because they escaped the burning. The burial areas were probably for the Romans who buried their dead, showing that there were two culture groups working alongside each other on the wall, and the Votadini also lived between the Tyne and Firth of Forth.

At one time the Gypsies had their headquarters at Yetholm, which is on the border of England and Scotland which, in all probability, connects them with the burial mounds, stone circles and single stones, cairns, 'cups', concaves and ring marks on rocks, which appear to have given the equinox and solstice at the time they were carved and may be connected with the weather, i.e. snow or water levels; the snow level being taken when snow is blown into a sheltered area from a certain direction, denoting climatic conditions.

The Northumberland sword dance is performed at the time of the winter solstice. The five Zoser men wear the white shirt and feather of justice in their hats. The dance steps are called the rant and at a given moment they interweave the double handled wood rappers (Sphinx) into a circle, which is then held aloft by the 'fixie' in the centre for Ra, and they perform backward somersaults over the rappers, representing the lifecycle, and move in alternate directions for the culture, science and initiation, etc. The Villain and King represent the Sphinx good and bad. The sword dance takes two years to perfect and seven minutes to execute.

The Northumbrian pipes are sweeter and smaller than the Highland pipes because of their straight, not conical, bore and can be made with 1-17 keys. They are played with only one finger released at a time instead of various fingers at a time, and are therefore more difficult to play than the Highland pipes. They can sometimes be heard at Alnwick Castle.

The fancy carved shepherd sticks have fish, animals and birds carved on them and represent an art dating back many centuries. Animals pertaining to Northumberland are the white-faced sheep, the Scots black-faced sheep and blue-faced Leister or Border Leister, a breed whose original home was in the Hexham district of Northumerland. A herd of wild goats roaming the Kedland Moors and the famous white wild cattle of Chillingham are ruled by a supreme bull king. They have white-tipped horns, on the inside and part of the outside of the ear is red, and they have black muzzles.

St. Aidan from Iona is said to have brought Christianity to Northumberland, the cradle of English Christianity. St. Cuthbert, his successor, was born around 634 in Northumberland and went to Ripon (658) to wash the feet of a visitor (John 13 v5). At the age of 30 he went to Lindisfarne Holy Island, where St. Aidan had been. St. Cuthbert died about 687 and, when his coffin was opened in 1104 AD, the body was found to be in perfect condition (enbalmed?). (See Saint Northumbria Ltd., Market Place, Corbridge-on-Tyne.) Longstone, Farne Islands, is completely surrounded by salt water but has a continuous supply of fresh water from a spring which remains at a constant level.

One of the oldest churches in England (700 AD) is to be found at Woodhorn near Newbiggin-by-the-Sea, just 17 miles north of Newcastle-upon-Tyne. The church has a square belfry, which in itself is a rarity, and one of the tower bells is believed to be among the oldest in England (1242) and identified with Wucestre, one of the Villas given to St. Cuthbert by King Ceolwulf when he gave up the Northumbrian throne in 737 in order to become a monk. Both bells are mediaeval.

The Uncletin Ice-age-stone at Newbiggin is in danger of being lost to the sea due to subsidence.

AMERICAN INDIANS, ESKIMOES, PACIFIC ISLANDERS

Greece, Crecia or, in Hebrew, Javan (2298 BC) (Aegean Sea) fourth son of Japheth (fair) (2449 BC) who was the second son of Noah and who had descendants and land in Ionia, Macedonia, Greece, Syria, etc. was probably Japetus whom the Greeks considered the ancestor of the human race.

The pyramids of South America (built by the Aztecs) at Teotihuacan are at 52° which equals the degrees for the earth cycle. The Aztecs worked out the calendar with the 52 and 72 year cycle and had 5 unnamed days every year (360 degrees in a circle and 365.25 days in a year), the equinox and solstice (Aztec Calendar Stone). The Mayas also worked out the 52 year cycle.

The Incas worked on the equinox and solstice, which accounts for the narrowing of the opening and entrance from base to apex. The chevrons are in various forms straight and diagonal. They terraced the mountains (Pisac near Urubamba Gorge). There are engravings and paintings near San de Atacama in the north of Chile depicting animals and llamas similar to those found in Tibet and China.

Some of South America's huge engravings can best be viewed from a high vantage point. The one near the Bay of Pisco measures about 820 feet. Engravings of this magnitude were probably done accurately by using the sun's or moon's shadow for the seasons and days of the year. Other designs could record eclipses of the sun and comets, etc. and denote where they were last seen in the sky. Some of the designs depict spiders, eagles, peacocks and other birds.

Europeans are reported to have been seen near some of the

ruins, but they returned into the bush and vanished. Contact has been made with Assurins who have Caucasian characteristics, two of the eight tribes are 248 miles south of the capital of the Amazon, Manus Pahakanas and Araras (Rhodesian Chronicle 5.2.1971). These people are probably remnants of the pure-blooded descendants of Thera, who closely guarded their ruins and cities to preserve the ancient sciences, history and ancestry. They have learned to trust no-one in their fight for survival among the heart-extractors, head and souvenir hunters.

The Assurins could also be connected with the Byblos (Phoenicia, Syria) who traded with Egypt and other countries and overseas, crossing the Atlantic and settling in the West Indies. Some probably crossed the mainland of America and the Pacific Ocean to the Islands. The Byblos could have been following the Thera people, overshot the islands and landed in New Zealand and Australia.

The North American Indians use bows, javelins or assegai and ceremonial spears with copper heads. They wear their hair long, similar to natives of India and China. They live in wigwams or coloured enclosures round a group of dwellings, which are similar to the Africans, and those of Ancient Britain, use a back-drop loom similar to those in Egypt at the time of the pharaohs and quarry their stone by similar methods.

The Incas used string, knots and beads of red, blue, white and green. The colours probably carry the same meaning as those of Egypt. Green for heart of the newly-married, blue for knowledge, white for justice and geometrical alignment, black for age and red for youth. They were called 'Big Ears' because of their extended earlobes (based on the ancient Sun kingdoms of America). The Spaniards approached the land from the east and therefore came in 'peace' as Gods and the legend came about as a result of their connections with the Mediterranean area of Thera and Egypt.

When the island of Thera (Santorini, Atlantis), which is beyond the Greek Pillars of Hercules, became overpopulated, some of its inhabitants chose the sea rather than face certain death as heroes of sport and legalised murder. The successful gladiators or slaves were probably set free, but the loser was thrown to the alligators. Some of the heroes took to the ships with their personal possessions of grain, maize and livestock. The methods are clearly shown on Egyptian wall paintings. The people of Thera sailed into the unknown, beyond the Greek Pillars of Hercules, because of its association with the superhuman task they faced in crossing the Atlantic, which was named after them. Some of the less venturesome could have turned north and followed the coastline until they were a safe distance from their homelands and stayed in Europe. Some settlers may even have returned to Thera and encouraged others to join them, taking a chance to live in freedom.

When the island Thera blew up it was probably the result of seawater reaching the erupting volcano, which sent a tidal wave of destruction in all directions, and contact with the voyagers was lost.

Legends relate to geysers on Atlantis which produced opals and obsidian, which has a fiery gloss and is resinous. Legend also has it that Atlantis blew up and disappeared below sea level because of the evil ways of its people.

The Apache Navajo Papago Indians say that the east is black, which represents the warm coloured people of Ham (Noah's son); west yellow, for mixed parentage; north white, European and Greek; south blue, Libya, Bushman, because they, the Arabs of Morocco and some of the American Indian tribes used a blue dye on their body to protect them from the sun and loss of moisture. Due to the lack of fresh water, moisture was obtained from vegetation and watermelons, which affects the pigmentation of the skin. The precise description of the Navajo Indians positions Thera exactly with the countries and cultures of the Mediterranean people and must therefore pertain to the original ancestral homeland.

The Labyrinth basket work of the Pima Indians date back to the Mediterranean and Egyptian cultures. The Pawnee Indians of the plains place their dead in frames above the ground and wrap them in such a way that the air does not get to them. When only the bones remain they place them in a rock crevice, similar to some African customs where chiefs are placed in rock crevices.

The serpent of the Mississippi represents the days of the year, age of initiation and the rise and fall of life together with metric measurements. The head is triangular shaped, as a pyramid, with above it the circle of Ra. The curves of the snake are for the Sphinx with four sections for childhood and two resting on the base line for knowledge and initiation.

The American Indians have knowledge of the equinox and solstice which is shown in their leather and beadwork. The number of beads to a design, or the number of rows, give the 52 year cycle, days of the year and the angles of the equinox and solstice. It is compatible with the Zulu beadwork of Africa. The crosses are for the equinox and solstice which are vital for the growing of crops, winter storage of food and hunting. The feathered headdress represents the heart and feather of justice, Zoser, Sphinx, science and culture.

The Sciences are based on the moon, sun, equinox and solstice and the elements fire, earth, air and water are vital for the existence of man and animal. The Great Bear and Little Bear represent Ursa Major and Ursa Minor, the former includes the north star. The Serpent is for the earth cycle, the bird and feather are for justice, and the dog the Sphinx and the triumph of good over evil. All these constellations are close to the North Star.

The carving on the Indian peace pipe reflects the culture of the Sphinx, Zoser and Ra, which is probably the reason for its name (see Tutankhamun's 'lighter'). The Indians raise their right hand when greeting, as a signal and sign of peace.

The feathered headdress box lid of the Chippewa Indian has the pictograph of the Sphinx (Wisconsin 1850-75). The American Indians have the cultures which originate from the Mediterranean area and are based on the stories pertaining to the Bible from Adam and Eve (3037 BC) to the Ark (2348 BC). The Giants were the Philistines of Caphor (Crete) and the land west of the Dead Sea, which took the brunt of the Thera catastrophe.

Amazons are a race of female warriors of Scythia, which is to the north of the Black Sea. It is possible that there is a connection between them and the Amazons of South America. The American Indians used fire as signals, which resulted in disaster for those who intruded on their sacred ground or ancestral caves, where they try and preserve their ancient cultures and traditions. Had the Europeans settlers respected or realised the significance of their fires, religious gatherings and animals (bison), the Indians may not have been so intolerant and would have retained more of their beliefs and sciences.

Zimbabwe was more fortunate in having rock formations which saved bloodshed, though the Africans still perform religious grass burning on the arrival of the rains to clean the lowland and promote growth.

The Tupilak Eskimos' soapstone carvings are of animal/man mixture. The position of the postures reveal the teachings of the Sphinx. One has the hindquarters and forefeet off the ground and a bald head for the child. The second shows the forefeet off the ground and is in a sitting position for youth, while the third has long hair with the forefeet off the ground for initiation. The fourth is for age which is shown on the face and has three feet resting on the ground.

The Igloo and the African hut are similar in shape. The walrus is treated as sacred because they say it is a reincarnation of ancestors. The diet of walrus and elephants is probably an indication of food and plenty. The tusks of both are of ivory and represent the lifecycle.

The Easter Islanders of the Tamuto Group in the Pacific Ocean have Mediterranean features. The small art treasures are of sculptured stonework and engravings of animals, some of which have human heads (Sphinx and Eskimo art). The large stonework is of the same magnitude as that of Stonehenge, the Pyramids and Wailing Wall, which is 1,550 feet in length and 58 feet high. The five lower strata date from King Herod, the next four are Roman and the upper strata, made of much smaller stone, the Mamelukes and Turks (Pupils calendar 1972-73 published by the Education of Youth Departments of the KKL Jewish National Fund, Jerusalem) similar to the Lion Gate walling of the Mycenae, Greece, the mural wall of Easter Island and the Inca wall of Sacsahuaman near Cuzco, Peru.

The islanders could only use the stones available locally and these had to be carried up the mountain from the valley below or quarried near the summit by fire, similar to the methods used in Africa. The ground would be levelled for building.

It is possible that some of the Byblos tried to follow the

Thera across the sea and were either repulsed, blown off course or sailed on to New Zealand to become known as Maoris, who do have the curly hair of the Africans. In contrast, the Australian Aborigines have the straight hair of the Indians. The Thera people could have hidden in the family caves of the island, which are underground and now hold the stone carvings and replicas made by their ancestors, which could be reconstructed, should the need arise for them to leave the island by building ships to cross the ocean.

New Zealand has the monoliths or 'totem poles' similar to the American Red Indians. The Maoris were not rediscovered until the Europeans found them hundreds of years later. Australia has rock art pertaining to Ra, the Sphinx, Zoser, initiation and astrology. They use boomerangs similar to those found in Tutankhamun's tomb.

The statues of Easter Island were probably made to represent the days of the year, science and culture, but not all of them had been completed before the 'Long Ears' War. Incas and Buddhists have 'long ears', Buddha and the red topknot are very similar, but long ears are also a sign of nobility in China. The Buddhists could have fled from China with the advance of Islam and Kublai Khan. The war ended in death for all but one of the 'long ears' in a ditch. The statues were pulled down and the 'short ears' reigned supreme. The 'short ears' are similar to the people of Thera and probably wanted the statues positioned for the equinox, solstice and 52°, because the three crosses were so close together they probably worked in with each other. The rock engravings on the south west side are not unlike the North American designs used for special ceremonies to do with the science of the universe, equinox, solstice, Sphinx and culture.

Easter Island is very roughly triangular. The equinox and

north/south equals the west side coast line. The 52° is from the south Rano Kao to the north east Katiki. The winter solstice is along the La Perouse Bay line on the north side of the island.

The huge stonework was pulled across the island on log rollers and then mounted by methods which placed stones under the principal stone as it was being levered with long poles and tipped into the hole.

Postcards.

A Zululand bride and bead work with 'warrior' husband in tribal dress.

B Zulu witch doctor with his knobkerrie and switch of authority.

C Married Zulu woman with her bead work on her hair.

Zulu rickshaw boys

Zulu dancers with ostrich feathered headdress.

A   Married Zulu woman in tribal dress with her love letter bead pedents. The colours used in the design all have their own specific meaning.

B   Zulu rickshaw boy.

C   Zulu warrior in tribal dress with shield and assagai.

Photo: U. M. Erasmus

Postcards.

Rickshaw boys and decorated rickshaw Durban.

Rickshaw boys showing their beadwork and headdress Durban.

Bushman table and head wood carvings from the Okavango area.

Herero women

AFRICA

The rock art of the Tasili Plateau has a painting of ladies with hairstyles similar to the Japanese riding cattle. Traditional brides wear a belt of knowledge at the waist and diagonal lines for the geometrical alignment. The headdress has an assortment of symbols of Zoser and the Sphinx. Hair protrudes from the centre of the headdress in the form of a curve for the lifecycle. The brides whiten their faces and wear symbols in their hair.

The religious, cultural and scientific knowledge of ancient Japan and Egypt at the time of the pharaohs appears to have had much in common. Japan means 'the source of the sun' and is written in a square for the word sun, the source is written in the form of a cross for the equinox and the inverted 'V' with the point at the cross intersection of the bar for the solstice, 52° and lifecycle.

The Japanese script is written up and down, the flag has the circle of Ra in the centre with the sun's rays radiating from it for the science of the universe. They study the stars and universe and have symbols and buildings comparable with the teachings of Zoser and the Sphinx. 'Haniwa' is a clay figure which used to be placed next to the graves in ancient times. It has circles for the eyes and mouth of Ra and the long equinox nose continues right down from the top of the forehead, very similar to some of the African carvings. The arms were carved for the lifecycle, one pointing to the ear and the other to the centre of the body.

Other paintings at the Tasili Plateau show foreign regalia of friends and foe, some with body shields and spears, the lines and dots representing Zoser and the Sphinx.

There is another painting depicting the choosing of a tulli, long horn bull, with the cows kept separate. This may have been the first introduction of pedigree animals. Some of the men have wide brimmed sombrero hats to keep the sun off their faces. The bulls were probably gathered for the choosing of Apis the Bull. This was done by the markings and was the start of cattle being bred to type. Longhorns do not seem to have been used for headdress and may, therefore, have been a form of recognition of the breed which was used in the fields to pull the plough and produce milk for dairy products. Longhorn cattle were also domesticated by the Red Indians. The tulli can withstand drought conditions and are indigenous to Africa. The markings help with identification and thus save branding.

The rock art of the Tasili Plateau was above the water level of the Thera tidal wave and has therefore survived the catastrophe. Other rock art may have been lost for ever because it was below the water and sand levels. It was probably the result of the tidal wave leaving the desert and sand in its wake which prompted the first southern migration of the North African people. According to Gen. 13 v10 Egypt was once a well-watered area. There are circular ruins at Jebel uri Darfur in the Sahara similar to those found in Zimbabwe.

An African Numbian from Numindea, bronze head jar found in Alexandria (bronze having been introduced to Egypt in about 1600 BC) has a high headdress similar to the headdress for initiation and marriage of the Guto people of Zimbabwe. This bronze head could pertain to the 'African' (Mediterranean area) because of the colour of the metal and the features. The Worozvi tribe of the Fort Victoria district of Zimbabwe claim that they are a branch of the people who migrated from the north and used to have picture writings similar to the Egyptian hieroglyphs. They dress in skin aprons back and front and wear a skin covering one shoulder, the same as the Bushman. They keep domestic animals as did the Lydians and claim they were connected with the building of the Zimbabwe ruins. Tribal laws and customs are based on the Old Testament and the Holy Bible and some of them are akin to the Jews' food laws (Lev. 11), circumcision (Gen. 17 v23) and Ten Commandments (Exodus 20). They despise the abuse of sex and lack of self-discipline. Hebrew script is written from right to left and so is the African and Bushman's.

The hairstyles vary between the tribes and are probably affiliated to the styles prevalent in the northern parts of Africa at the time of their migration. The Zulu women have their hair styled in the crown of northern lower Egypt. The maidens perform the snake dance at a specific time of the year, when the participating maidens have reached maturity and marriageable age. The snake dance represents the lifecycle. (Statues found in Greek temples show snake dances were performed there as well.) The black leather skirts worn by married women are made up of four-finger wide strips, the top being rolled at the waist so that the baby can sit comfortably. This roll represents the whirl of emanating knowledge and Ra. The length and width are correct measures.

The beadwork and colours all have their specific meanings pertaining to the Egyptians in design, scientific and geometrics. The men wear coloured discs in their ears which give them large lobes (Buddha). The warriors have black and white shields of skin in the shape of a tortoise with reinforcing squares for Zoser and the groupings for the Sphinx and science of the universe and knowledge.

The rickshaw boys wear head decorations made of cattle horns (Sphinx), feathers (initiation, heart and feather of justice) and coloured trimmings which make them very colourful as well as scientific. The decorations and seed rattles are similar to those shown on rock art paintings in the Sahara which are associated with maturity. The Bushman uses similar leg rattles.

Bantu stands for 'B' leg and foot for the geometrical alignment. 'N' chevron; 'T' 'D' lying on its straight side are for the lifecycle. The click language of the Zulus and Bushman denote the North African Mediterranean area because the click language set them apart from other tribes.

The Sandawe Tanganyika still speak the Bushman Hottentot language and resemble the capoid people, particularly the Hottentots (the Origin of Races).

The Modes Kry women of the Okovonga have a grass plait over the centre parting of the hair, similar to those depicted on Egyptian works of art where the snake is placed over the crown of the head and the hair hangs in very fine plaits or ringlets, held off the face by a loose bead chevron design band at the base of the skull.

The Ndabele have individual coloured rolls of beads on their arms and legs similar to the people of Uganda.

Xhosa have the light skinned faces of Nigeria (Niger) Ikoi Ikop society. The Xhosa use white for initiation into manhood and the head covering is similar to the top of the Kiaar (house) roof of Nigeria, where the men cover the body with ash to make it white for wrestling.

The Swazi have a similar hairstyle to the Mende people of the Sierra Leone.

Lesotoland (Basuto) is protected by mountains with a very steep ascent. The Basuto people use sure-footed horses similar to the Arabian horses. Basuto in hieroglyphics is 'B' a foot and leg 'S' similar to the hairpin bend ('T' 'D' lifecycle).

The non-click language suggests people from West Africa,

north of the equator, whose migration was affected by the slave trade and advance of Islam, resulting in a second migration.

The Ibo Nigera tell the story of when man became so greedy that he lost his land and God ascended into heaven. This story could pertain to the Herero of South West Africa, who fled from the north and kept their faith. They claim their land is no more, which probably relates to Islamic takeover. The Herero could have been connected with the pharaohs Hieros and On. This would explain their name.

Damra 'M' a bird and Ra God. Herero are very proud and tall people. The women wear a head covering in the shape of the hieroglyphics for 'sky' knowledge of the universe, which could incorporate the hairstyle. This head covering never comes off in public because the penalty is death by suicide or murder. They dress in full length dresses over a number of petticoats. The colours of the shawl and head covering match. They usually have small families of only two children, one for culture, the other for science and male and female.

Dumah is a tribe of Ismail. 'U' hand measure hieroglyphics (Greek triangle and pyramid) Dumah means angel who presides over the realm of the dead but also means 'silence'. Hebrew Amulets (Gen. 25 v14).

It is a common practice for African women to cover their hair as a form of respect. The colours are carefully selected according to the fertility cycle.

The Ethiopian cross decoration combines African culture below, Christian and African inside and Christian outside. The shank design is African with the number of designs Christian. The symmetrical is Christian and the geometrical, African.

The African musical instruments are designed with the science of the universe and culture of Zoser and the Sphinx in mind. Some are governed by the design, sound and trimmings, e.g. securing of skins over the top. Colours and designs cover the outside of the drum casing. The wind instruments start with the Kudu horn and Jewish Shofar or ram's horn (Gen. 4 v21, 22) and single notes which can be played with two fingers. The rest of the wind instruments are graded by the number of holes. The original bagpipes date back to the time of the Egyptian pyramids.

The string instruments range from the monochord to the lyre, guitar, zither, harp (Egypt, Irish) and piano (Gen. 4 v21 and 3870 BC Jubal).

The mbira (African piano) has the top and bottom set of twelve notes making a total number of twenty four for the age of initiation. The mbira is played by sounding notes on alternate sides of the centre note, it should not be played for more than a few minutes as the music is taxing for the player.

The Marimba (xylophone) has one or more players with their own set of keys to strike in sequence representing the Sphinx and Zoser. It is very pleasing to the ear when three or more different sizes are played in harmony.

The percussion and leg rattles are correctly made with the leg rattles having one set for the teachings of Zoser, the Sphinx and the age of initiation and the other for the lifecycle of 52 rattles.

There are families of drums, and up to five in a set. The language of the drums is emanated through the rhythm beat and represents the small drums for the child and animals, the large for the initiation and the bird, while the middle size is for the descent of the lifecycle.

The harmonizing, hand claps, repeats, etc. are all synchronised to give the correct interpretation and rendering of the whole for the science of the universe, initiation, Zoser and the Sphinx.

A balanced orchestra takes into account the first, second and third instruments per group, the number of strings, percussion trimmings, etc. The holes of the wind instruments are no longer taken into account. The movements and tempo pattern are derived from the Egyptian 2/4, 3/4 and 4/4 time. The Egyptians included musical instruments in their pyramids, which shows their age.

The African women plant the crops, carry the water and, with the exception of the Zions, make the beer for the menfolk to drink as they smoke and relate tales of bygone days and dream dreams of the future. A rich man has more than one wife to see to his needs and work the fields. The children stay at home with their mother until the boys are old enough to look after the livestock, while girls learn the domestic side of life until they are old enough to marry. The girl's father will expect a down payment of cattle when the marriage takes place and the balance when the first child is born.

The women use the quern or goyo* (Shona) to grind the mealies and grain. Querns are made by first heating the centre of the stone or rock and then striking it at a certain angle to shape and chip the stone, just as was done in the Stone Age. In September the querns are used for measuring the moisture content of the air. Water is poured into the quern after sundown and the level is marked and if it remains, there should be good rains. If the quern dries out there is little or no moisture in the air and the crops will be poor. An average is taken over the month and the verdict given.

---

*Shona

In the drought season of 1972/73 the quern measure dried out two or three times a day. In the wet season of 1973/74 water remained in the measures for two or three days before needing refilling.

Some querns are marked with two level lines for Ra, then 5 'V' marks positioned between lines 4, 5, Zoser, the Sphinx and pyramid. Two 'V' marks the line of the sun, one each for the mist, normal rain and heavy rain. Wind directions are also taken into account by dropping a handful of fine sand or soil next to the quern stone so that the wind can blow it.

The meg* is the spherical stone which is placed on the quern goyo when it is used for measuring the angle of the sun's shadow scientifically.

The hari* is the name given to a triangular stone of any size, such as the one on the Acropolis at Zimbabwe, or a smaller stone used as a marker with cultural or scientific meaning. Hari is also the name given to the earthenware jars or beaker cones, which are used geometrically. Shards of earthenware found at various sites are of cultural and scientific significance. When the hari earthenware is broken it shows that the area is no longer in use and it ensures that the science is not lost, because new areas have to be found and symbols have to be made. The colour used on the hari is produced from haematite stone. If the hari was not broken when its lifecycle was completed, people would not know if they were correctly placed or not. Consequently, if a place lies dormant for a while, everyone knows that the markers are out of date.

The Africans can tell the time by the sun, by placing a stick (obelisk) in the ground and then marking off the sun's shadow on the ground for the hours of the day, similar to the 'T' square of the Egyptian Merkhet. They also place 3 or 4 stones so that

Goyo stone

Goyo stone without meg, used to gauge the moisture content of the air.

Denonia Farm, Harleigh

GOYO STONE

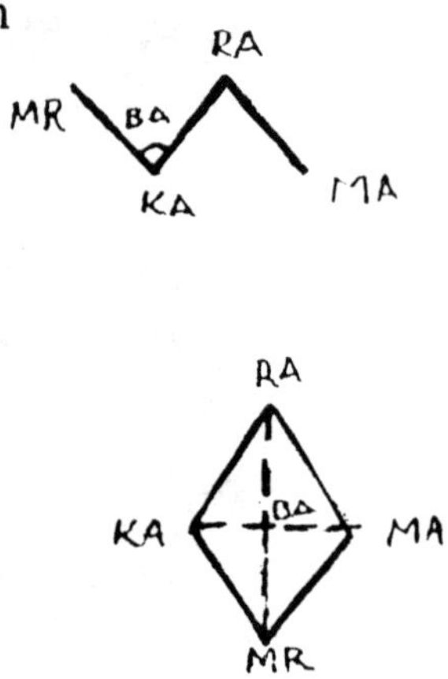
RA
MR
BA
KA
MA
RA
KA
BA
MA
MR

Importance of letters
in place names

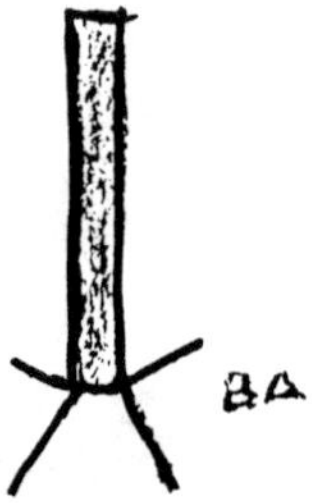
BA

OBELISK SUNDIAL

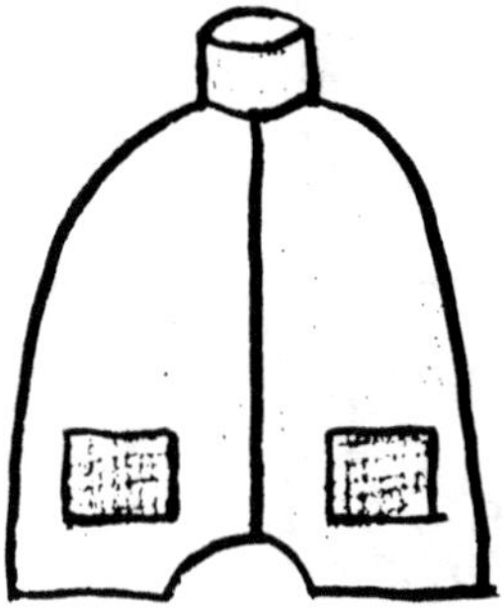

CHITURO

HARI STONE

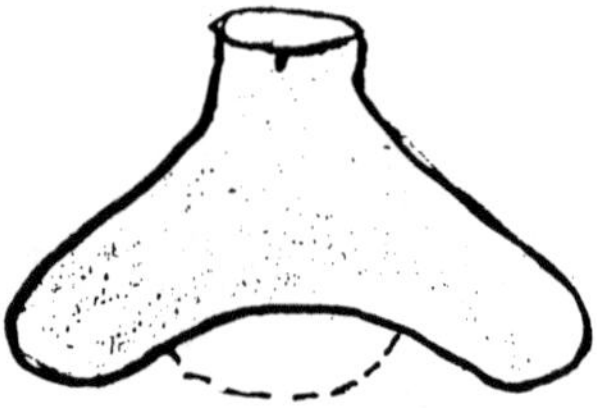

CHORONGO

MBIVA HARI

GROMON METAL

CHIPFUKO

DENGA,
EQUINOX MEASURE

Drawn by
U M Erasmus

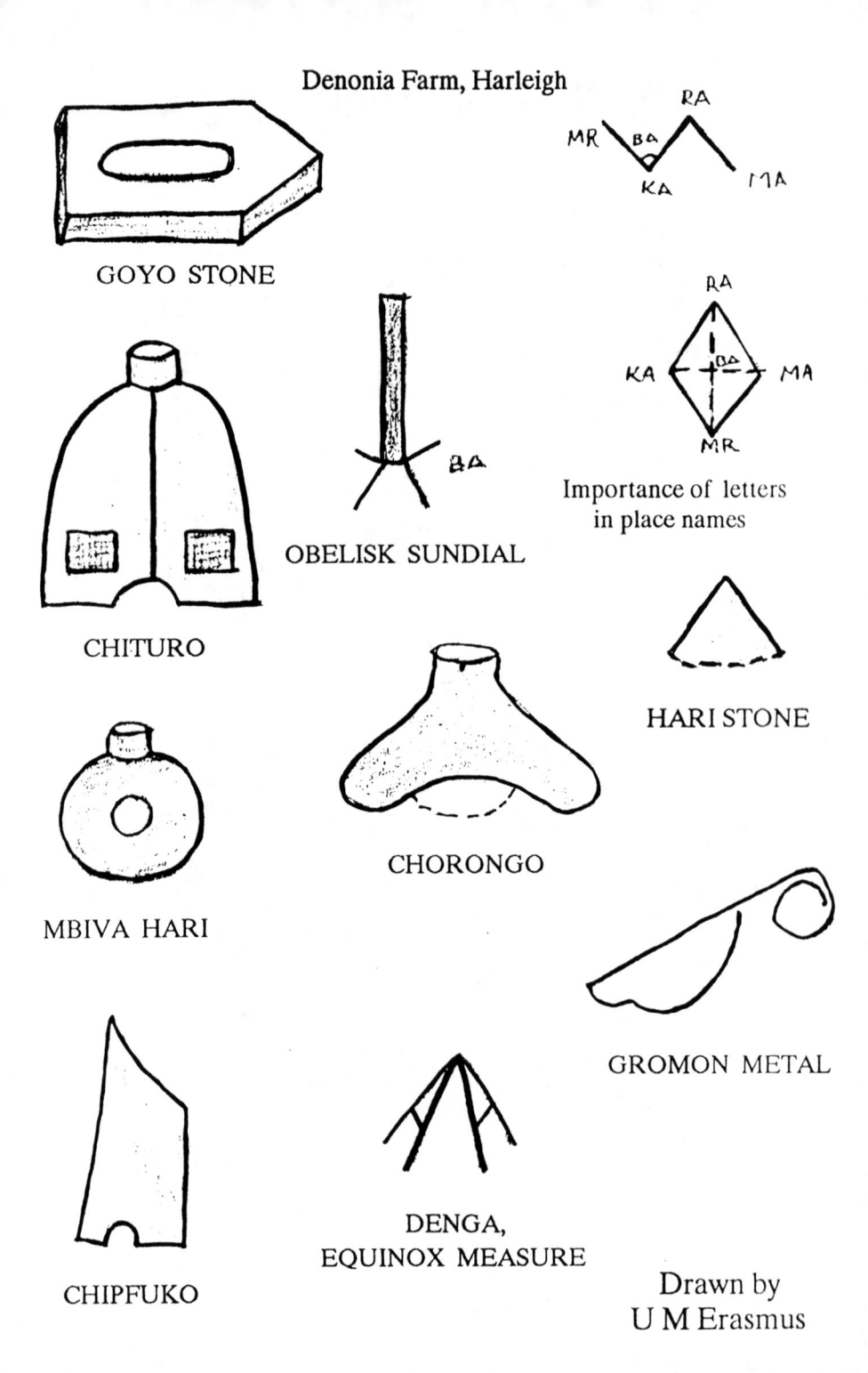

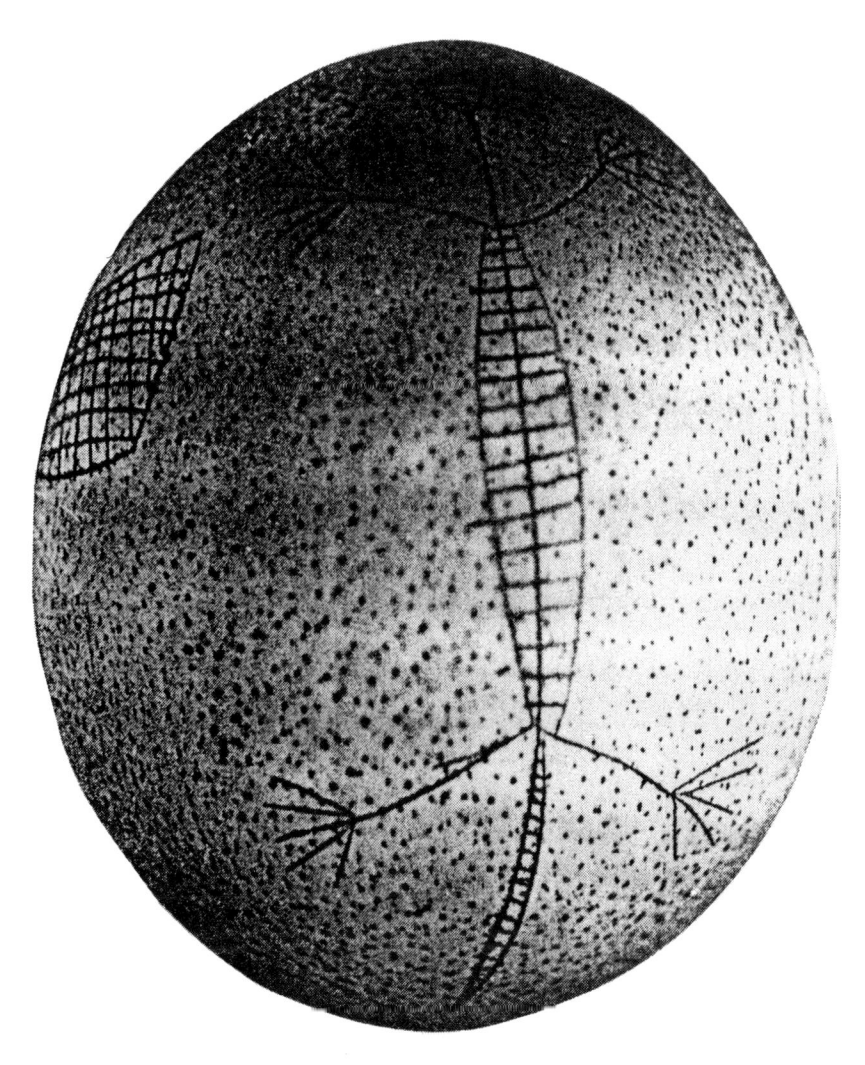

Ostrich egg engraved with a stylisation of a crocodile.
National Museum, Bulawayo.

Prehistoric Rock Art Book.

Prehistoric Rock art, Rumwanda Rock Shelter, Ndanga, Fort Victoria area

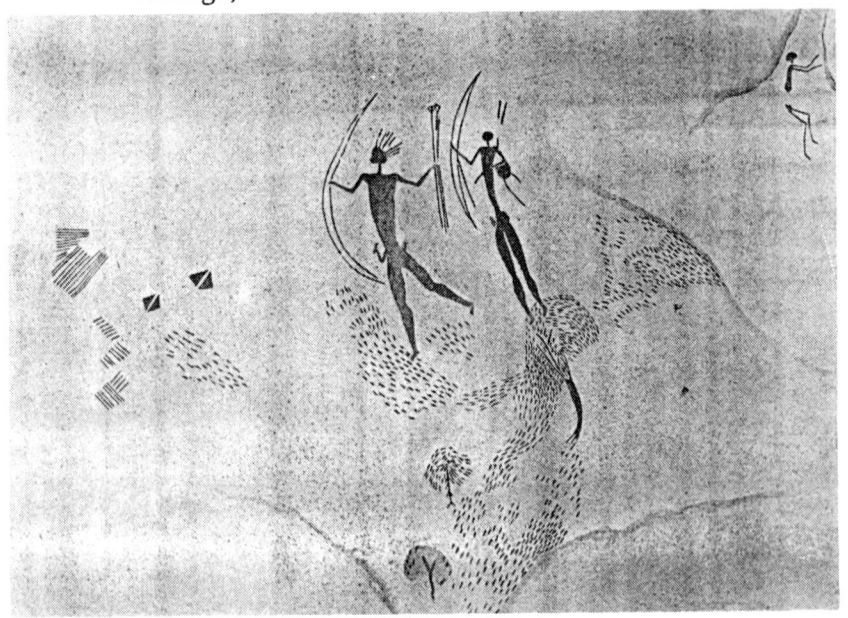

Prehistoric Rock art, Saffron Walden Farm

Prehistoric Rock Art

Rock painting, Diana's Vow Farm, Rusape

Prehistoric Rock Art Book.

Prehistoric Rock art, Mucheka Cave, Mrewa,

Drawn by U M Erasmus

Muromo Farm, Umtali, rock paintings

Drawn by U. M. Erasmus

Prehistoric Rock Art Book

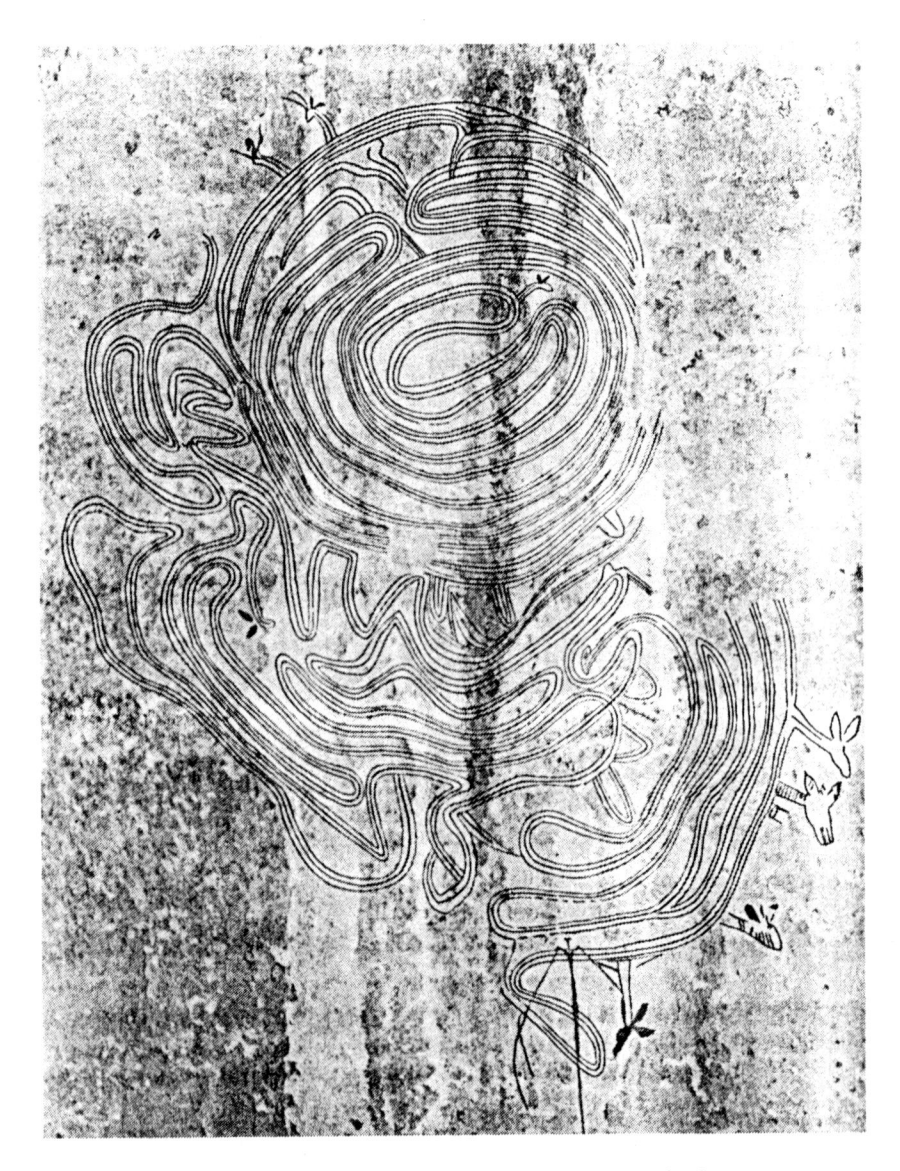

Muromo Farm, Umtali area, The Labyrinth.

Prehistoric Rock Art Book

A   Silozwane Cave, Matopos National Park

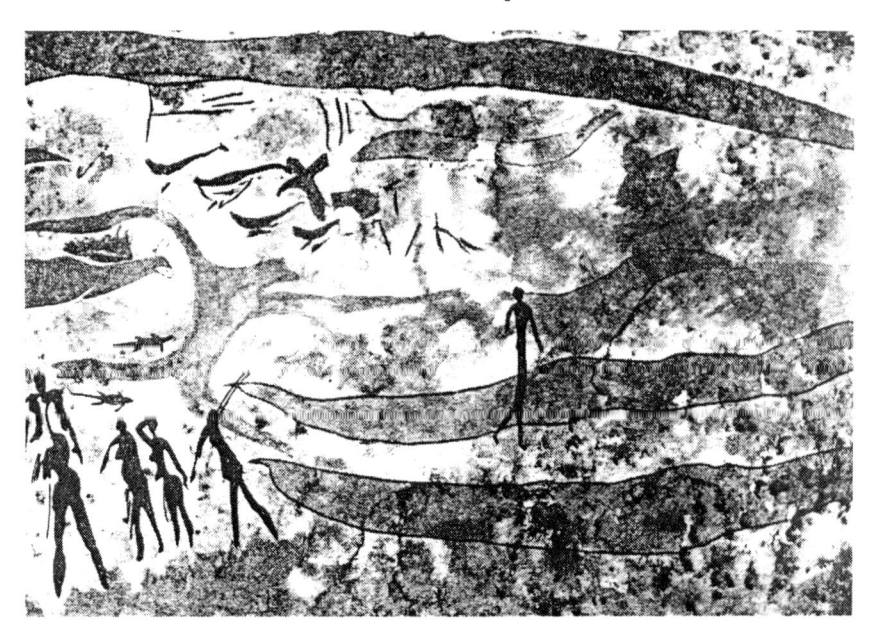

B   Silozwane Cave, Matopos National Park

Prehistoric Rock Art Book

Silozwane Cave, Matopos National Park

Rock Art of South Africa

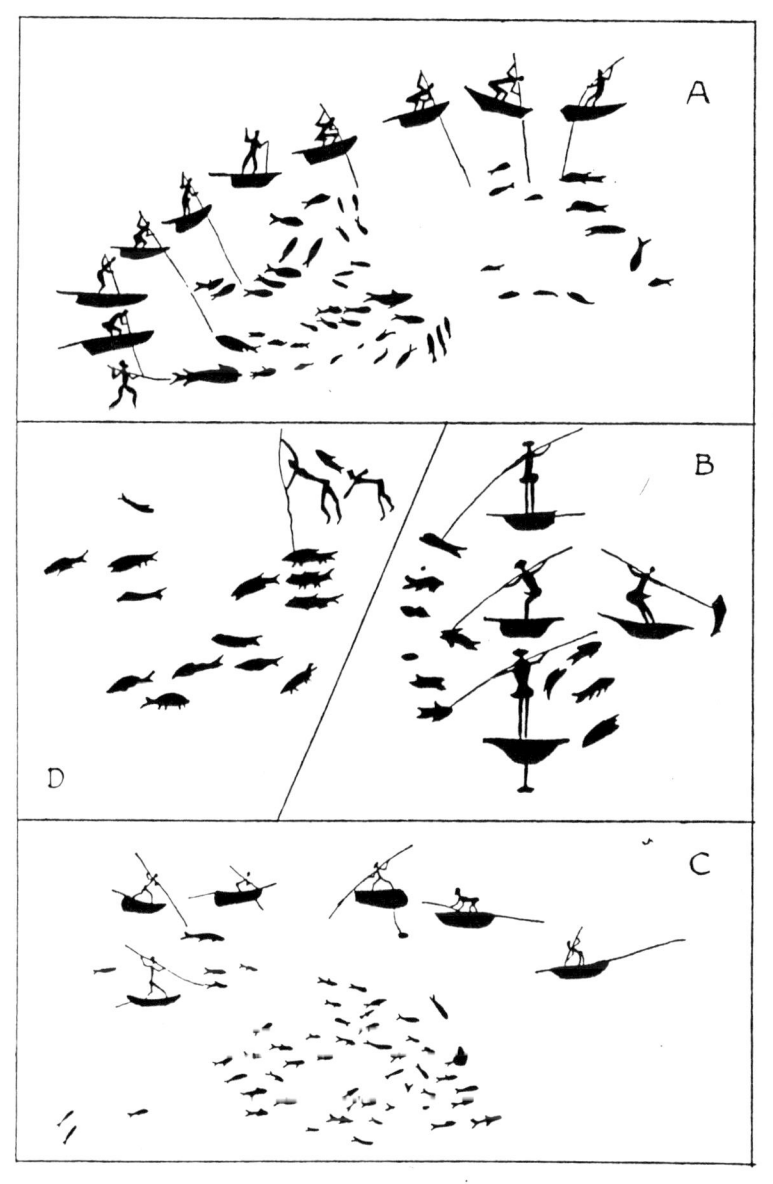

A   Mpongweni Mountains, Underberg, Natal. Harpooning fish

B   Kenegha Poort, Griqualand East - Harpooning fish.

C   Tsoelike River, Basutoland. Harpooning fish.

D   Uysberg, Ladybrand, O.F.S. Harpooning fish.

La Rochelle, Clarens, O.F.S. Animal under rainbow

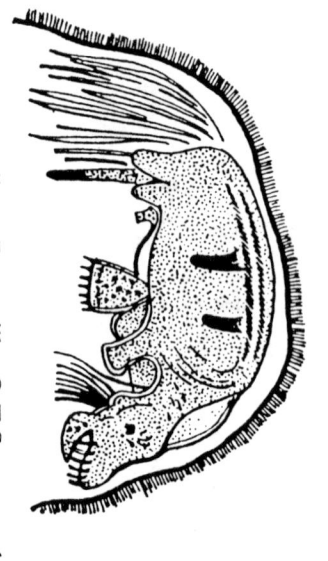

Klein Aasvogelkop, Rouxville, O.F.S. spotted animal under rainbow

Willow Grove, Wodehouse District, Cape Province, spotted animal with fish

Giant's Castle Game Reserve, Natal. spotted animal.

Rock Art of South Africa

Prehistoric Rock Art.

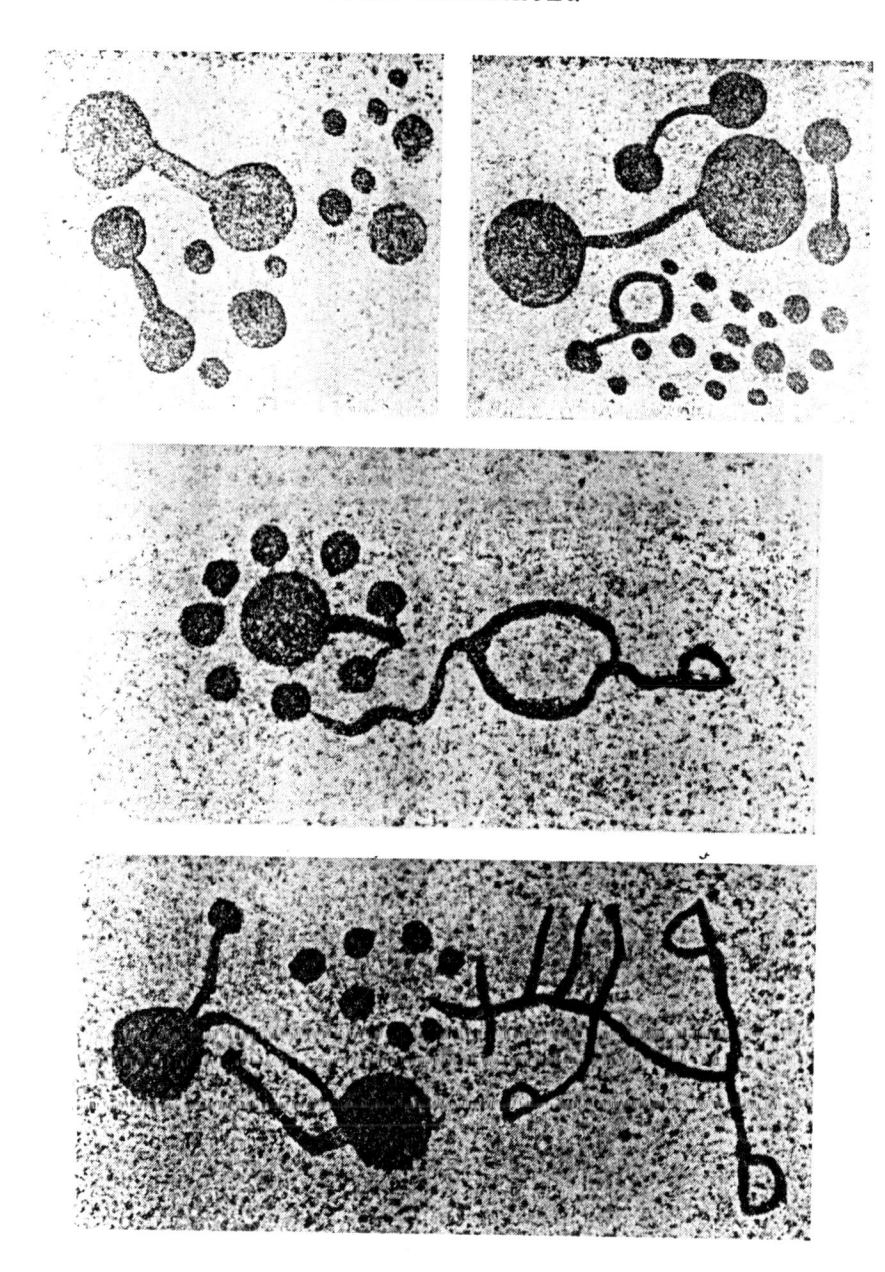

Rock engravings, Melsetter area, set lines and circles.

Mythical creatures

A   Barrow Hill, near Wepener, O.F.S. horned snake
B   Eland Cave, Drakensberg. winged buck.
C   Giant's Castle Game Reserve, Natal. elephant-like creature but with claws and extended trunk.
D   Harmony, Griqualand East.
    bogey animal and Bushman.
E   Kamberg area, Drakensberg, Natal.
    half human, half buck figure.
F   N'dedoma Gorge, Drakensberg, Natal. Sphinx of a praying mantis.
G   Giant's Castle Game Reserve, Natal. Sphinx chameleon.

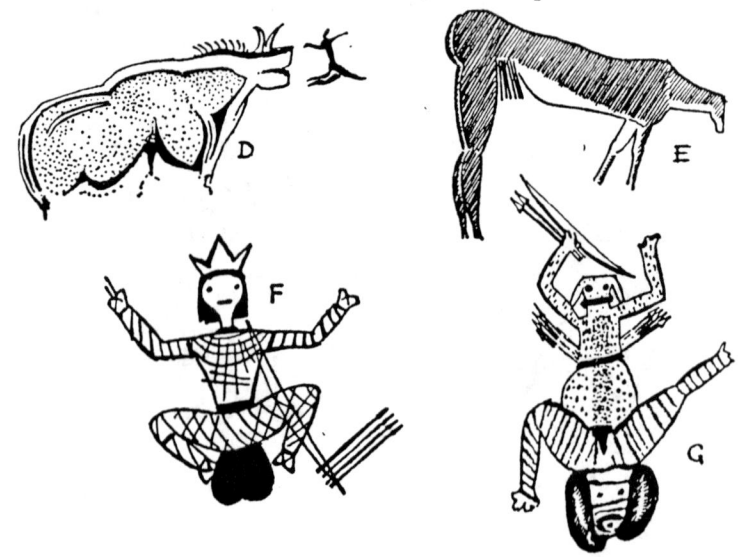

the sun strikes them at certain angles for midday and evening which mark the lunch and going home times.

The earth cement markers are also for the mutaro* which is designed by placing a stick or pole in a pakati* hollow in the ground and marking off the shadow of the sun at 6 am, 11 am, 2 pm and 4 pm. The design is derived from the Egyptian Ba, a duck with feathers on its head. The mutaro* resembles the duck's foot and so connects it with Egypt and hieroglyphics. The circle and asterisk are used for the design of the engravings.

The torso is for the equinox when the sun is directly overhead at midday, shines through the neck onto the hollow below, at sunrise and at sunset shines through the arch and equinox holes onto the hollow.

The torso chituro* of a female has the two halves for the Sphinx, the five lines for Zoser on either side of the arch totalling ten. The bust represents the pyramid, the lifecycle and passing on of knowledge to the next generation. The squares have seven lines across for the sphinx and five down for Zoser. The coned neck is for Ra and the hole at the base of the cone is for the equinox. The arch represents the lifecycle - when one ascends the pyramid and reaches the top, the new generation takes over, as the older generation passes on its way down the other side of the arch. The concave saucers on either side of the torso are for the geometrical designs and line up with the holes behind the saucer. The side of the torso and the arch represent the pyramid, the concave saucers Ra.

The Sphinx has the body of a lion and the upper part of a human and poses the riddle 'what animal goes on all fours in the morning and at noon (equinox) on two, then in the evening (solstice) on three? The answer is man, he crawls on hands and knees in childhood, walks erect in manhood and uses a staff in old age.

The front view of another Sphinx has the long vertical base with the lifecycle in the centre and on each side, above the arch, four short lines. The top cone is for Ra and the equinox. The bust is geometrical.

An oblong wall Mukombe* with the loophole in the centre near the base of the wall represents the pyramid and the climb to the top on the one side, followed by initiation, practice and then the passing on of knowledge and experience ending with the descent and close of life. The concave saucer, the wall and the hole give the geometrical alignments. The oblong wall measures the moisture content of the air. Grain seeds are placed in the hollow for three or four days and when they germinate it is the sign that there is water in the air. If the quern dries out, so do the seeds, and growth cannot take place and crops will fail if there is insufficient or no rain.

The prehistoric remains from the Hari Rotten Row Museum, Harare, are comparable with the Mastaba's of the Egyptians' first dynasty. The African earthenware pots are shown on Egyptian hieroglyphics. Africans break pots at the time of burial as a sign of death and the end of life, but also as a prevention against disease.

The word kaffir is probably derived from Khaba the pharaoh who is said to have built the Layer Pyramid in Egypt and pertains to a native of Kafiristan in Asia.

The line designs are called Imbwe* for all earth cement designs and shapes i.e. crocodile, tortoise, hollows, curves and straight lines, pointers, etc. The sun is aligned with them at 6 am, 11 am, 2 pm, 4 pm which gives the 52° and 72° for the lifecycle and universal evolution and lifespan at the time of the solstice, which is called chondo*. Imbwes often mark burial areas and should be treated with due respect.

The equinox chirimo* is worked out in exactly the same way as the Egyptian pharaohs, from at least the time of the Scorpion Pharaoh Menes who is shown holding an 'A' nhungo* (Canaan script 1000 BC) for a 'K' ox head, which was written as an 'A' and used in modern times for the gnomon of sundials for telling the time. At the time of the equinox the two 'A' symbols are made up as follows, each side is one and a half metres, a bar is placed halfway or a metre from the top, the 'legs' go half a metre into the ground and the feet of the legs are half a metre apart. The two 'A's are placed with the apex touching and the feet a metre apart. The sides and the space in between are equidistant, it then becomes known as denga* is positioned so that the sun shines directly through the legs so that the bar casts a shadow between the opposite 'A' at sunrise and sunset.

The geometrically designed headrests are used as direction guides and are probably handed down from one generation to the next as an heirloom. They are connected with the teachings of Zoser and the Sphinx. Tutankhamun had an iron headrest in his sarcophagus, iron having just come into use and therefore being of great historical value.

Some of the iron objects found at the historical sites appear to have weathered very well. This may be due to the method used in smelting, which preserves it and slows down the rusting process. Tutankhamun had an iron knife placed in his coffin which still shone when it was opened (this may have been the one that inflicted the wound on his face). He also had an ivory headrest and an opaque blue glass paste one. The headrest placed under the sleeper's head would prevent it being taken without the sleeper's knowledge.

The African tribes have 'iron gods', which are similar in design to the sections shown between the legs of Tutankhamun's throne and the ecclesiastical throne and the triumph of the upper over the lower mind. The 'iron gods' represent the declaration of war and are, therefore, not displayed except at such times, consequently they are kept covered in an animal skin which, in turn, may help preserve them. It is also a declaration of war, when the word 'iron' is used in connection with a person's name. A doll with metal has the same sinister meaning.

When the Africans move from place to place they take all their pots and bedding with them. They round up their cattle and livestock and leave little to show where they have once been. Moving frequently is necessary because they are self-sufficient and the earth must therefore be able to support them and their lifestock in food and water in order to survive.

The wide gap between the lasting structures which were built on outcrops of rock (kopje) 'Who built his house upon a rock and it fell not for it was upon rock' (Matt. 7 v24) does not affect the arable land or cause soil erosion. The pole and daga huts with the thatched roofs were only used for a short length of time and did not need foundations, and at the same time cleared the land for cultivation. Mud plaster was also used for the pyramids of Egypt, where there was also a great gap between the permanent site and construction site, the living quarters of the workers. The local Africans kept well clear of the ruins so that they did not attract attention to them, except when they were in use. The Africans appear to have buried some of the chiefs at the site of the ruins, the same as the pharaohs of Egypt, and this is probably why the ruins were ransacked by the Arabs, who were fortune-hunters.

When the chiefs want to test the young initiates and find

out just how much they know about the laws of science and culture, they send round word that the final test for the passing on of knowledge to the younger generation will be held at a certain time and place coinciding with the summer solstice and lasting about a month. The youths are circumcised and allowed to have the knobkerrie, which is a stick with a knob on one end. When they become old they have the iron head through it turned upside down to show that sex is of little interest to them as they are descending the pyramid of life. The Zions (African) are a religious group pertaining to Zimbabwe. The leaders of the local group have long loose robes of green, blue or white with the 'asterisk' for the equinox, solstice and 52° and carry the symbols of the pharaohs crook for culture. They use the langauge of the drums and musical instruments. The followers run around in circles in alternating directions for the appropriate number of times pertaining to the teachings of Ra, lifecycle and days of the year, Zoser and the Sphinx. Zuva* is the name given to the sun, Mrra is the name given to god (ascent to God). Their yearly initiation gathering was held at Zaka near the Zimbabwe Ruins for the 52 year cycle including the 1950s and each participant allotted to attend must attend no matter what the cost or circumstances, because it pertains to the initiation which must be completed before marriage can be entered into. They have retained their knowledge of rock art, stone construction and musical interpretation and rhythms of the original ancient cultures, proof of initiation being circumcision which is also a form of hygiene. The Zions burn the veldt (grassland) between the winter solstice and spring equinox** to promote growth, the ash puts nitrogen into the earth and controls the pests which need oxygen to live.

**Southern hemisphere seasons

The burning also clears the earth of waste matter so that the water does not get polluted when the rains come, a basic form of health preservation. The heat from the fires forces the hot air to rise and the cool air to rush in and, if moisture is in the clouds, rain or drizzle will follow. The grass will turn green and there will soon be plenty to eat for the animals, whereas the dry grass which was not burnt does not afford much nourishment.

The witch doctors are probably a remnant of the ancient herbalists, as traditions are handed down from generation to generation as a matter of family hereditary traditions. They use the switch of authority, the geometrical woods and small animal bones, which are paired for male and female, the male being the larger. Smaller pairs of bones are for children. Stones are red, golden/brown (tiger eyes are found in Africa and represent eyes). A chicken is used if the person is sick. The evil spirit is transferred into the chicken. If the person dies it becomes a form of last rites. Often, modern medical attention, had it been given at the right time, could have saved the life. Modern medicine, however, is often used as a last resort when it is too late so that the witch doctor's reputation is not challenged.

The chiefs are known as Shamba, lion, and the Egyptian pharaohs were also associated with the Sphinx. The chiefs are chosen by the people for their knowledge of the ancient sciences and culture, because it is they who must pass the young initiates, while the headman title is handed down from father to son.

The oblong piece of wood with diamonds, chevrons, curves, etc. are all for the equinox, solstice and the 52°. The diamond is geometrical and represents Zoser, the chevrons represent the Sphinx. If two or more are combined or represented they can be added to the meaning desired of one, two, three, four, five, the Sphinx and Zoser.

Twenty is the age to start initiation training and twenty four the age of full initiation. It takes four years to complete the course.

The following items were on display in the Bulawayo Museum:-

An axe with a wooden handle covered with copper 'cord' for the age of initiation and the rise of the pyramid. The connecting rods are for the geometrical design and the Sphinx. The circular markers are for Ra and the square is for Zoser. The all metal ceremonial axe resembles a small 'f' and 't' joined together. At the bar of the 'f' the base of the 't' is geometrically designed with the 'f' representing the pyramid and lifecycle and the handle of the 't' Zoser, the science of the universe and knowledge. The two sections represent the Sphinx. The ceremonial axe made of wood with the iron blade passing through the eye at the thick end has the pyramid at the one end for the lifecycle and 52°. The eye is for Zoser and the equinox. The upswept iron curve is surmounted with a spear for the passing on of knowledge to the next generation and the Sphinx.

The Bushman has a 'U' shaped bag similar to those shown on the rock paintings. These bags have the trimming for cultural knowledge of Zoser, the Sphinx and the pyramid. The two beads at the base of the bag are for Ra, the Sphinx, equinox and geometrical alignments.

A second bag is in the shape of a diamond with a pointed base and leather thong trimming for the science of knowledge. The rounded top point joins a square loophole for the equinox and the passing on of knowledge to the next generation, the pyramid and Zoser. The 'U' of the upper half is for the lifecycle and the trimmings all pertain to culture and initiation.

The string of seven rows of beads represents the science of

the universe, initiation, Zoser, the Sphinx, days of the year and probably the seasons and moon phases. It is, in fact, a complete work of science. There may also be a personal row of beads pertaining to history and ancestors.

The ivory symbols are similar to those shown on some of the rock art paintings and have the marks pertaining to the sciences of initiation, the circles of Ra, the curve shapings for the lifecycle, the 'face' for the pyramid, the three dots and lines for the Sphinx, the geometrical lines for the equinox, solstice and 52°. The sets of three, four and five lines and bands are dedicated to the Sphinx and Zoser. The geometrical diamonds are cultural.

The decorated ostrich shell is probably one taken from a deserted nest. The shell itself represents the days of the year because of its structure, the figure's head is 'U' shaped and has five chevrons and three short lines. There are five fingers and toes on the end of the lines. The body has twenty horizontal lines and so has the tail for the training and initiation. By adding the body and limb lines together it gives a lifecycle of 60, less the chevrons and head marks for the lifecycle of 52 years. When the head total is added it gives a total of 68 years for the Bushman's lifespan (shortened by the living conditions).

The love arrows have the chevrons for the age of initiation, geometrical alignments and culture. These arrows are pocket size and are directed at the rump of the bride to be as a form of proposal. Bushman are highly skilled scientific bow and arrow hunters, which is the reason why the oryx and gemsbok still exist in the arid country of the Kalahari but are extinct in other areas. The Bushman could be classed as the first game farmers of Africa, as it is thanks to them and their philosophies that Africa once had an abundance of game which roamed the land

and kept nature in balance. The gun will go down in history as the curse of civilisation because of its killing power, and use for greed, vanity and ignorance of survival of animals and man. Snaring of game is also a callous form of killing (Ecclesiastes 3).

Had the game been preserved and used for game farming it would still have been plentiful and profitable, as it requires little attention or financial outlay other than water holes, which by their existence would attract other game which would then remain within easy reach even on the poorest of soils.

The introduction of domestic animals, other than those needed for milk and dairy produce, is detrimental to the land. Erosion is caused by over-grazing, creating deserts, and the animals carry diseases contagious to men. Game is disease-resistant and therefore healthier than domestic animals. Under normal conditions and habitation, domestic animals should not have taken over the land at the expense of natural game because the game keeps insects and nocturnal life on the move at night, helping control their numbers, and gets small doses of disease, which builds up resistance and immunity. Domestic animals, however, rest at night in confined areas and therefore receive greater doses of disease and become ill. Where game has been shot to extinction, insects and vermin have increased alarmingly.

'Clean' animals (Lev. 11) have germs in the bloodstream, which is why they are bled, 'unclean' animals retain the germs in their body fat and the cholesterol clogs the blood stream which causes blood and heart conditions and increases the severity of other diseases. Some of these germs die with boiling, others by freezing.

The food laws were incorporated in the Bible. The Egyptian diet during the enslavement and certain foods eaten by the

Jews after the Exodus, caused upsets to the system and they were therefore classed as unclean food. Those that did not upset the system were considered clean. This applies to anyone who has abstained from eating 'unclean' food for a certain length of time and then partakes again, due to the chemical reaction. Jews, therefore, keep dairy produce, which is alkaline, away from meat, which is acid, and allow two hours between eating meat and dairy products. It is quite possible that the foods classed as 'unclean' are the cause of incurable diseases. It is also possible that 'clean' foods are a cooling agent and have a similar reaction on humans, which makes them suitable for the tropics, while the 'unclean' foods have a heating reaction which makes them more suitable for the colder climates. However, the two should never be mixed. Eskimos eat a lot of 'unclean' food and do not feel the cold, but if they changed to 'clean' food they would feel severe cold.

Doctors may one day diagnose and predict prolonged sickness in patients by their blood group, which is prevalent to certain diseases such as cancer and other incurable diseases. This could help people to guard against certain diseases pertaining to their blood group and for doctors to prescribe preventative medication, bearing in mind that those who eat 'unclean' food are more vulnerable to disease than those who do not.

Some Indian doctors take an interest in the medical science of astrology, which assists them in their diagnoses. The blood groupings and astrology could be included in medical practice and deter unscrupulous people from taking advantage of the less fortunate.

India suffers from overpopulation and desert conditions, while Brahmin cattle are considered sacred, which allows them to roam the streets for food and tit-bits without which they would surely die. The milk can be used for dairy produce. Their dung is collected in baskets, put out to dry and used as fuel for fires or for plastering walls and floors. Flat dung can be stacked and made into a wall and save wood and other materials which are costly or in short supply.

Women whose horoscope shows that they will not marry are married to trees so that they can water and look after them and so afford protection from those who would use the trees for firewood, the construction of homes, or cremation.

South African Zulus also use dung for the floors of their kiaars. They work it until it is quite smooth and their bare feet make it shine. The kiaars are kept spotlessly clean and are circular and domed like an igloo. Long grass is selected and cut, then bound together with natural twine strips of bark or reed from the river to build the structure. Other tribes place poles in the ground, plaster over the gaps with mud and place a circular wooden cone frame roof on top of the walls and cover them with selected long strong grasses.

Bushman build similar constructions when vegetation allows, otherwise they will make do with a lean-to against a thorn tree and a few bits of grass for a roof. The sleeping area is just a depression in the earth where they rest their head on their bent arms and hands to keep the insects off the face and out of the ears.

BUSHMAN

The first historical records were those of the pyramids, because the art and hieroglyphic records, the culture and hierarchy of the pharaoh's. The first religious Hebrew texts appear to have been written after the Thera catastrophe, between 1300 and 165 BC, under the adverse conditions of 30 years in the Wilderness at Petra, cut off from outside interference concerning the laws, statutes and code of life of the Ten Commandments.

There may have been a connection between the Queen of Sheba's wealth and her gifts to Solomon 1033-975 BC (Kings 10 v10 and Kings 11 v1) and the payment of the scribes Bible (Bilan el Moluk, Valley of Kings and Biban el Harim, Valley of Queens). Solomon was the tenth son of David and second by Bathsheba (Queen of Sheba from Mareb - South Arabia).

The Laws of Moses are based on the principal teachings of Zoser. The days of the week are derived from the four days of Zoser and two for the Sphinx with the seventh day rest, so that knowledge could be passed on from one generation to the next.

Abraham instituted circumcision (Hagar, his wife, was Egyptian) because in the desert and wilderness there is a shortage of water which creates hygiene problems. Where water is abundant bathing is considered healthy and a form of purification resulting in baptism (Lev. 16 v1-13).

The Lydians, originally from the Mediterranean, became known as Bushman who, when faced with extinction and only a remnant of their former nation, vanished into the Kalahari where they have been able to exist by utilizing the liquid from watermelons and roots. Because they know how to work out the equinox and the solstice, giving them accurate directions, their knowledge of the stars and 52° year cycle gave them an indication of when to expect good and poor rains. Their diet and climatic conditions would affect their stature and skin pigmentation (Numbers 11 v5) and sleep and rest also affect stature.

The word Kalahari can be split into Ka (Egyptian for descent, down Africa) and hari, the equinox and geometrical alignments. Sahara has the Ra ending. The tidal wave of the Thera catastrophe left desert in its wake 'wrath of God', The reason why so few skeletons have been found is that Bushman no longer able to keep up with the struggle for survival, endanger the lives of the younger people and the rest of the group who have to move on because of the seasons, food and rainfall, and leave their old people behind protected by a shelter with as much food and water as can be spared. Eventually the hyenas take the occupant of the shelter. The Bushman use ostrich eggs to store water. When the shells break they are used for making beads. The ostrich can live in arid country and can make the difference between life and death for the Bushman.

The praying mantis (Hottentot god) is so named because of its four animal legs and two arms which show the ridges of Zoser. The head is triangular, it has wings to fly as the bird of initiation. Some are green coloured, representing the heart, others are brown for knowledge. They have a blue waist underneath with a dot in the centre. The fact that this creature is so aptly named shows that the Hottentots and Bushman had a lot in common.

The pastoral Hottentots probably consisted of young Bushman, wives, children and old people, while the Bushman hunters were the fleet-footed youths. The Bushman and Hottentots were therefore one and the same people divided by habitat and probably the two migratory periods.

The red-skinned people of Thera, Lydia, Asia Minor and

the red pigmentation of the African Lydians (Bushman, bowmen) adhere to the ancient teachings pertaining to the Ten Commandments and Zoser, middle and end (Rev. 1 v8).

Four, a perfect square, 10 the quaternary system which was their method of counting. Zoser also taught silence with only more advanced pupils permitted to make decisions after initiation. 'Children should be seen and not heard', 'honour thy father and mother' (Exodus 20 v12). To know everything is to be called Ziva* and to know nothing is to be called Zero* Shona.

The Sphinx taught four - the crawl; two - initiation (bird); three - the stick of age. To know, dare, act, keep silent, the heart and feather, the measure of justice by which all humans are judged and weighed in the balance. Hunting was forbidden 'Thou shalt not kill' (Exodus 20). Male animals were later exempt due to necessity and so the balance of nature was preserved. The use of the crocodile and tortoise as direction markers the Sphinx and Zoser. Culture, science, Ra cones and circles worked in with the optic equinox, solstice and 52°, the days of the year, seasons, female fertility, astrology and astronomy.

On, Heliopolis, was the original home of the Sinaitic script from which the writings and records are derived. It also formed the basis for art, engravings, sculpture and paintings which are interpreted from right to left, the same as the Hebrew script, and from bottom to top for the ascent of the pyramids, lifecycle and hieroglyphics.

Pyramids are found all over the globe and belong to the ancient cultures and sciences. The Zimbabwe ruins have a circular layout with decorated walls for culture and geometrical alignment. Stonehenge has the circular layout and the upright stones and lintels for alignment.

The Bushman avoid the use of graven images (Exodus 20)

in their rock art by nondescript features with only the sex indicated, animals are clearly shown because they represent culture and science and incorporate the Ten Commandments. Animals see, hear and speak no evil.

Whenever humans have been denied animal company, delinquency has resulted, as they have not learnt to share their love and care or accept responsibility for themselves and others.

Bushman are pink coloured when they are born (Numbers 11 v5) and darken as they grow older and with living conditions, vegetation and liquid. (Birds' plumage can also be affected by their environment and diet.) They have the Mongolian spot on their skin over the sacrum. To mention only two of their visible characteristics, their dental bone structure and climatic adjustments are comparable with the genus of Mongols, American Indians and Eskimos. The hair is spiral while the Africans' is woolly. The African is of a different genus. The Bushman's posture is probably due to their sleeping curled up against the cold. They have not become acclimatised to the extreme temperatures. Sleeping on one's back usually results in a flat posterior.

Bushman are the only people of Africa to have lived in various areas between the Mediterranean and the Cåpe, where various art treasures were found, including those at Tsodilo Hill and the Balancing Rocks of the Eirdrop Kopjes and the horizontal parallel line on the Dolerites boulder near Rietfontein, Eierdorp (Mier), north west Cape Province.

Before a painting is undertaken the artist has to find the right rock surface, a sheltered position and correct direction, preferably facing north west for the more equable climate, as the weathering of the rock will darken and eventually obliterate the painting. A cave is formed by making a fire against the rock surface in order to peel the rock for their requirements. The firing of the caves denotes the direction of the wind and indicates the coming of the rains. The Bushman become noted as weather prophets. They took into account the direction of the prevailing wind and rains, as well as the direction from which heavy rains could be expected.

The artist then had to know his subject and collect root vegetation, shrubs and trees for the dyes, and have the necessary tools. He would paint with a feather brush on the hard, not yet weathered, surface. It is, therefore, certain that the rock art is part of the initiation training undertaken by the art instructor or the youth. The actual painting was virtually a religious work of art pertaining to God, culture, science and code of survival. It is, therefore, possible that father and son worked on the same painting, figures being undertaken by each set of youths. This could account for the varying qualities, colours and proportions as well as the overpainting.

The dyes for the rock paintings were taken from ground roots, shrubs and trees, some of which seem to have been incorporated in the paintings. The bark of the tambootie (spirostachys africanus) tree is taken off and cooked in water until it produces a red colour (youth) it has the thickness of ordinary paint and is ready for use after 24 hours. The wood of the cork (commiphora glandulosa) tree of the 'never say die' species is cut and allowed to dry for three to four days. Then the sap is collected and cooked with water to produce a white paint. Roots are taken from the young trees of the mountain seringa (kirkia willmsii) and, after cooking in water, give a yellow coloured paint, blue is produced from the leaves. The leaves of the palm produce the green. The trees themselves are depicted on some of the paintings. There is a monkey's tail (vellozia retinervis) which grows on kopjes, the leaves collected from the stem provide a yellow paint. If overcooked it becomes black, the colour of age. The fibres of the monkey's tail can be separated to provide a brush.

The euphorbiaceae, euphorbia family, produces a milky latex which is probably used as a preserving agent for rock art and, therefore, was an important factor to take into account when paint dyes were being prepared and used.

The sweet thorn tree gives the red preserving dye which is used for fishing equipment.

Ruins and art are marked by the vegetation of the cabbage tree (cussonia spicata), Kaffirboom (erythrina caffra) and aloes (Psalm 45, Song 4, Numbers 24, Proverbs 7). The latter is used by the Bushman for bows. The aloes' resins of volatile oil of balsam and olibanum and aromatic gum resin were probably used as incense at the time of initiation, as was the case with the pharaohs of Egypt. It is also used as an insect repellant in areas where smoke from the fire has been eliminated. The red aloe and trees show up against the landscape and the 'red' season coincides with the initiation. The solstice is for the male and the equinox for the female and crops. The summer equinox and solstice virtually coincide with one another in Zimbabwe, because of the distance of the equator.

The Ilala palm Hyphaene Crinita can be used for food by tapping the trunk and raw materials. The flame lily (gloriosa superba) is predominantly red in the low veldt where the rainfall level is low, but is yellow in the mountains where there is plenty of rain. Vegetation around the ruins was chosen or planted for its colour, significant use and characteristics. (Technical names taken from 'Trees and Shrubs of the Kruger National Park' by L. E. W. Cood.)

The rock engravings are preferred to rock paintings in the

mountainous areas of Inyanga, Melsetter, Victoria Falls and the Drakensberg, because of the high rainfall, mist and dampness which weathers and darkens the stone and would soon obliterate any paintings. The engravings are usually well out of the way of intruders. The stone constructions and rock art appear in conjunction with each other and were in all probability undertaken as part of the initiation training. The stone constructions were maintained by those undergoing training so that the art and buildings were preserved from generation to generation.

Painting and engravings can easily be dated to within 66 years by the positioning of markings, the equinox and solstice of the original creation and present day equinox. White markers, white figures or natural formations to give the alignments are always there.

The Lydians, Bushman, worked their way down through Africa or settled in Zimbabwe, making their homes in the Inyanga district where the mountains provide the temperate crops, rainfall and cold winters. The valleys, on the other hand, would provide the tropical crops and would be hotter in the summer. The North African coast is just north of the Tropic of Cancer and Zimbabwe is just north of the Tropic of Capricorn. They terraced the mountains, conserved the earth and rainwater and grew their crops as had been done in Egypt along the River Nile in 4000 BC. The terracing would also protect the crops from the cold wind and force them to grow quickly as the stone would retain the heat of the sun and keep the plants warm.

Terracing was probably done by the sun's shadow, the same way the pyramids were squared and built. The culture and scientific knowledge was also used as a guide for the design and layout of the constructions.

Ruins in Zimbabwe are sometimes marked by a triangular

hari stone at the highest point of the construction, such as the platform area of the Acropolis at Zimbabwe Ruins and Nyahokwe Ruins. Both are positioned at the highest point of the ruin area for the ascent of the pyramid and lifecycle, they also act as markers for the trained eye to see.

They were skilled in positioning big boulders such as the Balancing Rock of the Giant's Playground, Epworth Mission and Zimbabwe Ruins and dressing them into geometrical alignment.

There are too many spherical boulders to mention but a trained eye can see them and pick them out among the ordinary rocks and boulders, as they are usually in prominent positions and geometrically positioned or serve a specific purpose pertaining to culture and knowledge. It would appear that these stones replace the larger constructions dating from the advent of Islam and it is, therefore, possible that this marks the period of slavery, tribal unrest and the advent of European civilisation.

It was the Lydians, Bushman, who imparted their knowledge to Africans who were friendly towards them. They respected those who respected them. Purity of character was an important factor in their culture. Sex was treated with respect. Disrespect or making fun of the Bushman or his stature could lead to trouble. 'Love thy neighbour as thyself' (Matt. 19 v19, Romans 12). The short stature of the Bushman and Pygmies gave them a better survival chance as they required less food than taller people.

When first approached, or when leaving domestic, cultural or religious areas, direction rules must be observed. From the east is a token of peace, birth, life, sunrise and youth (Moses approached the Promised Land from the east). From the north represents God, light, midday, knowledge will be passed to the next generation. From the west is a sign of death, sunset, war or destruction and from the south silence, unknown, hidden darkness, midnight. This is why there are so many entrances and exits to an area. A weary traveller would be seen accorded the correct reception and fed if appropriate.

The raising of the right hand, clapping with the right hand uppermost, right over wrong, good over evil. The Egyptian engravings and paintings pertaining to death have the figure facing the west with the left side, shoulder and foot forward. Those pertaining to peace, if they face to the west with the right side, shoulder and leg showing forward, good over evil. Hence the front facing shoulder of Egyptian art. Egyptians cut off the right hand of their oppressors, but saved those who showed humanitarian courage in the face of danger.

"Z" in the first position of a word - Zoser had his pyramid built in his lifetime. "Z" in the third position - Giza, the pyramids here were built after the pharaoh died. The Layer Pyramid indicated that the Pharaoh died unexpectedly. The letter "Z" is used in the word Mitzraim, which was the name of upper Egypt until Pharaoh Egyptus (1485 BC) just after the Thera catastrophe. Zion (African) Zion (Hebrew) Zodokite Sect (Hebrew) Zoroastrian (Zend Avesta) Aztecs, Zimbabwe, Zulu, Zeus, Zodiac, etc. The "Z" of the Bible and the chapter, verse and numbers all pertain to the teachings, culture and science of Egypt and mark the important sections.

The Matabele names with the letter "Z" denote characteristics pertaining to Egypt such as birds, colour, feathers, nesting times such as the Wahlberg eagle which has a hatching period of 72 days, the grey and brown hawk also have "Z" names. Makalanga (Shona) words also have "Z" (Zvimandivonerepi mufananidzo (Bushman paintings) Kukwira (ascent) Kudzaka (descend) note the 'ra' and 'ka' and meanings.

Place names can be seen easily by looking at a map because they are too numerous to list here. The positioning of the letter "Z" gives an indication of the importance of the place. Zimbabwe has the first letter "Z" because it is an important place and is revered by all, which is the reason why Rhodesia was renamed Zimbabwe after the famous ruins. The "Z", when placed on its side, outlines the pyramid with the start of the "Z" for Ma, birth, Ra, apex - God - followed by Ka, death, the last leg forming the angle for the respective degrees Ba. Should the line go down, forming a square diamond, it becomes Mr for the unknown, or up and across the equinox. The direction of the Ba angle gives the Mr meaning through the 360°.

Matchstick lettering from Pyramid and Sphinx can form a square, or triangular shape. The letters remaining constant are YAMIHNX, what is learnt in youth is built upon during initiation. Other letters are EFKL TVWZ numbers are 147.

The stone buildings usually have their own characteristics such as Zimbabwe with its soapstone and high conical towers; (and cones rounded and on the ascent) Nalatale with its square cones on the top of the main wall and the double alignment and earthmarkers used in conjunction with each other; the Nyahokwe Ruins and the square niches and raised platforms; Chawomera and its two vaults and loopholes; Harleigh and its loopholed wall with the central cave features; Khami and its boulder cones and passage construction.

It is possible that each tribe of chiefs has its own design by which they are known and, so one section did not encroach on the others' land, they were virtually land and boundary markers. The art of construction was guided by the population, weather, vegetation and materials found in the area.

In Zimbabwe the optic alignment for construction of the ruins and markers is governed by the sun being directly overhead at midday. The choice of stone kopjes gives a firm 'fixed' lasting base for foundations and they do not take up valuable arable land, nor are they in the way of tribal warfare or easily accessible. One must be going to the area for a specific reason as there are no other diversions on the way. Stone kopjes were not defiled by previous occupation, the imported soil being undefiled means burials, etc. pertaining to the ruins are there by design. The boulders are usually bold (Motopos, bold head) (distant view of the hills) this type of boulders gives an indication of the surrounding being preferred for caves, paintings and burials.

It will be interesting to see if the ruins and art treasures maliciously destroyed in Zimbabwe and elsewhere are governed by the pharaohs' curse, because it breaks the links between the groups. There was a ruin on the Chigarapasi Hill at Chireszi with geometrically curved walls and loopholes, but the stones have been removed and used for the construction of a modern building close to the area. The symmetrical hill, Datanga, has baobab trees growing on one side only and there are hot springs in the area.

The Egyptian pyramids and artworks work in conjunction with each other and the same is applicable in Zimbabwe, where the ruins and rock art go together. Dhlo Dhlo actually has the painting adjoining it, Harleigh Farm has the painting close to it, so has the Labyrinth near Umtali. Bushman Point Ruins near Harare are too dangerous and disintegrated to warrant further mention, there are also ruins in the Matopos complex.

The rock art of Africa is undertaken at the time of initiation, when the young initiates participate in decorating the stone face of caves. The theme of the artistic work is based on the ancient teachings of Ma, Ra, Ka, Ba, Mr culture and science needed for survival. Rock art is, therefore, a lesson for all to see as tablets of knowledge and serves as a written word.

The symbols of initiation are used at the time of the equinox and solstice. The merging of extremes and the equilibrium of the equinox and knowledge of the night sky helps with navigation, the seasons, and serves as a calendar.

The items of gold, wood, bronze, ivory, pottery, stones and colours, with the exception of iron, are used as symbols for science and optic alignments.

The number of lines, dots etc. of animals, birds, calls, feathers, eggs, the hunter and hunted all have their meaning. For instance, the giraffe sees all, hears all and says nothing. The elephant is vegetarian and, because of its size, is a sign of plenty. The hippo grunt, buck markings, horn and spoor impressions represent science and culture.

It is only through observing and learning about the laws of nature that humans can learn the laws of God and survive in coexistence. When vanity and greed take over, the heart becomes empty and life extinct.

ROCK PAINTINGS OF MASHONALAND

The majority of the following descriptions and recorded numbers are taken from plates shown in Rock Art of Central Africa and, wherever possible, I have tried to complete the painting and, by so doing, create a greater understanding and depth of meaning portrayed by the artist/s.

The Chikupu Cave, Masembura Reserve, Northern Mashonaland No. 5.

The group of figures with the headdress numbering five for Zoser and seven for the Sphinx 4, 2, 1. The front figure appears to have a bird head and a body shield covering the body and is receiving the stick of age and retirement after putting the newly initiated through their training. The knobkerries and symbols of initiation are being passed from one to the other down the line. The 'rocks' are divided for red, youth; yellow, initiation; dark red, age. There are two colours for initiation and two for age with the yellow for passing on of knowledge before the final descent. The yellow line marks the 'rocks' for Zoser.

(a) Domboshawa Cave. 34 - 422 - 1

The complete painting has a set of five Zoser buffaloes followed by a horse, which is slightly higher, and showing an elephant under them. There is a branch with four leaves and a giraffe's head beside it for Zoser and silence. Under these are a black and red buffalo for age and youth and two sets of men. There is a watermark and a section of figures in mirage. The new graduates in units of four, five and seven hunting bows and animals are as follows.

(b) Has the red line which represents the lifecycle and the figures holding their symbols of initiation represent the heart, feather and Sphinx. The colouring also denotes initiation.

Under this section a rhino is shown and, to the right, are kudu. The two in front and above are complete and there are two half kudus. In the next section, above more figures are a set of wildebeest followed by another rhino, but this one facing towards the earlier mentioned one.

(c) The dashes under one arm represent initiation. The bird has a circle of Ra and, from the shoulder, the teachings of Zoser and hunting. On the other side of the figure the heart and feather with the stick well off the ground is a reminder that age requires a stick. There is a fire hole on the south east side of the cave giving the optic alignments of the equinox, solstice and 52°, and the slope of the entrance is for the lifecycle. The hole itself turns into the rock but is well guarded by bees (section C is just above the painting and the geometrical fire hole).

Makumbe Cave No. 192.

This has the elephants representing Ra; the pink, youth; yellow, initiation and the dark colour, age. The Ra dots are for Zoser and the Sphinx. The figures have the symbols of initiation with the stance and colour indicating age and achievement.

Howickvale Farm, Umvukwes area.

The buffalo has the outline of the lifecycle and above the front legs are the figures of initiation. The head has the square of Zoser and the bird Sphinx is on the neck. Above the buffalo is the spotted animal with the dots of the universe and the outline for the lifecycle. The zebras are for science of the universe and lifecycle.

Mashonganyika Farm, Goromanzi No. 200.

The animals are for the Sphinx, the birds for initiation, and the three claws are for age.

Robert McIlwaine National Park No. 515.

The dark buck is for age and the dots are for the lifecycle.

The legs of one buck divide the quern ovals into groups for Zoser and the Sphinx. The yellow kudu gives the geometrical alignments with the head and ears. The yellow is for initiation. A buck is an antelope which does not shed its horns every year.

Somerby Farm No. 193.

The elephant represents Ra. The double animal has four legs, then matures onto two lighter legs. One buck has a figure overpainted to represent the Sphinx. The figures next to it are learning to stand upright for the initiation. The three hippos represent age and descent down the pyramid of life, leaving the younger generation on the other side of the dividing line. The snake at the top of the painting stands for the lifecycle and geometrical alignments. The tree gives the teachings of Zoser; the Sphinx and the leaves represent the 52 year cycle.

Caroline Farm, Robert McIlwaine National Park No. 194.

The bird dashes are for the geometrical alignments and the science of the universe. The fish have the fins for the lifecycle, the pyramid and the Sphinx. The dashes of the fish are for Zoser, the Sphinx and the initiation. The lines from the fish are parallel for the Sphinx and the set of ten are for Zoser. The elephant Ra is balanced on three legs for age. The dots are for initiation. The animals in the foreground have the dots of knowledge, the figures of initiation and the line of the lifecycle. The bird-animal in front of it represents the Sphinx. From animal to bird and returning to the three legs of the animal.

Kisanzi Farm, Darwendale No. 441.

The animals are for the Sphinx. The top one is 'flying' through the air for the bird of initiation. The fence lines are for the science of knowledge, Zoser and the Sphinx.

Robert McIlwaine National Park No. 529.

The crocodile has on its body the ridges for the age of

initiation and youth, which are divided by the figure of the initiation holding an animal in its hand. There are initiated figures overpainted on the crocodile, which has 24 dashes on the tail for the age of initiation. It has two feet on the lower side with claws for Zoser and the Sphinx.

The second crocodile has a ridge of 52 miniature pyramids on its back and is balanced on two feet and the tail. The head gives the geometrical alignment. The figures are the newly initiated, with the odd-coloured one giving the geometrical alignments.

Robert McIlwaine National Park No. 530.

The dots are for the science of the universe. The trees and leaves are for the age of initiation, lifecycle, Zoser and the Sphinx. The mountain mahogany trees are below the animals and a buck is beside the palm tree. The rest of the trees are seringa and peppers. The pathway is for the Sphinx, the markings on it for Zoser, the dark colour for age. The Chief may have been old and had his own idiosyncracies. The rock has the yellow tree section for the beginning, middle and end, with the clear parts dividing the section. The fourth 'rock' has the lines for Zoser, Sphinx, age of initiation and the 52 year cycle. The two bands are for the Sphinx and the four sections are for Zoser. The men have the feathers of initiation. The animal has the bird on its back and bird-shaped ears. The tongue has the lines of Zoser. The yellow is for knowledge and initiation.

Waltondale Farm, Marandallas No. 284.

The youthful figures go on all fours, then learn to walk upright, are initiated and receive the bow. The five 'feathers' shown on the shoulders represent Zoser and from the elbows two for the Sphinx.

Manemba Cave, Mtoko No. 511.

The downfall of age and the rise of youth is shown by the animals. The natural line represents the entering and leaving of the world, the line of initiation and the passing on of knowledge.

Lion's Head, Msana Reserve No. 225.

The young initiates have four arrows in the hand and the fifth gives the geometrical alignments, while the bow acts as the lifecycle. The second figure has two arrows and the bow for the geometrical alignments and a single arrow protected by an X. The buck is female, and therefore protected, so the arrow misses it as it stands balanced on two legs for the Sphinx.

Frees's Plot, Hatfield No. 82.

The buck stands balanced on two feet, which denotes initiation and gives the geometrical alignment. The centre buck is old, which can be seen by the length of the horns. Two are for the Sphinx with the three lines for age under the nose. One is also connected with a curved line for the lifecycle. The figure catches a staff of knowledge as he climbs up the pyramid of life.

Chinamora Reserve, Makumbe Cave No. 148.

The Ra elephants have the 'ribs' of knowledge and age of initiation, Zoser, the Sphinx and the lifecycle, the total giving the days of the year. The figures holding the heart and feather are yellow for initiation. The sable represents the Sphinx, Zoser and lifecycle and gives the geometrical alignments.

Zwimba Reserve No. 98.

One figure has two feathers for the Sphinx, the age of initiation and Zoser. The feathers on the back of the head are for the descent of the pyramid and the passing on of knowledge to the next generation.

Makwe Cave, Inoro No. 105.

The hunter and his mercy-killing of a buck with a broken leg. The animal below it has four feet on the ground and the second has two feet and a tail denoting age.

Lion's Head, Msana Reserve No. 224.

An old hunted rhinocerous on two feet has arrows balancing it. The rhino may have been destroyed because it was a rogue or dangerous.

Near Christopher's Kraal, North of Makumbe No. 186.

The graceful lines of a buck on the point of death show the reverence and compassion of the hunters, who compare it with the Sphinx walking on three feet, the horn indicating the completed lifespan.

Rodedede Cave, Mtoko No. 513.

The elephant represents Ra and when Ra dies so do the Sphinx and Zoser, which is shown by the dead buck under the elephant. The moral of the story is that one cannot live without the other. Therefore, both must live and keep to the laws of the universe and teachings of Zoser and the Sphinx, or all is lost.

Rodedede has the three 'de's for the beginning, middle and the end, death.

Inoro Makwe Cave No. 264.

There are five white lines for Zoser and seven for the Sphinx. The ridges from the head down the back to the parson's nose are outlined in white and mark off the pre-initiation age, initiation and the final descent ending with the geometrical alignment between the ears, representing the Sphinx. The head is a mixture of bird and elephant for Ra and initiation. The ridges are for Zoser, pyramid, Sphinx and give the geometrical alignment.

Mrewa Cave No. 481.

The elephant is for Ra, the ribs on the top are for the Sphinx. The square head is for Zoser and the trunk is for the lifecycle. The two short and two long legs represent the Sphinx and the tail, old age.

Mrewa Cave No. 466.

The bushman tell a story of Ra's elephant wife who was killed by two brothers. The foetus died in the womb and the fluid brought the other elephants to investigate. The one elephant has the vertebrae on the top and two short and two long legs for the Sphinx. However, the tail and trunk are being used for balance. The lines from the elephant show the 52° and the descent of the pyramid. The second elephant also has the very high vertebrae above its back and uses its tail and trunk. The bird-man near the elephant has the three fingers for death and is using them for balance. The parallel lines are for the Sphinx and are on the line of the solstice.

Chinamora Reserve, Makumbe Cave No. 238.

The Zebra represents the Sphinx, Zoser and initiation. The top animal gives the geometrical alignment from the face. The front legs are of human form, the back legs are those of an animal with the tail for a stick of old age and descent of the pyramid. The animal represents the Sphinx. The figure wearing the initiation apron has the 'Sphinx' parallel arms, the bow of Zoser and the lifecycle.

Ruchera Cave, Mtoko No. 391.

The zigzag 'lightning' is for the age of initiation, Zoser and the Sphinx. The river has the days of the year and the science of the universe. The curved line is for the lifecycle.

Ruchera Cave, Mtoko No. 220.

The front female figure's arm gives the geometrical alignment, and dots and dashes for knowledge. The central animals represent the Sphinx, with the 'ears' for Zoser and the horns for the lifecycle. The male in front of the animals has the lines for the age of initiation around his head. The dots on the wrists are for Zoser and the Sphinx. The dashes are the age of initiation and the lifecycle, the stick is for the descent of the pyramids and the objects protruding from the chest are the next generation in training for initiation.

Ndobe Hills, Mazoe No. 266.

Has the three red animals in front and the yellow-fronted animals behind for the initiation. The rear half of the same animal has black feet and tail for age. The animals give the usual geometrical alignments.

Ruchera Cave Mtoko No. 221.

The crocodile with two legs on one side is for the Sphinx. The other two legs are for age. The animal at the crocodile's head is for youth. The standing figure surrounded by animals has two feathers on the head. The animals pertaining to the Sphinx, circumcision and initiation represent the different stages of man from conception to death, (the fish and the flexed animal). The figure with the dark body is for the heart, feather and Ra. The bag is for the teachings of Zoser and the Sphinx, as are the large animals. The objects are for the initiation and knowledge.

Enkeldoorn Mangene Reserve No. 419.

The snake represents the 52 year lifespan and the animal type figures at the top of the painting are for the Sphinx and effort of learning to stand upright and then descend the pyramid of life.

Dengeni Cave, Zaka area No. 407.

The one white figure holds the Bushman's hunting weapon in his hand and the Egyptian flail in the other. He also has a feather in his hair. The four lines on his calves are for the Sphinx. The lines above the knee are for initiation and the ten dashes on the body for Zoser. The other white figure with the javelin has the lines of initiation and knowledge on the body, arm and javelin. The dark figure (shown facing), arm and stick give the geometrical alignment of the equinox. The two short Sphinx lines are on either side of the stick for the solstice and 52° on the lower trimmings, as are the sticks carried by the other figures. The white figures are geometrically positioned to give the optic alignment.

Theydon No. 132.

The figures are learning the Law of Knowledge and are graduating from the crawl to the upright posture.

Chikupu No. 22.

The right hand side figure has just received his animal skin apron to remind him of the Sphinx and the circle of Ra. The next top figure has the tools of knowledge and the one showing on the left, with the head of the bird emerging, has the arms off the ground and stands on two legs. The lower centre marks the group who do not take an active part in hunting, but make the tools and see to the training of others still to be initiated.

Rakodze Farm, Marandellas No. 401.

This rare painting probably represents the initiation and installation of a Queen as Chief (e.g. Queen Victoria or Queen Elizabeth II) and shows the initiation of women at the time of the equinox. It was probably painted by females and shows the bag of geometrical tools of office, the laws of Zoser, Heliopolis, Ra and the Sphinx.

Prospect Farm, Harare South No. 52.

The sexes, wearing their regalia and showing their knowledge of the sciences and marriage, mix for the first time after initiation.

Marangoa Hill, Darwendale 472

Has the ladder with 52 full rungs and dashes for the age of initiation. Four rungs are separate for Zoser. The picture suggests unfinished training or exfoliation of the rock face.

Cairnsmore Ranch Umvukwe Range

The animals represent youth up to the time of the initiation. The figures with animal (Anubis) heads show age, followed by the descent down the passage (Sphinx), burial and return to Ra (the circle). The thorn tree is for the tree of life and the red colouring for youth. The dots below the tree are for the lifespan. The white figures are geometrically positioned and represent the Sphinx, Zoser and Ra.

Carolina Farm, Lake McIlwaine No. 215.

Four figures in the lower group represent Zoser and the eight in the top section the Sphinx. The arms of the centre dividing figure give the geometrical position, the head is for Ra. The two figures in the foreground are for the Sphinx, with the three objects for the alignment and initiation.

Gambarimwa Cave, Mtoko No. 434.

Courtship of the newly initiated is shown by the lines on the body and the upright figures.

Glen-Norah Farm No. 2.

The dashes are for the days of the year and the science of the universe. The elephant represents God. The different stances of the elephants are for the stages of the Sphinx. One is standing on the two front feet and trunk for age, another is on four feet for youth. There is an animal/bird for the Sphinx. The triangular section of the painting has the parallel lines for the Sphinx, with the four figures ascending the pyramid of life, while there are three other figures displaying the 'pronged' headdress of age and descent of the pyramid of life. The snake represents the lifecycle, Zoser and the Sphinx. The dark figure at the top is ready for descent to the relaxed group, while the youth is ready to ascend the pyramid. The square section has the Sphinx parallel lines at the bottom with the three large and two small figures connected with it. The tree of initiation is at the side of the square and the objects above it are for Zoser, 4, 10. There are 10 'feathers' on the head of one figure for the quarternary.

Makabusi Farm, Harare East No. 20.

The male figure with the heart and four-piece headdress has four dots on his hand and holds the stick of descent. Youth is represented near the middle section of the body. The female descends the pyramid with the birds representing the heart and feather down the arm and another going down the three sticks.

Dengeni Cave, Zaka area No. 405.

The giraffe represents silence for Zoser and the position of the feet for the Sphinx. The white initiation apron gives the geometrical alignment. One figure has the Sphinx lines from the shoulder and body divisions. A second figure has Zoser lines from the shoulder and Ra eyes. The covered heads are for the lifecycle and Egyptian afnet. The pink face probably shows the three have not completely grasped the science of the universe and knowledge, which only the clear faced figure has for the difference between theory and practice.

Rumwanda Rock Shelter, Ndanga, Fort Victoria area No. 445 (Fort Victoria has changed its name several times since African rule).

The lower section of the painting has the white and yellow figures 'emerging' from the animals to represent the Sphinx. The second figure has the lines of the hair giving the age of initiation. The figure of this group has three marks for the Sphinx and the dots on the arm are for Zoser. The position of the limbs suggests the descent of life. Above this group there are white and pink figures duplicating the same scene, showing the next generation being taught the art of the Sphinx (the parallel legs).

The crossed arms of the first figure give the geometrical alignments, whilst the second figure has the symbols of initiation and the lines of Zoser. The third also carries the lines of Zoser and the bird head for the Sphinx, while the body displays initiation. The feather of justice is held in the hand, emphasising its importance, and, clearly shown Egyptian afnet headdress.

The yellow seated figure is being installed with the symbols of knowledge. The sceptre is handed on to the next generation. The design he is seated on is for the science of the universe, Zoser, Sphinx and lifecycle. Above the sceptre are 10 lines for Zoser. The bird figure represents initiation, the heart and feather and justice. The lines of the hair denote the age of initiation, Zoser, the Sphinx and the pharaoh's kerchief of Egypt. The theme of the painting is that the yellow figures represent theory and practice, while the pink show theory only. The dark quarters of an animal on the shoulders of a dark figure shows his independence of others. The artist probably based his colours on the scops (otus scops).

Mrewa Cave No. 450.

The kudu and buffalo represent the Sphinx and the figures have the feather on the head for Zoser, the swollen arms from bending the bow and the knowledge of walking upright for the initiation and the Sphinx as the older generation descends the pyramid.

Gomokurira Hill No. 86.

The elephant is for God, with the back for the ascent of the pyramid and lifecycle. The descending figure is holding the symbols of initiation on to the next generation, those ascending and walking upright. Other figures also hold symbols of knowledge, while those of age look on, probably instructing the younger generation. The stick gives the geometrical alignment and shows the method for working out the equinox, solstice and 52°. The heart and the feather of justice are shown on either side.

Bushmans Point, Robert McIlwaine National Park No. 230.

The lower figures on either side of the rock quern are for measuring the moisture content of the air. One has the heart and feather in the hand, while the other is sighting for perfection the measuring stick of age. The top figures are preparing their tools for the initiation. One holds the geometrical symbols while the other prepares an apron. The falling figure makes way for the new generation.

Bushmans Point, Robert McIlwaine National Park No. 479.

The yellow-lined figure is for the Sphinx and Zoser with the youth crawling under the weight of knowledge. The top striped figure has the tree of life on each arm, representing the dyes used for the painting, and the dot of Ra on the bottom and the animal crossing in front for the Sphinx. A tree grows from a seed, the flower blooms and then the seed forms, drops to the earth and grows, thus continuing the cycle of life.

Gambles Cave, Duhwe Hill, Makaha.

The lined figures represent the science of the universe and days of the year, age of initiation and give the geometrical alignments representing the lifecycle, the Sphinx and Zoser. The square apron is also shown for initiation. The leg decorations are similar to those shown on the Sahara painting with the sombrero hat.

Rakodze Farm, Marandellas No. 103.

The figure has the heart held in the hand, the tree of life and the dyes used for the painting on the shoulder. The points on the knee and elbow are for the pyramid and Zoser and also give the geometrical alignments. The toes are for the Sphinx while the head represents the lifecycle.

Zwimba Reserve No. 79.

The figures are seated for the descent of life with the dandelion flower for the completed lifecycle. The lines from the shoulder are for the Sphinx and pyramid, with the heart and feather next to them.

Frees's Plot, Hatfield Harare No. 53.

The cork tree (commiphora glandulosa) is of the myrrh family and the fruit has the two split sections of flesh exposing the seed for the Sphinx. The dots are for the age of initiation, the lifecycle, Zoser and the Sphinx. The corner gives the geometrical alignments. The colours are yellow for initiation and dark red for age.

Mimosa Farm, Harare South East No. 423.

The river is for Zoser with the descending lines at the top for the pyramid. The dots are for the days of the year, initiation and the lifecycle. The cork tree leaves are for the tree of life and the fruit for knowledge. On one side of the river is an ascending figure, while another descends. Some distance in front of him the lone figure has the stick of age and the symbols of initiation.

Ruchera Cave, Mtoko No. 243.

Only a small section of the full painting is shown in the Rock Art Book. The circular shape represents the unit, two the parents, three the offspring who learn to crawl on all fours just like the animals. Then the human matures and learns the art of walking on two feet and the laws of the universe. The figure has the bands of successful hunting and the lines add up to 52, 14, 10, 25 and 12. The trunk of the elephant represents God or Ra and the three rocks the decline and death. The funnel represents the tree of life and the growing up of the individual, who opens out when fully initiated. The white elephant dominates the painting.

Zombepata Cave, Sipolilo Area No. 521.

The Ra circle is shown with the lines, five on one side and two on the other for the Sphinx and Zoser, on the outside of the circle. The five line divided circle has the dashes for the days of the year within the circle. The migration from one section to another is shown by the white dashes leaving the circle and going to another. The animals represent the Sphinx, who learns to walk on two feet instead of four as the other animals.

(a) Zombepata Cave No. 521.

The arrows are used for the geometrical alignment. There are 52 arrows in each direction and there are 10 in the bottom group with the age of initiation at the top. The teachings of Zoser are shown by the pyramids. The tenth one is on the line of the equinox and has burst open the top for the passing on of knowledge to the next generation. The plain circular dots are for the 'bricks' stacked on top of each other, indicating the passing on of knowledge. The white dots represent the science of the universe and knowledge.

(b) Macheke No. 424.

One animal stands on all four feet. At the top of the overpainted section is another animal with three legs. The yellow animal at the bottom is taking it easy after imparting knowledge to the newly initiated. The overpainted figure has the feathers and heart in each hand and is made up of the science of knowledge. The thorn tree is for the lifecycle and Zoser. Another tree is probably the myrrh cork tree and the objects are fruit of that tree. The overpainting could represent wild oats.

Ventersburg Farm near Harare No. 88.

The terracing is in the form of rows of dashes for the 52 year cycle and the days of the year. Because the buck is female and must not be hunted, one figure carries the feather and heart of mercy.

Saffron Walden Farm No. 427.

The newly initiated are clearly shown with the symbols of initiation, Zoser's ten feathers, quaternary and the two Sphinx parallel lines among the dots of the universe and knowledge. The double pyramid in front of them represents Zoser, the geometrical alignments and the Sphinx. The Sphinx near the pyramid has 10 (5, 5) lines for Zoser as well as the lower section (2, 4, 4) which make up the upper section of the Sphinx for the age of initiation. The separate diagonal grouped seven lines are for the Sphinx and Zoser, then four and three for the Sphinx followed by four lines one way and six the other, again for the Sphinx, with the total number of lines giving the final age of initiation. The yellow mountain seringa tree is for the Sphinx, Zoser, the lifecycle and initiation.

Epworth Mission No. 65.

The newly initiated feel very tall and proud of themselves in spite of swollen arms from bending the bow.

Bonn Farm, Macheke No. 459.

The dashes are for the science of the universe and the branches of the mountain mahogany trees are for the Sphinx. The four tree fruits are for Zoser. The crossed stems form the shape of the pyramid and geometrical alignments.

Mrewa Cave No. 85.

The figures are young initiated who are overtaking the older generation. The animals are descending towards the dot quern in the centre of the dashes which represent the science of the universe, days of the year and the geometrical alignments.

Epworth Mission 64

The figures denote the initiation and descent of life. The snake of dashes represents the science of the universe and the tree of life is for the Sphinx. The snake has a bird-shaped head at one end, followed by a square for Zoser and the curve for the lifecycle. The mountain seringa tree in the centre denotes the source of the paint for the picture.

Beta Musami No. 166.

The dashes are for the science of the universe. The mountain seringa trees are for Zoser and the Sphinx. The tree roots also supply the paint colours for the picture. The last figure has the symbols of initiation, the second the heart and feather, while the third carries the symbols of the pharaoh and wears the regalia of the chief and crown of feathers.

Gomokurira, Chinamore Reserve No. 77.

The palm tree has the three branches of seeds on one side, of which two are joined together and the other is separate. The branches on the other side are for Zoser and the Sphinx. The top branch has the 'pod' open with the black dashes forming a pyramid and number the age of initiation. The black branch behind the red ones denotes the passing on of knowledge from the older to the new generation. The smudge at the end of the red and black branches denotes inferior fruit, not all knowledge is good fruit. The black wild palm represents age, and the leaves between the trees the passing on of knowledge. Vegetable ivory is a round seed of the palm tree and is so hard that it has to germinate 'naturally' inside the digestive tract of an elephant. The dark figures look back to see the young horse of the future generation. The red figures below the horse repesent the close of life and death, nearby are the initiation symbols, heart, feather, Ra for God and justice.

Macheke Cave, Mrewa No. 467.

The rocks are for Zoser and the ebony (ebenaceae) tree is for the science of knowledge, with the rusty 'pupsecene' on the young leaves which represents the dots for Zoser and the Sphinx. The stems of the leaves and dots total the age of initiation. Not shown in the Rock Art Book is a buck behind the tree and, close by, a set of circles and other game animals.

Bushmans Point, Robert McIlwaine National Park No. 76.

The group of initiated figures are looking at the figure cutting the pepper tree of life and Zoser, the Sphinx and geometrical alignments, which are now in the hands of the younger generation. The five top Zoser figures are initiated. The hanging down aprons will serve as the 'stick' of age. The trees give the dashes for the science of the universe and days of the year, as well as supplying the red dye from the bark for painting.

Runanga, Domboshawa No. 314.

The stick gives the geometrical alignments and represents the Sphinx and Zoser. The circles represent Ra and are a darker colour for age and quern moisture measures. The twig is on three legs for age. The yellow objects are four on one side, two on the other, with a double one for the centre of Ra. One has three tails for the Sphinx and there are ten roots, including the double one for Zoser. The objects are monkey plants, which give the yellow paint.

Makumbe Cave No. 196.

The baobab seeds are for the age of initiation and lifecycle, with the lined 'pyramid' for the teachings of Zoser. The Sphinx is represented by the double pyramid. The carried pyramid is for the stick of age.

Howick Estate, Concession No. 203.

The first object has two Sphinxes, with the zigzag for Zoser and ending with the dots for Ra. The second is on its own for the ups and downs of life. The third is split into three for age and the Sphinx, with the end for the lifecycle and rise and fall in life. The fourth is the same, but suggests the passing on of knowledge at the time of the solstice. The sprouting Ra seed represents Zoser and the Sphinx. The direction of the lines gives the geometrical alignments and the ascent and descent of life, while the squared sphinx neck is dedicated to Zoser.

Surtic Farm, Mazoe.

The animals represent the Sphinx, the lines the teachings of Zoser, age of initiation and geometrical alignment. The figures are descending the pyramid of life after the initiation of the next generation. The dots are for Ra and Zoser with the top for the Sphinx.

Madzangara, Mtoko No. 396.

The circles represent the gathering together of the young initiates who are of age to begin their final training under the retiring master, shown with a short stick in the hand and the hair of Zoser at the back of his head. The Sphinx in front and the bird's beak represent the feather of justice. The top objects are the young taking shape from birth to the descent of the lifecycle. One the crawl, two and three the preliminary knowledge, followed by the upright stance of initiation and, finally, the descent of those who are not for initiation. The circle is also a quern stone with moisture seeds.

Epworth Farm No. 21.

The long-legged animals are for the acme and base of the pyramid. The figure on long legs has three fingers, pyramid legs and the stick of age in the hand, the next is sitting at the base of the pyramid, shown by the angle of the legs and knees and a figure beside one foot. The figure standing at the top of the painting has the feathers of Zoser on his head, the two sticks of the Sphinx and geometrical design. Beside him is the bow for the lifecycle. The central figure holds the heart and feather in each hand. The animals are for the Sphinx. The dashes give the geometrical alignments and represent the lifespan. The animals in resting position represent the close of life. The figure with the three fingers and in a flexed position represents death.

Chikupu Cave, Masembura Reserve number 302

The elephant represents God and the double line the Sphinx. The animals are red for youth and yellow for initiation; the figures are walking upright with their cloaks of initiation over their shoulders and three of the figures have their arms forward ready for the descent.

Ruchera Cave, Mtoko No. 390.

The newly initiated give the geometrical alignments and represent the Sphinx, the limbs and tail are for Zoser.

Oatlands Farm No. 41.

The Sphinx men have the feathers suspended from the arms for Zoser, the lifecycle and age of initiation. The kudu and another lighter animal are descending the pyramid of life.

Glen-norah Farm No. 40

The transformation from youth to initiated is clearly shown by the lines of Zoser, the Sphinx and the lifecycle. The line is for the lifecycle. The darker figure with the heart and feather in each hand starts the descent. In the hand of one of the two descending figures is a bird with its head hanging, which could be a hunting trophy. The lower small figure has the wings or double pyramid with the head for Ra and the neck for the equinox and the close of life.

Glen-norah Farm No. 286.

Circumcision and the symbols of initiation and the gradual upright stance of the red figures.

Arlington Road, Hatfield Harare No. 112.

The elephant is for God, the objects for Zoser, and the pairs for the Sphinx. Then animal heads are grouped for the age of initiation, Zoser and the Sphinx and represent the lifecycle. The snake is also for the lifecycle, and the dots the age of initiation. The white animal gives the geometrical alignments. Under the rhino's chin is a bird, representing the heart and feather of justice. The red rhino has a dark camel on its hind leg representing the pyramid. The elephant standing on two legs and trunk is for the close of life.

Mshaya Mvura Cave Mtoko No. 512

The lower line is for the age between birth and initiation. The figure is holding the heart and feather with the lines of Zoser and the Sphinx hanging from it. The figure on all fours is the initiate ascending the lifeline to the top, where another figure is preparing the descent at the end of the lifecycle.

Mrewa Cave No. 449.

The two Sphinx figures in the lower part of the painting have white dashes on the legs, arms, body and heart for Zoser and the Sphinx. The tree trunk with a descending figure on each side represents the Sphinx. The heart shaped pregnant figure has a feather beside the arm and is red for the new generation and the Sphinx. The leaves of the tree are for the science of the universe and geometrical lines.

Mucheka Cave, Mrewa No. 469.

Only two of the four polychromatic figures have been reproduced in the Rock Art of Central Africa. One figure has the white underside and front of the leg representing maturity and instruction, the yellow on the arm is for knowledge and the Ra eyes give the geometrical alignments, with the ears and white headline. The figure carries the feather of justice and divining rods as well as the forked stick of the equinox in the hand. The second figure has the yellow front underside of knowledge with the tail representing the rise and fall of man. He carries a boomerang with parallel Sphinx lines in his hand. The head has a red 'U' with the dark shaded 'nose'. The whites on both heads give the alignments and the white chest represents the lifecycle. Both these figures have the legs and feet of a lion and one has a tail. The heads of the figures have pointed ears of the scops owl (bubonidae family) which stands about 18 cm tall with yellow eyes and bill. The legs are bluish horn. When it is alarmed during daytime it makes a purring chirrup at intervals. However, at night the chirrup becomes a real trill. As a rule, the bird perches in grey bark trees matching its plumage for camouflage (Roberts Birds of South Africa). There are four colour phases, which explains the four similar figures on the corner of the cave. The 'U' shaped head and centre dividing line could be associated with the inverted 'U' and dividing centre similar to the spoor of a cloven hoof seen on other painting and rock art engravings. Both lion and owl are hunters and the domestic cat feeds on similar food as well as making a similar purring noise. The animal/bird combination pertains to the Sphinx and the lion to the Chief. The colour combination is for the owl colour phases and the markings represent the science of the universe and the owls eyes are for Ra.

Chikupu Cave No. 91.

This represents the rise of man onto two legs, which have muscle lines for the Sphinx and Zoser. The figure's hair is also dedicated to Zoser and the Sphinx, while the arms are ready for the return to the animal stance of old age, the fall of man. The feet represent the Sphinx and pyramids, the upper arms the wings of a bird, and the head the initiation. The Ra tortoise has the lines of knowledge in the centre.

Nyahuvu Farm, Headlands No. 3.

The top four figures from right to left: the head of Ra, the legs of the pyramid, equinox, solstice and 52°. The next two figures are for the initiated and, finally, the larger figure is for the passing on of knowledge to the next generation. Below these figures are shown the four Zoser Ra dots for the beginning, the middle and end. The bird and thorn trees are for the lifecycle, with the roots and branches for Zoser, the Sphinx and paint dye. The bird trunk of the tree is for the heart and feather. The rocks are for Zoser and the Sphinx. The two-tone figure has the yellow for knowledge and the dark shades for age. The double head is for the passing on of knowledge. The arrows represent the solstice and 52°. The two legs are balanced against a tail and between the 'legs' is a yellow cross for the equinox and solstice. The four Ra 'dots' are for Zoser and the Sphinx. The elephant represents Ra, and the figures around it the lifecycle. The upright figure at the apex of the pyramid and the one next to it hold the heart and feather of justice in each hand.

Epworth Mission No. 301.

The dashes are for the science of the universe. The pepper tree of life has the initiated descending and beside it the elephant and the circle for Ra and heliopolis (On). The animals are for the law of the Sphinx and knowledge.

Mucheka Cave, Mrewa No. 463.

The animal with Sphinx skin has white knowledge arm bands, three centre bands and five dashes above them. The two legs are balanced by the tail (age). The male figure stands on two legs of initiation. The female wears the hunting apron and the hunting bands around the arms and body and three white lines around the head for beginning, middle and end. The last figure without an apron has the five bands of the face hanging down the lines of the hair for Zoser and seven arm bands on one arm and five on the other.

Waltondale Farm Marandellas No. 273.

The climb up the snake of knowledge, science and laws. The snake corners have pyramid points representing initiation and the ups and downs of life, with the dark figure passing on his knowledge before finally descending the path to the close of life.

Muromo Farm, Umtali Area No. 519 The Labyrinth.

This painting has a dark red baboon and buck on the west side of the water mark, which runs down the rock face. At the bottom of the next section are two dark red sable antelope. The figure between them is holding an Egyptian flail, while the figure in front of the second sable antelope has the two Ra dots at the back of the head, similar to those shown on the Brandberg Mountains in South West Africa, and resembles the eye markers used in Egypt on the 'Stela of a Musician of Amon' which retains the initiation and the playing of the harp. The Pharaoh's head and initiation crown are on the main stem representing the Sphinx. Above the sable antelope is a 'black' rhino painted in a white/pink colour with a human animal on its rear section for the Sphinx. The figures in front of the 'black' rhino show the initiates training to stand upright. One of them has the three feathers on his head, similar to the Votive (Louvre Museum, Paris). Above them is an animal and a figure with bent legs and arms on the head for the equinox and descent. The next group has an elephant at the base of the painting with a young calf between its trunk and forelegs. Everything comes from God. Above the elephant are two stick figures, one holding the heart and feather in its hands giving the geometrical alignments, while the head is for Ra.

The Labyrinth shows the meandering of youth as it passes

to and fro over the white and black of knowledge (the plate shows yellow and black). The animal heads give the lines of Zoser and the Sphinx. The total number is for the age of initiation and the angle of geometrical alignments, equinox, solstice and 52°. There is only one path of ascent to the top of the pyramid. There, the bird and the Sphinx denote initiation and equinox when knowledge is passed on to the next generation, followed by the descent. The background of the Labyrinth is natural rock followed by the white/pink paint and lastly the black water mark, which represents the beginning, middle and end. A centipede is phosphorescent and lives under stones. It makes similar labyrinth lines while hunting at night. The slave traders hid during the day and hunted by night, so the Bushman marked this area as a warning for others of the potential dangers which could ensue from the slave traders.

Close to the labyrinth is a group of yellow figures representing the newly initiated in their aprons. The dark figure at the top of the group represents the equinox, while lower down another dark red figure looks on as the youths perform an initiation dance.

To the east of the main picture is another very small painting of about a metre and this depicts the close of life and the descent of the pyramid.

To the west of the painting and quite high up is another small separate painting, probably a giraffe of silence. The snake is ascending the picture giving the equinox at the start of life, then the solstice with two Ra dots on either side of the snake for the geometrical alignments and Zoser. The snake turns for the 52° and forms the equinox with the dots and squares for the passing on of knowledge. The head and animal beside it represent the Sphinx.

On a completely separate rock face is a painting of a black buffalo with a lighter-coloured head. The animal is about half a metre long. In the centre of its body is the lower half of a figure representing the Sphinx. There are other well-defined buck in dark red and two dark squares for Zoser and geometrical alignments.

The funnel-shaped 'horn of plenty' at the top of the painting has a yellow point at one end, then a dark red curve for the lifecycle. At the wide end of the horn section are five lines radiating from it for Zoser and a proteaceae flower. Below the bevelled edge is another funnel-shaped 'horn of plenty' without the lines of Zoser (Votive Group from Egypt in the Louvre Museum, Paris) with beside it a dark red buck.

The next bevel of the rock shaping shows a yellow outline design with two 'legs' at one end and three at the other. Two of these are joined to the upward curve line for the ascent of Mr. At the top the line levels out and gradually curves down and passes a red smudge to join the two black 'legs'. One of the black legs is joined to a yellow circle, filled in with white for everything comes from God and returns to God. On the roof near the above painting is a small area where the rock has peeled with a dark red painted area for Zoser, while the yellow animals represent the Sphinx.

Dengeni Cave, Zaka Area No. 368.

Here the ups and downs of life are shown and the overlapping of knowledge, so that the laws are passed on from one generation to the next. The Ra dot at the end of the painting represents, as on the above described painting, that everything comes from and returns to God, and the heart and feather are also depicted. Some of the lines are geometrical and give the age of initiation, Zoser and the Sphinx as well as the pyramid of life and lifecycle.

Domboshawa No. 57.

The seven quern dots are together. The ten for Zoser are on the other side. A red figure is crossing the palm of the hand which is used for measuring (Egyptian). The hand represents the five and four of Zoser, while the span between the thumb and fingers is 24 cm., representing the age of initiation. The animals are not shown in the Rock Art of Central Africa.

Cherewa Cave, Mtoko.

The figures have their initiation symbols with the elephant representing God. The geometrical cross of blossom (Sinaitic script) is next to the trunk and represents the rise and fall of man through life.

ROCK ART OF MATABELELAND

White Rhino Shelter, Matopo Hills.

The white rhino has a square lip for grazing while the black rhino has a pointed lip for browsing. It is more aggressive and slightly darker in colour (the Afrikaans 'wide lip' was probably mistaken for 'white' when translated into English). The young back-to-back wildebeest have the lines and mane for Zoser and the Sphinx. The resting animal is looking at the next generation running past with their symbols of initiation. The top figure has the Egyptian flail while the others carry a number of arrows equal to the age of initiation, Zoser and the Sphinx. The total number of arrows carried gives the lifecycle. Above the figures the animals are descending the pyramid. One has the three lines clearly shown on the neck, with the others for Zoser and the Sphinx. The lion gives the geometrical alignment. The tail is curved upwards for youth and the mane for the Sphinx and Zoser. The young Sphinxes at the base of the painting have the central lined animal representing the Sphinx and the initiation. The lined animals have their own specific meanings which are for Zoser and the Sphinx.

The rhino ascending the pyramid has uneven horns so that it can balance on them for the initiation. However, the figure on its back is standing on two feet. Man and animal are interdependent on each other for survival.

The next rhino's horns give the geometrical alignments. The front horn is for the lifecycle and the second for the pyramid. The young hippo can only remain on all four feet and gives the geometrical alignment. The running figure below it carries the bag of symbols on his back and knowledge on his head. The retired figure is preparing for his descent down the pyramid.

The figure with the Ra shield has the stick of age and a Zoser square and the Sphinx lines. To the side of the feet a young buck ascends to take his place.

Another rhino head is geometrically aligned and represents the Sphinx and Zoser. The kudu has the lines of Zoser, the Sphinx, lifecycle and initiation. The lined figure, 75 cm in size, is by far the largest single picture in the group and the stick suggests that retirement is imminent. The hair is in a 'pyramid' style. It carries two birds on the shoulders (four legs) and on the hip the square of Zoser. The figure is at the height of knowledge and must pass this on to the next generation so that they can learn from his experience.

The five birds have the ten legs and four heads (one is headless) between them for Zoser and the Sphinx. They also give the geometrical alignments between them and singly. The elephant represents God.

(a) Nswatugi Cave, Matopos National Park.

On the west side of the cave is a yellow lion. In the corner is a 'palm of the hand' and serpent symbols of the Sinaitic script. At floor level, in a corner of the cave, are two earth cement circles, which are geometrically designed to give the optic equinox, solstice and 52°. These work in with the white section of the painting on the cave wall. The cave can be dated by the original markers and equinox.

(b)

The buck have the lines of the Sphinx and Zoser. There are more lines between the buck, beside the first buck's hind legs are a pyramid, Sphinx lines and the curve of the lifecycle.

(c)

The group of dark figures have three white bands around their necks and are in the same position as the buck above them.

The upright figure has the heart and feather on his head and a tree of life on the shoulder. The three yellow animals have the dark colour of age underneath and the white on top, representing the retirement of the older generation and the passing on of knowledge. Near the buck's neck are two figures helping each other along. The dots of the universe are on the 'rocks' and the seven white squares are for the lifecycle, Zoser and the Sphinx. The white and red object has the lines for the lifecycle and marks the 52° from the earth cement in the corner. The white roan antelope gives the teachings of Zoser, the Sphinx and initiation. The giraffe's neck has the lines for the age of initiation and represents the lifecycle and silence.

The squares are for Zoser, the yellow dots for initiation, the dark dots the lifecycle and the total number of dots the days of the year. The reedbuck gives the solstice and geometrical alignments. The kudu has the lines of Zoser on its back and is on two feet for the Sphinx. The lines beside the dark figures are for Zoser and those between the dark red figurers are for the Sphinx; the pink youth and the older generation ride while the red youths walk. The dark group of figures mourn the departed whose symbols are shown on the ground near the mourners and the giraffe moves away in silence. The red figure is directing the yellow figures undergoing training and initiation. The red figures with their symbols of knowledge have the yellow lines and markings of the initiated. The dark figures on the buck are looking on from a distance. The front kudu has the lines of Zoser on its back. The animal head gives the geometrical alignments. The zebra gives the science of the universe, age of initiation, Zoser and the Sphinx.

Isotja Cave Matopo Hills.

The yellow giraffe looks on silently as the birth of the next generation becomes imminent. The lines between the pregnant figures indicate that the children will attain the age of initiation, ignorant of the science of the universe and culture of their forebears. The dark figures of age look at the ignorant younger generation, indicated by the true yellow for those who look back for support instead of forward with confidence.

Isotja Cave, Matopos Hills.

The white circle with the dot of Ra in the centre, sun sign in astrology. The geometrical shaped torii of the Shinto shrine headrest are poorly made. One has the symbols of initiation and a bird though it is not of upright stance, however, the darker figures walking towards it are upright. The other headrest has the figures trying to balance on two feet. The dark figures represent the close of life, with the next generation not ready to replace them. The white gives the geometrical alignments on the cave.

(a) Silozwane Cave Matopos National Park.

Near the entrance are the legs of an animal, the lines for the 52 year cycle and the age of initiation. These are followed by an elephant for God and three sets of mountains (Sinaitic script) with three and four peaks to each set. Above the entrance on the ceiling of the cave a very tall figure can be seen, carrying an animal and feathers. The shape outlined in red next to the figure is to show that it is not a water mark (similar to the one at Bombata Cave) and by using the points and indents it gives the geometrical alignments.

On the east side of the cave a tailed figure is depicted with a stick in his hand and a chicken at his feet. The tail shows the fall of life and advanced age when knowledge is passing on to the younger (chicken) generation. The next stick figure has the heart in one hand and a bow in the other. The other two figures have legs, and all three are headless, half knowledge is like someone without a head. The snake under this section is marked for the science of the universe and culture. The next section shows figures who are learning from each other so that they will have some idea of what knowledge will be required of them at the time of their initiation.

(b)

The next section depicts a pregnant Bushman woman who makes a place in the bush for her confinement and is faced with the life and death decision of the expected child, which could affect tribal survival. The three hearts represent the beginning, middle and end and the feather of justice. Silozwane, means the death of mother and child. This painting therefore shows how great the responsibility is for the young mother in the struggle for survival and the hardship the Bushman must endure. The lines and the quern's watermarks show the lack of moisture in the air, with the figure in the centre making a quern moisture stone which means famine and sorrow.

If a baby is born and lives during the dry season the survival of the whole tribe could be endangered, therefore births and survival must take place only when food and water are more plentiful. Bushman are a very humane and gentle people who only hunt in order to survive in the formidable Kalahari desert.

(c)

The evolution of man through life as he observes nature. The birds learn to fly, fish with the pyramid shaped fins fly and insects fly. The buck has a dark colour on the outside of the legs and the light colour on the inside and under the tail. The animal matures and shows only two legs for the Sphinx. The two chameleons have independent eyes for self-assurance.

The signs of the zodiac are Aries, buck; Taurus, bull; Gemini, bee; Cancer, white fish; Leo, lion; Virgo, the birds; Libra, the buck which is near the bird; Scorpio, crocodile; Sagittarius, fire which is near the head of the snake; Capricorn, the snake; Aquarius, the chameleon and Pisces, the red fish.

The next set of figures are undergoing training and are learning the art of balance on two feet. The square objects represent the cave and seclusion; the dots of Ra are close to the objects. The 'cave' has two legs of the Sphinx superimposed and showing the heart and animal, there is also a bird with the feather of justice. The two giraffes remain silent and do not reveal what they have learnt. On the other side of them are the initiated with their symbols of initiation and knowledge. On the root section just above the symbols of Zoser and Ra are two figures, one holds an animal and heart, the white figure next to him holds an ostrich feather in the hand and has another feather on the head; the face is that of a bird, thus justice of the heart and feather remain uppermost at all times.

The frieze below the painting already explained is indistinct and appears to have been painted over many times, probably by each set of initiated, adding only to the lower section, taking care not to spoil the upper one.

One to two metres above floor level are some white circles, oblongs, dashes and a 'T' shape. These are all for the optic geometrical alignments from the north and south to the side and cave flooring. The solstice is from the west corner to the circular designs on the west side of the cave. Another alignment is between the east corner and the white circle. The others give the 52°, etc. The white sections on the ceiling are geometrically positioned.

At the north end of the cave are some fire holes which have been burnt into the rock with dry grass. These holes are also an indication as to how the caves were formed. The hollows on the equinox side are connected with the rains and female initiation. The fire holes on the solstice are connected with the male initiation. The combination of fire holes, white mark, equinox and solstice should make it possible to date the cave.

At the time of the initiation the sexes are segregated. The penalty for intrusion by the opposite sex is death, so the fire and smoke act as a warning signal to all concerned. The cave is positioned so that there is a very steep climb up the rock face, Mr. The descent has a slightly easier gradient with a fairly level pathway along the rock representing the descent of the pyramid and close of life.

(a) Mucheze Cave, Gwanda District.

This cave has three types of hand prints; One group has the actual handprint method, the second a painted hand and the third elongated prints. These are for youth, initiation and age. The fingers and thumb represent Zoser and the Sphinx and the groupings are the same. The yellow figure is for initiation and the animal represents the Sphinx.

(b)

The elephant represents God. The giraffe is for silence. The dots are for the science of the universe while the lines are for Zoser and the Sphinx. The ostrich represents the initiation and the eye dot, Ra.

(a) Bohwe Cave, Matopos Hills.

The lion represents the Sphinx, the mane is for the age of initiation, while the front is for Zoser and the back for the Sphinx. The figure in front of the lion has fallen due to age, indicated by dark red. His staff is on the line of the equinox and solstice. The spear gives the three geometrical alignments for beginning, middle and end and Ma Ra Ka Ba Mr. One of the larger figure's arms form the circle for Ra with his head serving as the dot.

(b)

The older hunters are showing the way to the faster moving, lighter coloured new initiates. The pyramid funnel shape represents the rise and fall of man and Ma Ra Ka Ba Mr, the animals are for the Sphinx. The snake is for the lifecycle and prevents the older generation taking part in the hunt, so that they may only stand and watch the results of their pupils' initiation, which will represent a sad but proud day for them as their life is drawing to a close.

Springfontein Farm, Figtree, Bulalima-Mangwe District.

The initiates of both sexes dance wearing their aprons and carrying their symbols of knowledge. The yellow represents knowledge and the colour of youth. The buck shows only two legs, and the resting animals are for the Sphinx. The half circle is for the lifecycle, the dots and feathers, the heart and Ra.

(a) Bambata, Matopos National Park.

The 'lined' animals are for the lifespan, the leg lines are for the Sphinx, Zoser and initiation.

Ba m ba ta suggests that the joined figures are for the optic alignments and passing on of knowledge. The pursuing hunting figure with the animal head probably depicts death.

Bambata Cave seems to have a lot of incomplete paintings. Starting at the right side there is a horse saddle (see Isotja Cave), half a metre of whirl imprints. chevrons and figures, the shrouded figures depicting death before their task was completed.

(b) Has the red for youth on the first 'rock' and by the edging shape gives the geometrical alignments. The dark red is for age and green top for the heart. No. 2 has a dark red outline and is red and green. No. 3 has a yellow section and red top with dark red lines of a giraffe for silence, the lifespan and geometrical alignments. No. 4 is red with two bands for the Sphinx and Zoser. No. 5 has a lower half and a band of 4 rows of red dots. The top has four to five rows in the one band for the Sphinx and Zoser. The sandwiched rock is yellow and pink with dots on the pink for the age of initiation. No. 6 has a small bottom section of yellow and the rest pink with the dots of science of the universe. The rows are for the lifecycle, age of initiation, Zoser and the Sphinx. No. 7 has a red top and bottom and a red outline with an orange centre. No. 8 is green at the bottom followed by orange and the remainder is pink with dots for the lifecycle, ascending the pyramid and protruding above it at the top. No. 9 is mainly green with red dots at the bottom and is pink 'rock' with rows of spots which are all for the lifecycle, Zoser and the Sphinx, while the outlines are for the geometrical alignments. The elephant smudge mark represents Ra or God and has the pyramid ears. The colours used show that the artist knew his vegetation by using tambootie, mountain seringa, palm and monkey tail.

There are two back to back elephants, one white, the other yellow, which are followed by a buck and figures. The horse has a three pronged, two banded stick from its shoulders and in front of it a three fingered figure. Next to the horse is part of a giraffe also with a two branched three pronged staff from the shoulder and two fingers above it. The figure depicts the appearance of man with his horse and gun of death - slave hunters? The Mzilikazi legend relates that Bambata means 'pat' probably pertaining to the sound of horses and guns.

Amadzimba Cave Matopo Hills.

This is a painting of a red oblong with darker red lines for the Sphinx, Zoser and age of initiation shown on the yellow section. A crocodile represents the Sphinx, Zoser and geometrical alignments. The figures have bird-like feathers. The upper pink section joining the top of the oblong is for youth and is subdivided into squares for Zoser and the hill for the lifecycle. The lines above the pink are also subdivided for knowledge. The lines on either side of the oblong box are for the Sphinx and lifecycle.

On top of the box are some hari shapes representing the equinox symbols; one is very clearly a pyramid while the others are shaped like tree stumps and termite hills, varying in height representing each person's different level of maturity, intelligence and capabilities. The dots are for the days of the year and the science of the universe.

Sibafo Shelter near Sibafu Hill, Matopo Hills.

Here the pink circles of Ra and Zoser with the dark mark for the age of initiation are shown. The pink figure is groping towards an animal on three legs, which gives the impression that the full initiation was not attained and old age has overtaken the figure. He has not mastered the science of the universe and culture. Other pink lines are also anaemic and there is one misshapen headrest. Two others are shown with a single horizontal line and the vertical lines 'hanging' from it while the top one has five 'legs' hanging from it. The dark animal beside the one symbol is resting and denotes old age. The pink is changing to white which is associated with youth turning to the European or foreign ways of life and forgetting the tribal traditions and sciences. The dark figures are passing on knowledge to the running initiated of the next generation, painted in yellow.

The painting of buck near Kyle Dam is done in a geometrical pattern. The buck's head faces north west and, in the second row, the buck's hind legs give the equinox. The solstice is to the west facing the buck's hind quarters and the 52° is to the front of the buck's front legs in the second row. The second set is formed by the bottom row buck's head facing centre south. The nose and back are for the equinox. The centre animal's rear, and the top fore-section of the north-east facing buck in the top row, give the solstice. The 52° is shown from the ears of the bottom row south facing buck to the front of the central animal and the hind legs of the top row north-east-facing animal's hind leg.

The third set is formed between the buck's nose in the south side bottom row and the front of the legs of the animal standing in the top north-east row. The solstice is formed by the same animal's legs, while the 52° runs along the neck and body joint from the south buck.

The Mtoko painting (Rhodesian Herald Nov. 14 1968).

The figure is 1.5 metres high (two royal measures), the legs represent the sphinx and the arms are off the ground. The lines give the geometrical alignments. The waistband has five lines and gives another set with the solstice down the front and top of the band. The 52° is the bottom line of the band while the top of the leg and the body give the equinox. The chest gives the geometrical alignments with the line endings. The lines themselves are for the Sphinx and total the age of initiation. The curved section is for the lifecycle. The head, nose and hair give another set of geometrical lines. The eye is for Ra and the head represents the lifecycle. The bird men on either side are for the initiation and the animals represent the Sphinx. The oval shapes are probably for geometrical alignments, science, culture and quern moisture measures.

The rock painting at Goromanzi (Sunday Mail, Rhodesia Dec. 7th 1969).

The buck represents the Sphinx and gives the geometrical

alignments. The elephant's trunk is for God and the giraffe's head and neck are for culture and the lifecycle. The trees are grouped for Zoser, the Sphinx and the lifecycle. The lioness next to the palm tree has human hands and small feet; it would appear that the lioness Bushman (genitals) is pregnant and represents the Sphinx. The palm tree has four Zoser leaves forming a pyramid with the angles of the leaves giving the equinox and 52°. The tree trunk gives the equinox.

The large outline of an animal with three toes represents the Sphinx, the beginning, middle and end. The five zigzags forming the chevron for water, Zoser and the geometrical alignments.

The figure lying under the animal 'apparently milking it' indicates man's dependence on animals and the Sphinx. The child is holding a bowl, probably a moisture measure or geometrical marker.

The lioness among the trees represents the Sphinx and the trees the paint dyes. The other object marks added to them represent the science of the universe and culture.

Near the Tuli River, Matopo Hills.

The younger generation are on their way to initiation and the bontebok (buck) changes into adult colours. The older generation watches the transformation, as any change takes time to fully implement.

Nanke or Majenje Cave, Matabeleland.

Here the symbols are surmounted by a white section for the lifecycle and Zoser. Above the white are two birds, the young one is upright and shows his new colours, while the other one is leaning towards the descending slope. The dark giraffe looks on as the young bird enters the rock of knowledge and emerges with the colours of knowledge. In front of him are seven figures with their initiation symbols.

The Tsodillo Hills of Botswana and Matopo Hills have circular motifs. The circle at the top of the painting has been divided into three across and two down. Below this are two crocodiles for the geometrical alignments, which are similar in outline to those on the carved dishes from Zimbabwe. These line animals represent the Sphinx and Zoser.

THE ROCK PAINTINGS OF ZAMBIA AND MALAWI

Mwela Rock near Kasama, Northern Province, Zambia.

The square is geometrically designed. The markers at the base of the square and the side sections represent the teachings of Zoser, the Pyramid and Sphinx. The lines are the units of Zoser and the outside shape the rise and fall of man (Kabbalistic Alphabet).

Zawi Hill, Fort Jameson District, Eastern Province.

Has the Ra circle and lines of Zoser. The inverted 'Y' is for the geometrical alignments. The animal represents the heart and Sphinx. The bird standing on two feet has the tail and feathers indicating the teachings of Zoser, while the body represents the rise and fall of man.

Rocklands Farm, Fort Jameson.

The animals represent the Sphinx. The lines of Zoser are under the neck and the circle of knowledge is on the side. The short dashes represent the days of the year and the science of the universe.

Nachitalo Hill Western Province District.

Here the animals represent the Sphinx and Zoser. The dots are for the laws of knowledge and geometrical alignment.

Nachitalo Cave.

The artist of these paintings was probably old, which would account for the choice of subjects. The black colour dye used is in sharp contrast with other works of art and may well serve as an epitaph to the elephant because of slaughter for ivory. The paint was probably made by cooking the leaves of the monkey tail until it became dark.

The top figure shows a male striding down into the picture carrying a container on his head. He carries a bow and stick in one hand. The stick figure has a broken cross, giving the equinox and solstice with the dot of Ra in the centre. The turban (house, palm or hand) is for Zoser and the Sphinx (parallel lines). The elephant tusk (or goad, Sinaitic script) is for the Sphinx and the descent down the pyramid of life. The middle figure has a knobkerrie which gives the 52 year lifecycle. The arms give the solstice and equinox. The lower figure has the pyramid head with the arrows for the equinox, solstice and 52°. The elephant is old and uses his tail, trunk and one hind leg for balance.

(a) Nachikufu Cave

This is an old elephant. The tusks have grown as long as the trunk and the tail reaches the ground. The tail hairs are numbered for Zoser and give the equinox, solstice and 52°.

(b)

This figure has a line from the groin (umbilical cord) round to the back representing the lifecycle. On the back the square for Zoser. The arm is outstretched to the stick, which has lines totalling the age of initiation, Zoser and the Sphinx.

(c)

The figure is sitting down to draw the bow, because of age. The branches of the trees are for Zoser and the Sphinx and give the equinox, solstice and 52°.

(d)

The figure's legs are bent with age. The feathers are falling off the back of the head, three on each side, a further sign of age.

(e)

The reed buck, giving alarm, has the horns of age and represents the Sphinx. The horns are made up of two dashes for the one and four for the other, representing Zoser and the Sphinx.

(f)

The figure of a praying man has the bird on the Ra head for the heart, feathers and justice. The bow gives the solstice, equinox and 52°, while the dashes are for Zoser and the Sphinx.

(g)

This figure is bent with age, but still strong enough to balance, carrying the stick or spear for the lifecycle and the solstice.

(h)

The line represents the lifecycle and the rise and fall of man from conception via the passing on of knowledge to the end of life. The figures are looking back, reflecting on youth and initiation. The position of the arms gives the geometrical alignments. The square is for Zoser, the bust for the Sphinx and the feather of justice.

The Nachikufu cave painting shows the degeneration of man and contempt for life.

(a) Nsalu Cave, Serenje District, Central Provence, Zambia.

Here the red represents youth, the yellow knowledge, and white for special markers. The yellow has the teachings of Zoser and Ra. The snake is for the lifecycle and the red arch is the rise and fall of man through life. These should be compared with the Kabbalistic alphabet.

The white lines and arch give the geometrical alignments. The lines and dashes are for the science of the universe and the days of the year. The 'U' shapes are for the 'palm of the hand', the Sinaitic script and the rule of ten for Zoser.

(b)

The ship of life shows the different aptitudes of knowledge and the close of life. Some learn quickly and die, while others learn slowly and all the time. A few never learn to climb the pyramid of knowledge.

(c)

Here one set of lines is for the 52 year cycle. Individual groupings are for Zoser, and the crocodile the Sphinx. Some of the boat shapes are similar to those used to transport the dead pharaohs down the Nile to the pyramids.

(a) Nachitalo Hill, Ndola District.

The long lines are for the teachings of Zoser and the Sphinx. The Ra dot is for the age of initiation. The curved lines represent the lifecycle and give the appearance of fingers and the 'palm of the hand'.

(b)

This one is geometrically designed and has the teachings of Zoser.

(c)

Again the teachings of Zoser are shown, but now including the 'ladder' on its side for the square base of the pyramid and Canaanite script.

The whole of the next group are of quern moisture measuring lines. The dots are seeds and the lines germination, a sign of good rains.

Figure 48 Nachitalo Hill.

The purple section represents age and the lines from it the handing down of knowledge to the next generation. The animal head represents the Sphinx, while a 'praying man' indicates the South Arab script, Zoser and the points between the horns of the pyramid.

The oblong shape and quern moisture measures include the Sphinx and Canaanite script. The lower section of the picture shows the rise 'Mr' of man from birth to initiation when he reaches the Ra circle with the lines of Zoser radiating from it and the justice of the heart and feather which lead to Ra (God). The dots represent the age of initiation and radiating from it are germinating seeds.

The other sections are connected with the teachings of Zoser, the laws and science of the universe. The measures and dots are seeds.

Nachitalo, Ndola District.

The colours used represent the age and the symbols the teachings of the pyramid and Zoser. The circle of short lines is for the start of life, the teachings of the pyramid and initiation, practising what has been learnt; the handing down of knowledge and the close of life. The ovals are moisture measure quern stones and rain dowsing sticks 'eye' (Sinaitic script). The long double line represents the beginning, middle and end and is comparable with the causeway between the River Nile and pyramids, the route taken by the boats of the pharaohs.

Nachikufu, Northern Province, Zambia.

The schematic painting resembles the ground plan of the Egyptian pharaohs' tombs and is also similar to the special quern stones and measuring stick, the number of circles giving the age of initiation and teachings of Zoser. The red is associated with Bushman art. It was also used as markers on the pyramids. The Zoser square, Sinaitic script, and the Ra circle date from 1300 BC. The double outline of the boomerang 'throwing stick' (slightly altered), represent the Sphinx. The 'U', Phoenician, Greek and Canaanite script.

Nachikufu Caves.

Here the 'M' stands for the Sphinx. The 5-line 'M' is for Zoser while the Ra circle has the dot in one section denoting the passing on of knowledge to the next generation and the close of life. The retiring generation turns more to God. The 'U' represents the lifecycle. The three spaces are for the Sphinx and the four lines for Zoser. The 'ladder' with the four spaces is similar. The extended lines give the geometrical alignments. The oblong 'ladder' has four complete sections for Zoser. The 'U' area gives the total for the Sphinx. The dot on the outside of the oblong is for Ra and the geometrical alignments. The square is for Zoser and the double outline represents youth and initiation. It is also a quern moisture stone.

Nachikufu.

The inverted four-lined 'E' represents the palm of the hand, Zoser and the Sphinx. Above it is an oblong divided into enclosed sections to give the geometrical alignments. Above these is a pyramid with the Ra dot surmounting it, the square at the side is for Zoser. On the other side of the painting a double 'U' with a tail is shown. This is similar to the South Arab script of the Iron Age. The parallel lines next to it are for the Sphinx. The inverted 'E' above it with a circle at the bottom and a dot, represents the Sphinx, Zoser and Ra as well as the geometrical alignments. The large square is for Zoser, the divided oblong the Sphinx and the yellow represents the initiation.

Nachikufu near Mpika Northern Province, Zambia.

The two creatures at the bottom of the all-white painting represent the Sphinx and the passing on of knowledge from one generation to the next. The crocodile represents the lifecycle, pyramid, Zoser and the Sphinx. The tail has the outline of a bird and gives the geometrical alignments. The geometrical design has the square for Zoser and the space for the Sphinx. The triangle is for the rise and fall of man as well as the alignments (Sinaitic script). The white dye is probably from the cork tree.

The Pulpit Rock, Mwela Rock Kasama.

In its original form the 'T'-shaped rock appears to have been similar to the pharaoh's ankh or crux anstra. The pyramid base represents the lifecycle, ascent and descent of life. The balancing rock across the top of the pyramid gives the geometrical alignments.

Mwera Rocks Kasama.

The lines are for the Sphinx. The dots and sets are for Zoser, initiation and the days of the year.

Zimbo Hills near Merwe Mission, Petauke District, Eastern Province, Zambia.

The flower has a set of four petals for Zoser and initiation. The other two are for the Sphinx. The petals give the geometrical alignments. The loose petal and lines give the geometrical alignments and represent Zoser and the Sphinx. The winding path has the dots interwoven for initiation. The white shield has the divisions for Zoser and the Sphinx with the pyramid triangles at the point. The circle is for Ra and the beginning, middle and end. The 'ivory' symbols are similar to those used by the Bushman. One 'U' is for Zoser and the other for the Sphinx, while the oval stone and circle marks are used for measuring the moisture content of the air.

The line with the five and seven cross bars works in with the Canaanite script which has a marked influence with the rest of the painting because script and other symbols are depicted and figures and animals are omitted, which is in keeping with Islamic Law, showing there are cultural changes but the rock art traditions continue. The Ra circle is for 'eye'. The 'K' and 'Y' red shapes are for the 'ox goad' and 'palm of the hand' which are the hieroglyphic equivalents for the Sphinx, Zoser, the measurement and the Bushman's bag. The red rake 'KAW' hieroglyphics have the ten Zoser crossed lines and the two Sphinx vertical ones. There is also a small set of red lines for the geometrical alignments and the curve of the lifecycle. There is another set of white dots close to it. When all dots are added together they total the days of the year and science of the universe and knowledge (compare with Kabbalistic alphabet and condensed 'el').

Zingalume Village, Chadiza Area, Fort Jameson, Eastern Province.

The oval gives the lines for Zoser, the Sphinx and initiation and represents the Canaanite script 1000BC, the square is subdivided into 24 squares. There are seven Sphinx divisions at the top and five at the bottom for Zoser. There are four divisions on the side and two rows of six for Zoser. The total number of squares gives the age of initiation, similar to the oblong. The squares are for Zoser and the triangle for the pyramid. The horizontal division lines represent the Sphinx. The small oblong below is for Zoser and the Sphinx. The geometrical alignments are to the side. The circle is for Ra and the lines for culture.

Nbangombe Village, Chadiza Area Fort Jameson District.

This painting appears to use the Iron Age South Arab script. The quern circle with the line down the centre gives one letter, a circle on its own and a dot with a line joining it to another. The figure with the toes and finger is for the age of initiation and geometrical alignments. The Egyptian duck of Ba has the head, neck, arms and body forming one letter and the legs another (house). This figure probably represents the hieroglyphics for the Sphinx and Zoser, while the dot is for Ra and God (compare with Kabbalistic alphabet).

Mpunzi Mountains Dedza District, Malawi, Central Province

The biggest motif is in the Canaanite script. The oblong

'house' and 'palm of hand' are for Zoser and the Sphinx. The circles are for Ra, the equinox and eclipses.

Mwalawolemba Shelter on Mikalongwe Hill, Malawi, Southern Province.

The Canaanite script is clearly shown in an inverted 'V' and 'U' and the 'palm of the hand'. Sinaitic script and design are comparable with that in the burial chambers of Ammenemes III at Hawara and the quern moisture measuring stone. The lines and dots represent Zoser, the Sphinx, Ra and the age of initiation. The curved line is for the lifecycle. The pyramid is on the inside to give the geometrical alignments. The ovals are comparable with the pharaohs' rock boat pits of the Valley of Buildings and mortuary of Chephren and moisture quern rings. The foot could also represent Pisces and 'M' Aries for the equinox.

Mwanambavi Hill, Mzinba District, Malawi.

The lines are for the teachings of Zoser, the Sphinx, age of initiation, lifecycle and the days of the year. The circle also represents Zoser and the Sphinx with Ra in the centre. The 'palm of the hand' has the lines for the Sphinx and Zoser. The same principle is used for the oblong.

The whole group represents the querns and moisture measures.

Pahl, Tanzania has white symbols of a 'U' and cross for the 'palm of the hand'. There is also a vertical line with horizontal lines crossing it (Canaanite script 1000BC) and 'F' on the back of 'praying man' Sinaitic script. All these represent Zoser, the Sphinx and the rise of man. There are snakes with 'bones' showing for the age of initiation, Zoser and the Sphinx. The flower head has the Ra dots which are loosely grouped into twos and threes for Zoser and the Sphinx. The sunflower is for the age of initiation, Ra and the lifespan. A quern moisture stone has seeds for the germination test. The ankh, Sinaitic script, alignments and lifecycle of never-ending knowledge.

Kukoma Kefete, Zambia.

This painting is coloured red and white. The comet head is for Ra and the tail germinates Sphinx seeds, a sign of a good crop and a time of plenty. The seeds also give the geometrical alignments. The square Zoser house, Sinaitic script, has the horizontal line next to the 'cup', KHP, Egyptian hieroglyphics. The 'E' represents the 'bow', Canaanite script 13th century BC, the beginning, middle and end. The inverted 'U' on horizontal lines is for the 'ox goad' Zoser, the Sphinx, the rise and fall of man and the sign of Libra. The quern represents the measuring of moisture content of the air. The 'cup' and 'E' the dowsing stick. It is a good sign if it dips into the water as this promises rain for the crops.

It is just possible that some of these paintings were undertaken when Dr. David Livingstone and Henry Morton Stanley were discovering Africa. The symbols could pertain to the character and strength of purpose of the explorers as seen by these African friends.

British possession of Cape of Good Hope 1795.

Livingstone 1813-1873.

Rhodes 1853-1902.

ox goad - strength of purpose

house - comfort of home

'U' palm of the hand - capable

man praying - religious

eye - far-sighted, straight eye, honest

schematic painting - daydream meander, African logic, resourcefulness

M - ladders - climbing, another start.

SOUTH AFRICA AND SOUTH WEST AFRICA

The Brandberg Mountains of South West Africa are also known as the White Lady because the central figure for ceremonial occasions has been whitened.

The figure on the right has a symbol similar to the mandrake flower on the painted ivory plaque from the lid of the coffin showing Tutankhamun and Ankhesenamun in the garden. The funnel symbols at the elbow are similar to the 'Votive Group'. The skin bands on the arms and legs are hunting trophies and the bangles are for Zoser. The body dots and groups are for the science, Zoser and the Sphinx. The stick is for the handing on of knowledge to the next generation. The figure below the Sphinx has near its heel the 'L' stick for the equinox and the bar of the 'A' for the solstice with the curved line for the lifecycle. On the other side of the figure are dots and a 'papyrus'.

The Sphinx bontebok (damaliscus pygargus), which is one of the world's rarest buck, is only found in the game park at Swellendam, east of Cape Town. At the top of the painting the buck's forepart, the bird's hindquarters and human legs and feet are for the geometrical alignments. The pyramid can be seen behind one leg for the lifecycle. The horizontal bands are for Zoser and the Sphinx. The lighter parts around the tail are for Ra. The back has a bird's head and the wings are on the underside. The animal and bird are one. The front of the Sphinx has the horn of the equinox and 52°. The ears are for the lifecycle with the lines on the back for the Sphinx. The animal in front of the Sphinx descending the pyramid of life has an animal body and a bird head, the reverse of the previous Sphinx.

The main figure below the Sphinx has the ten Zoser lines

beside the head and a line of the equinox for the passing on of knowledge. The face of the figure has the eye of Ra. The chin is for the geometrical alignments and the three locks of hair for the Sphinx. Near the shoulder of one arm is the dark outline of a symbol, the centre of which represents the lifecycle and Mr. The initiation of hunting trophies is on the arms and legs. The arrows are for Zoser and the bow is for Mr and the Sphinx. The lines on the body are for the age of initiation, Zoser, the Sphinx and geometrical alignments. The dots are for the days of the year and science of the universe and culture. The proteaceae flower (Exodus 25 v33) is clearly shown in the hand of the figure with the stem and petal sheaf giving the equinox, solstice and 52°. On either side of the flower stands an animal - one has a bird, the other not. This last one represents the Sphinx. This figure gives the human aspect of the Sphinx, while the one with the bird gives the animal.

The portly figurine with the stick of age is descending the pyramid of life and has the lines of knowledge on her head. The lower figure carries the symbols of initiation with the dots of Ra on the head. These are similar to the ones shown on the Labyrinth near Umtali and the Stela of a Musician of Amon from Egypt. The inverted 'U' and 'I' are similar to those on the schematic engravings at Chifubwa Stream Rock Shelter, Solwezi district, Zambia.

The figure next to the one described above wears the initiation apron on the chest in a half white moon. Both hands are white, while one is holding arrows. Above this is another bontebok in adult colours.

Frikkie Friars se Kliphuins, Boskloof, Clanwilliams Cape.

Here the fat tailed sheep are divided into groups for Zoser, the Sphinx and initiation. The lines are for the geometrical alignments and there are three feathers of justice on the Ra head.

Mangweni, Drakensberg near Underberg.

The domestic animals are placed firmly on the ground with three feet to show that they are not fleet of foot like game. They have the markings on the side for the beginning, middle and end. The introduction of domestic cattle meant the end of the game.

The Pioneer Painting of South West Cape.

Here the Herero, which is an African tribe, are depicted in their long dresses and aprons of squares. The under garment shows the lines for Zoser and the Sphinx. The circle of dots is for initiation. The woman in Victorian dress has on her apron the vertical lines for the beginning, middle and end, or the beginning of the end. The figure next to her has a horse head, as man and his horse are one. The horse and rider below it show a pathetic horse that obeys the rider with a cross for a head and hat. Due to his hat the man cannot see where he is going, which means the blind leading the blind.

The unfamiliar cross displayed by the Christians must have puzzled the Africans, realising only later that it heralded a different system of culture from their own. The harnessed animals (often up to 16 oxen are used) represented to them the same pathetic sight as the seated figure lacking culture. To them youth should go afoot and not ride in a wagon. The wagon wheels have three and four spokes. Both draught animals and man have much to learn. Youth should walk, and without the help of a stick.

This painting depicts bygone memories of Egypt when chariot warfare took place and the Africans moved south to get away from those who did not understand or fit in with their culture.

Orange Springs, Orange Free State.

Three females are grouped together for the beginning, middle and end. One has a Ra head, the middle figure carries half an arrow head and five fingers for Zoser while the third has a triangular head and three fingers on each hand for the Sphinx, age and Zoser. There are two figures near them, one sitting for age and the other dancing for youth. Above them are four figures grouped together, three females are clapping with the fingers for Zoser and the Sphinx, the group of fingers gives the age of initiation. The fingers of the other group total 30 for the age of discretion and responsibility.

N'Kosisana Stream, Drakensberg, Natal.

There are three figures looking over their shoulders, the back of the heads are clearly shown. The second figure has the square head for Zoser and low arms. The figure at the end has both hands at waist height. The other five figures, diminishing in height, show the bending of the body and the lowering of the arms while looking backwards. There is a human Sphinx mimicking an animal with human legs. The head with two horns is geometrically designed.

Able's Cave, Drakensberg.

Here seven sitting aged figures are portrayed, five in one group and two in another. The hands have three fingers for age and the body clothing denotes inactivity. The Sphinx figure descending the hill of life divides the group, which collectively shows the initiation characteristics. The Sphinx faces the buck which is standing with the hindquarters higher than the shoulders so that the back slopes downhill.

Beersheba Farm Griqualand East.

There are red horses and riders and black and white pairs. There are also pairs of red horses and black riders, white horses and black riders and black horses with white riders. One red figure is on foot and another dismounting with rifles pointing at fleeing figures. There is a red and black figure near the base of the painting (red = youth, black = age and death) which has a falling figure in front of him. The animals looking on are ignored.

Some of the running figures are holding bows which are no match to the guns. It is only their speed that saves them. The Arabs were known for their horsemanship and slave trade which may indicate that this painting was as a result of their raids.

Europeans wanted to herd their cattle and hunted down the game. In desperation for food the Bushman hunted the cattle which inevitably led to trouble.

Kwartelfontein near Smithfield, Orange Free State.

One figure has a white chest, white trousers and dark arms within a red outline for youth and a black head for thoughts of death. A white symbol outlined in red is hanging from his waist. The next figure has white feet and legs up to his knees, and red above. His hair and moustache are white, but the beard is divided into three sections on each side of a red (youth) face. There are yellow outlined guns on each side of him, denoting that a gun should only be used by those who use it wisely and preserve and maintain life.

Another white symbol, outlined in red, is hanging from his waist. Knowledge and power should not be entrusted to people who use it indiscriminately. The red horse has a dark mane and the marks of knowledge are on his coat. There are also dark circular marks on either side of him for knowledge. Under the horse and the figure are three yellow and white lions, yellow for knowledge and white for science.

Mpongweni Mountains, Underberg, Natal.

Here boats with extended ends are shown, but two are

without. The figures are divided into groups of four by one figure standing upright in one of the boats, probably representing the older generation in charge of operations. The stick reaching the top of the boat gives the geometrical alignments. There is a figure at the bottom left hand corner with a stick held aloft, very close to the biggest fish of all. There are, in all, 52 fish in the painting, two of which are being hooked by the nose, one group is swimming free and another four which represent the lifecycle (52), the Sphinx, initiation and Zoser.

Kenegha Poort, Griqualand East.

The equinox is represented by the two upright fishermen while the other two give the solstice and 52°. The bottom of the boat is geometrically designed on its stand and represents the beginning. The central figures with the geometrical fish are for the middle and initiation. The fisherman at the top is for the end, the passing on of knowledge and the descent of the lifecycle.

Tsoelike River Basutoland

Shown according to age, the different methods of fishing. There are 52 fish in groups of one to four, small and big ones representing Zoser and the Sphinx.

Uysberg Ladybrand, Orange Free State.

This painting shows swimming fish, four with legs and two growing them, representing Zoser, the Sphinx and the initiation. Fish replace the animal Sphinx and must be fairly treated as they also represent life. Lung fish have limbs which enable them to bury themselves in the river sand and survive in the air bubble during drought conditions.

La Rochelle, Clarens, Orange Free State.

The animal (Sphinx) is standing on a 12 pattern chevron, 7 and 5, representing Zoser and the Sphinx. Above the animal are three rows of ten chevrons 10x3=30 the age of maturity, 10 for

Zoser and 3 for the Sphinx and the beginning, middle and end. Beside the rear of the animal are some elongated dots and encircling the animal is a single line ending at the lower rear in 5 chevrons with two round the 'corner'. Above this line is a row of vertical lines following the circle around the animal. These give the geometrical alignments for the equinox and solstice. They total 52 for the lifecycle. Then there is a line of chevrons with forty patterns 4x10=40 and 30+10=40. Above and at the side of the chevron is another single line representing the descent of the lifecycle. There are in all 72 dots, 52 of which are around the chevron. The three chevrons give the year of initiation by counting the number of apexes.

Willow Grove, Wodehouse District, Cape Province.

The animal has 180 spots on its side 180+180=360. It has four legs and two fishes between the legs 360+6=366, which stands for the days of the year. The fish are geometrically aligned.

Klein Aasvogelkop, Bouxville, Orange Free State.

The Sphinx, very likely a hippo, has six teeth, 3,3. A hippo grunts four times (sounding like hu, hu, hu, hu) when in the water and signals the herd 6+4=10. It has the Ra eye and seven uniform and two odd whiskers. The hippo has two ribs showing beneath a double row of diagonal lines 30, 40. There are 10 double tails and the one balancing with the chin for initiation. There is an apron under its tummy representing Zoser, the Sphinx and the geometrical alignments. The hippo is enclosed within a single line and vertical lines radiating from it give the geometrical alignments and the days of the year.

Giants Castle Game Reserve, Natal.

The buck has 52 vertical dashes, 40 dots. 182 dots for half the number of days in the year. The buck's breath (which turns to steam in cold weather) denotes 2x4 rows of dashes and equals

8. Two ears are geometrical and represent the Sphinx and the initiation.

Another painting shows an elephant, whose trunk gives the geometrical alignments and the rise and fall of man. The toes are for Zoser and the Sphinx.

Barrows Hill near Wepener, Orange Free State.

Here a snake is shown with an animal angled head and two horns. The tail appears to be of a bird for initiation. The body markings consist of lines and dots which represent Ra and the age of initiation. The head and tail give the geometrical alignments.

Eland Cave, Drakensberg.

The buck has wings for the Sphinx and initiation. The wings have 12 and 7 feathers for Zoser, the Sphinx, justice and mercy.

Harmony, Griqualand East.

The Sphinx has ten lines for the mane and two geometrical initiation horns. The body appears to have a big heart indicating the animal's behaviour. The small figure in front of the Sphinx probably escaped death.

Kamberg Area, Drakensberg, Natal.

The Sphinx has the hindquarters of a human and the initiation apron of 7 lines. The geometrical alignments are taken from the human feet.

N'dedema Gorge, Drakensberg, Natal.

The Sphinx is a praying mantis with two fingers for the initiation and geometrical alignments. The body markings are for Zoser, the Sphinx, age of initiation and geometrical alignments. The eyes are for Ra and the crown is for the geometrical alignments, beginning, middle and end. The bow and 4 arrows are for the lifecycle, Zoser and the heart and feather of justice. The heart-shaped inverted seat is for balance.

Giants Castle Game Reserve, Natal.

Represents the Sphinx of the chameleon. Both chameleons and initiation change colours. The arms have the marks for the age of initiation and give the geometrical alignments. In the hand are the bow and two arrows for the heart and feather of justice. The eyes are for Ra and the mouth is for the never ending knowledge. The legs represent Zoser and the Sphinx and give the age of initiation. The feet are for Zoser and the Sphinx. The figure is balanced on geometrically aligned rocks with the divisions for Zoser and the Sphinx. The dots are for Ra.

Another painting shows two elderly men sitting with sticks of age in their hands. One of them is a bowman, while the other with a hat represents a European, showing that age and memories can bring different ethnic people together.

A figure dressed in cloak and caftan suggests a "foreigner". On one side of the cloak is a white bird man, his size is comparable with the figure's knowledge of the heart and feather of justice. The small bowman figure in front is the same size as the bird. The two 'African' hunters are double the size of the cloaked figure which is two hands in size, denoting initiation, and the hunter has learned culture and the Sphinx. All have buck heads.

The cloaked figure could learn from the bowmen who are willing to impart their knowledge and culture to others who are interested in learning.

Tynindini Herschel District near a Krans.

The slaughter of so many pregnant female buck is a great loss. Add to this that there are not enough mouths to use the meat so that much will be wasted. Consequently, the laws of nature and its preservation have been breached at time of plenty.

Wright's Shelter, Kamberg Area, Drakensberg, Natal.

The Sphinx is a mantis of Hottentot God. The mantis itself represents the animal and human legs and its wings the bird. This one is geometrically designed and has the dots of knowledge on its body. The two streamers form the back of the head and are similar to the royal diadem of the Egyptian pharaohs. At the same site are two oribi in profile and a foreshortened front view. Both give the geometrical alignments.

Ezelzacht near Oudtshorn, Cape Province.

The mermaid represents the fish Sphinx. Fishermen are subjected to the laws of fishing. Wherever there is life, hunters and fishermen are subjected to the laws of life and preservation. The painting shows the diversification is in accordance with the natural 'life' food of the area and must therefore conform to the laws of culture and survival.

One mermaid holds the symbol of the rise and fall of man and the knobkerrie which is a symbol of initiation and circumcision. One figure is shown pulling his line in with mermaids. The first pair of these denotes marriage after initiation, the second the geometrical alignments, while the third group of three stand for the beginning, middle and end. The following mermaid is swimming. This is equivalent to the flying bird of initiation as is the next animal balanced on two legs. The following symbol is indistinct. The laws governing the seas were those of the fish harvest and were to be observed, and only fish sufficient for the need were to be caught, eliminating waste or greed.

Natal National Park, Mont aux Sources

The seven figures return from their initiation. The leader has a buck covering his shoulder. The third from the right is from the older generation as he carries the stick of age. The other figures carry their own symbols of initiation and knowledge.

Game Pass, Kamberg Area, Drakensberg, Natal.

A frieze of game and a figure in Arab caftan dress with the head of Ra, the wing of a bird. The one wing and leg show incomplete knowledge. There are other figures among the game. The blind leading the blind. The 'bowman' figures seen at the top of the frieze are moving in the same direction as the game.

Kranses, Kamberg area, Drakensberg.

An influx of immigrants is shown bringing with them their new way of life. The game and hunters are migrating. Some of them are old and descending the hill of life and can be seen below the new arrivals, while the younger men above them select and hunt for food.

Ikanti Mountain near Sani Pass, Drakensberg.

The figures are moving from left to right denoting migration, while the older generation rest with the young ones by the wayside.

Martinskoek near Rhodes, Cape Province.

The introduction of dogs and men hunting together shows that females are taken while the fine male goes on his way. This way of hunting shows that the game has little chance of survival, as the hunting is done indiscriminately and selection goes to the nearest and easiest animal regardless of sex.

Makhetas, Basutoland.

A bird Sphinx with an owl head, eyes and nose. The eyes are for Ra and the face shows the geometrical alignments. The feather lines are for Zoser and the Sphinx. The quiver and feathers are for the age of initiation. The human Sphinx on the side has the ends of Zoser. The lines on the body are for the age of initiation. When added to the quiver and head feathers the total gives the lifecycle.

Makhetas has a Sphinx seal comprising the Ra eye, whiskers of Zoser and initiation, and the body shows the rise and fall of man in life.

The Rose Cottage Cave, Ladybrand, Orange Free State.

Two lungfish with legs show the similarity to an animal Sphinx.

Caledon Poort, Fouriesburg, Orange Free State.

The fish have noses for balancing and initiation. They also give the geometrical alignments and represent Zoser and the Sphinx. The coastal fishermen may have moved in from the coast and taught the local people how to fish in fresh water and maintain the balance of nature.

Lorraine, near Clanwilliam, Cape Province

A full size buck is shown on its own. After a big space a figure which is about to throw a boomerang across the river (represented by a watermark on the rock), followed by another space with a small buck in the distance. This denotes that game is scarce and when found only in small groups not herds. So in order the preserve the game the laws must not be broken and therefore the female, though nearer, must not be taken. The boomerang denotes that the justice of the heart and feather will be rewarded and offenders punished.

Able's Cave, Cockomb Mountain, Cape Province

The hand print measures, the breaking of the law on judgement day and the animal elephant God, lion chief have become as nought. The birds with their boomerang wings gliding overhead waiting to clean the land of its dead and dying animals. A sight only seen when the lion makes a kill for food and the wild life around it is waiting for the scraps from the lion's table. It looks as though there are vulture wings under the lion's table. There are also two hand prints below the animal giving 10 for the quatenary.

North Brabant, Fram Waterberg, North West Transvaal.

The hand print is a measure and represents Zoser and the Sphinx. The boomerang is for justice. The figures appear to be carrying symbols for the heart and feather of justice.

Rockydrift, near Nelspruit, Eastern Transvaal

There are a lot of young animals moving from right to left with a tall figure near the young elephant. They are ascending the picture, denoting youth in search of knowledge.

Andover, Wodehouse District, Cape Province.

The domestic animals are moving from left to right. In the centre of the picture the sheep are moving from right to left with the Sphinx figure leading the way. This shows the arrival of the domestic stock and the exit of the sheep and shepherds. The shepherd is probably a very young or old Bushman who is unable to go out hunting and is therefore of the pasture people.

Ebusingata, Drakensberg Natal

The birdman has the Zoser feather on the head. His knees have a triangular shape on the one and two squares on the other knee for the equinox solstice. The bow gives the geometrical alignments and represent the lifecycle.

Mpongweni, Underberg, Natal

The figure and animals are moving from right to left. At the top of the picture is a Sphinx with two hind legs, a long face and a horn as long as the body, representing that man and animal can coexist in peace because the buck is facing the immigrants. The Sphinx stands between the two ways of life.

Another picture shows the older generation starting to descend down the hill of life. Some are bent and others appear to be resting and watching the passers by.

Battle Cave, Giant's Castle Game Reserve, Drakensberg.

The running figure has the geometrical bands on the legs.

The quiver has the arrows for the initiation. Just below is a second quiver in the same colour as the hair of the runner. His face is white for knowledge and his well-defined hand is for Zoser.

Makhetas, Northern Basutoland.

The figures are closing in around the game animals as they are merging into the Sphinx, which has a chevron pattern in front of it. The cone shape represents the rise and fall of man. The red youth on the right side ascending and the yellow figure on the left descending. A shortened life is denoted by the curving line of the descent, loss of culture and science of the universe and survival. The quiver divided down the centre has the age of maturity 10, 5 for Zoser. Feet protrude from the chevrons, which are geometrical for the Sphinx and Zoser. The pattern on the cone is for the days of the year and lifespan.

The Meads, Griqualand, East Cape Province.

This painting is of buck in a confined dark space. The one at the bottom of the picture is just standing. Above it is a foreshortened rear view of a male buck with black horns, white face and two brown hind legs. The next one is a female and above her is the brown-coloured back of a resting animal. This shows how game has been cornered into a small area with little hope for the future as they look right to left for the descent of the pyramid. Death is the only release from starvation or being hunted to extinction because of indiscriminate hunting which gives no thought to survival and kills on sight for vanity.

Mpongweni, Underberg, Natal.

This is a painting of figures dancing after their initiation. Some have the headdress of birds (ibis of Egypt) and feathers in their hair. At the top of this group is a monkey man with the round head and tail of knowledge, probably depicting the instructor who, having reached the top of the lifecycle, is about to start the descent.

Drakensberg, Natal.

This is a picture of three horses and dark-faced riders in Arab dress and head coverings, carrying guns over their shoulders. The horses stand on three feet denoting death.

A Lion Shoulder Blade Bone Painting, Knysna.*

There is only one known bone painting found in South Africa and it is on the shoulder blade (scapula) of a lion. The white of the bone represents knowledge and the curve of the lifecycle. The ridges are for Zoser and the Sphinx. The geometrical alignments are taken from the base line between the two ends for the equinox which is also to the centre ridge of the bone. The 52° is to the jutting bone on one side and the painted object. The solstice is to the head of the object. The painting is for the initiation (on two legs) and the birdhead, justice and the heart. The Sphinx is for the descent of life as it passed the equinox of life. The shape of the bone itself is not unlike the wing of a bird and the bone, being animal, clearly represents the Sphinx.

---

*Now in the British Museum

Rock Art of South Africa

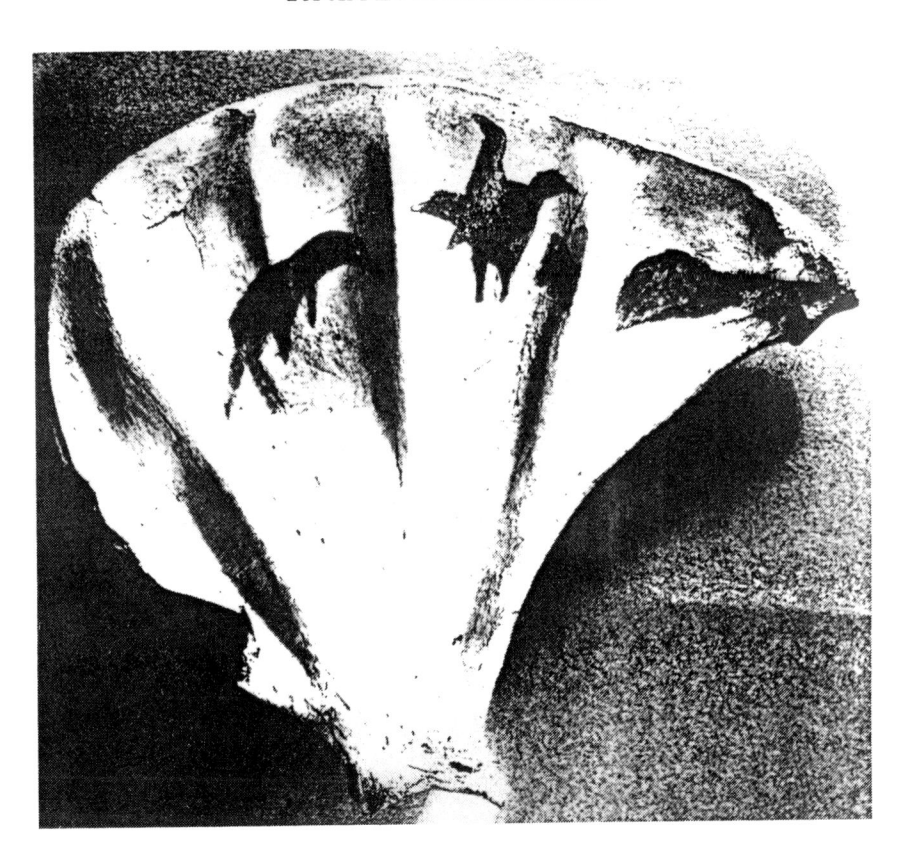

A lion shoulder blade bone painting from Knysna, represents the Sphinx.

Prehistoric Rock Art

Mtetengwe River, near Beit Bridge, Zimbabwe.
The petrograph of a giraffe.

Prehistoric Rock Art

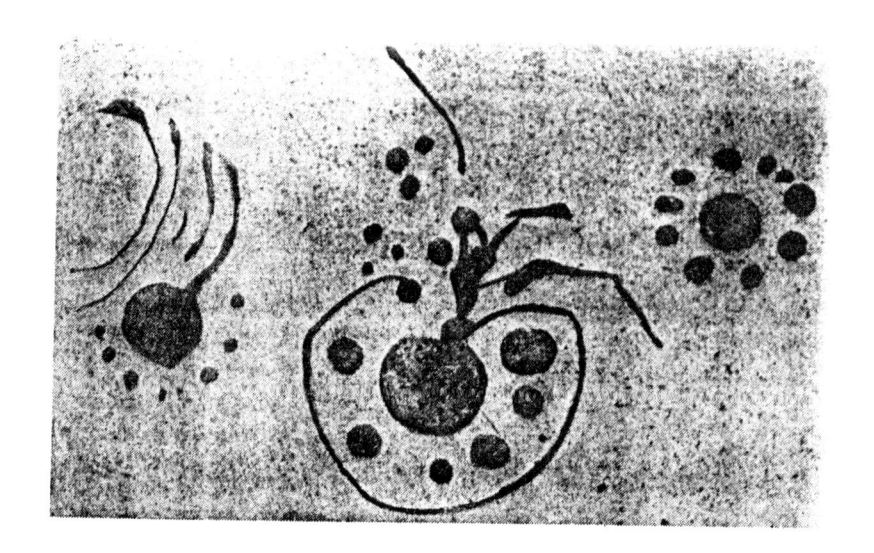

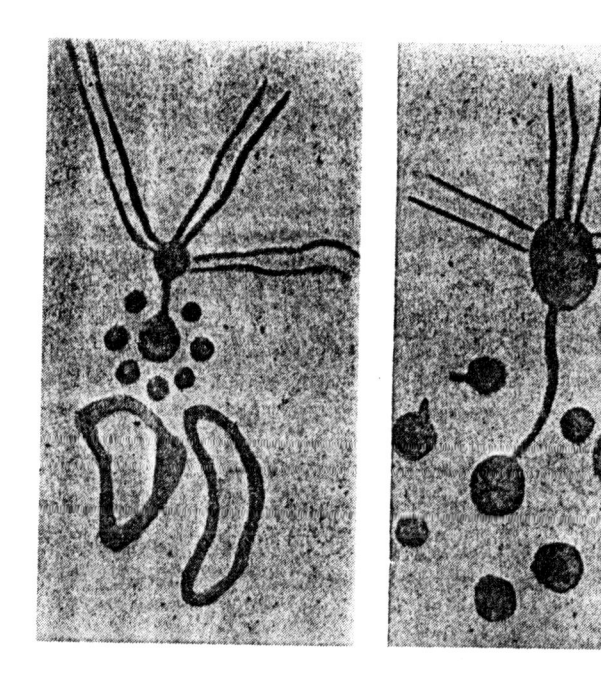

Rock engravings, Melsetter area, an 'ant' circles + lines.

Prehistoric Rock Art.

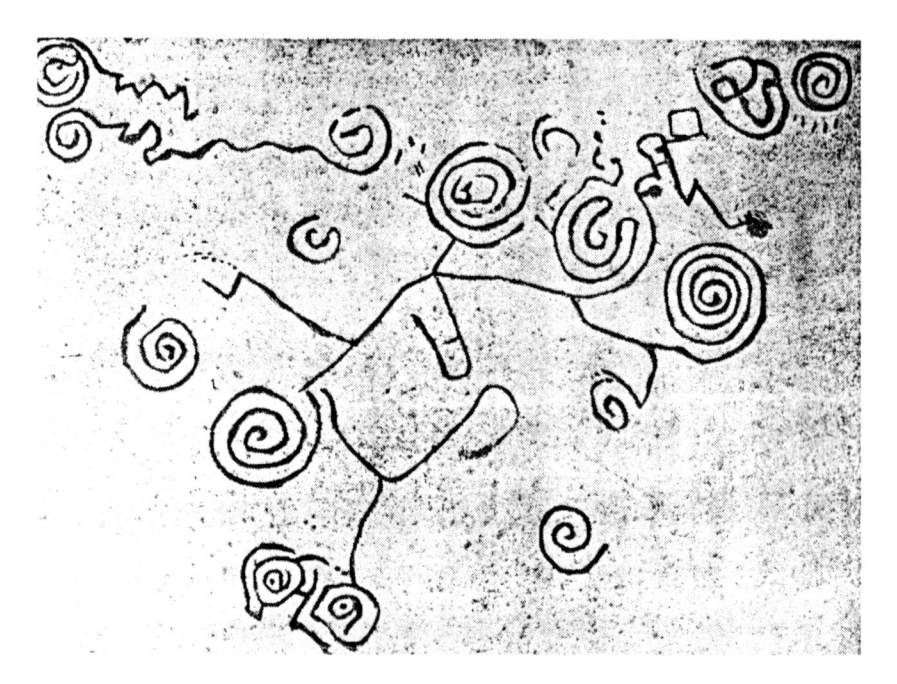

Rock engraving, Ingorima Reserve

Rock engraving, Inyanga Downs

SOUTH AFRICAN ENGRAVINGS

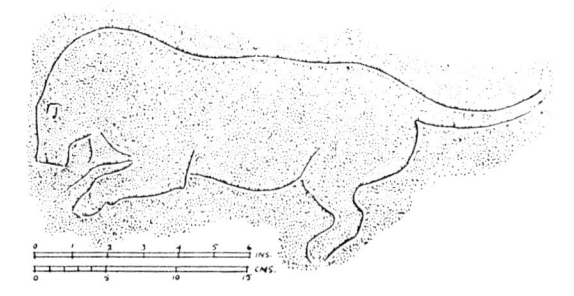

Doornkloof Krugersdorp District, (petroglyph lioness)

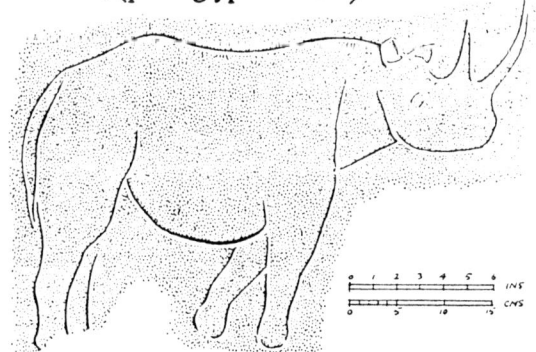

Doornkloof Krugersdorp District (Rhino)

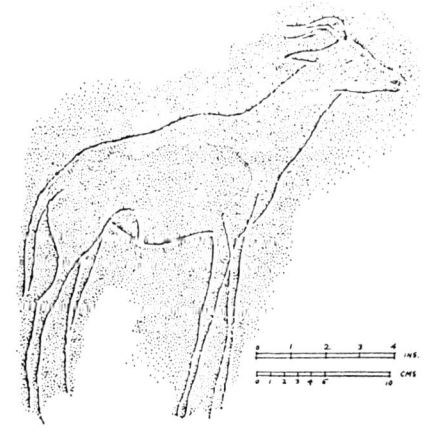

Groot Moot Krugersdorp District (Roan antelope)

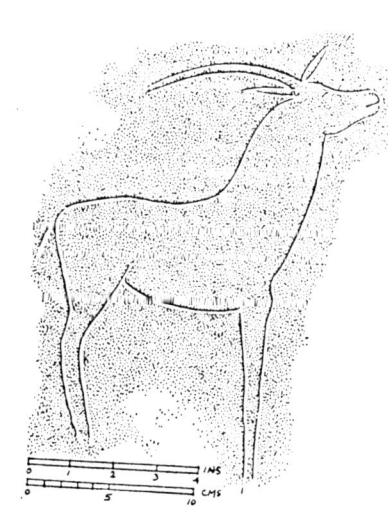

Groot Moot (Sable)

Rock Art of South Africa

Sweitzer Reneke District (Vulture)

Sweitzer Reneke District (Giraffe)

Groot Moot (Hippo)

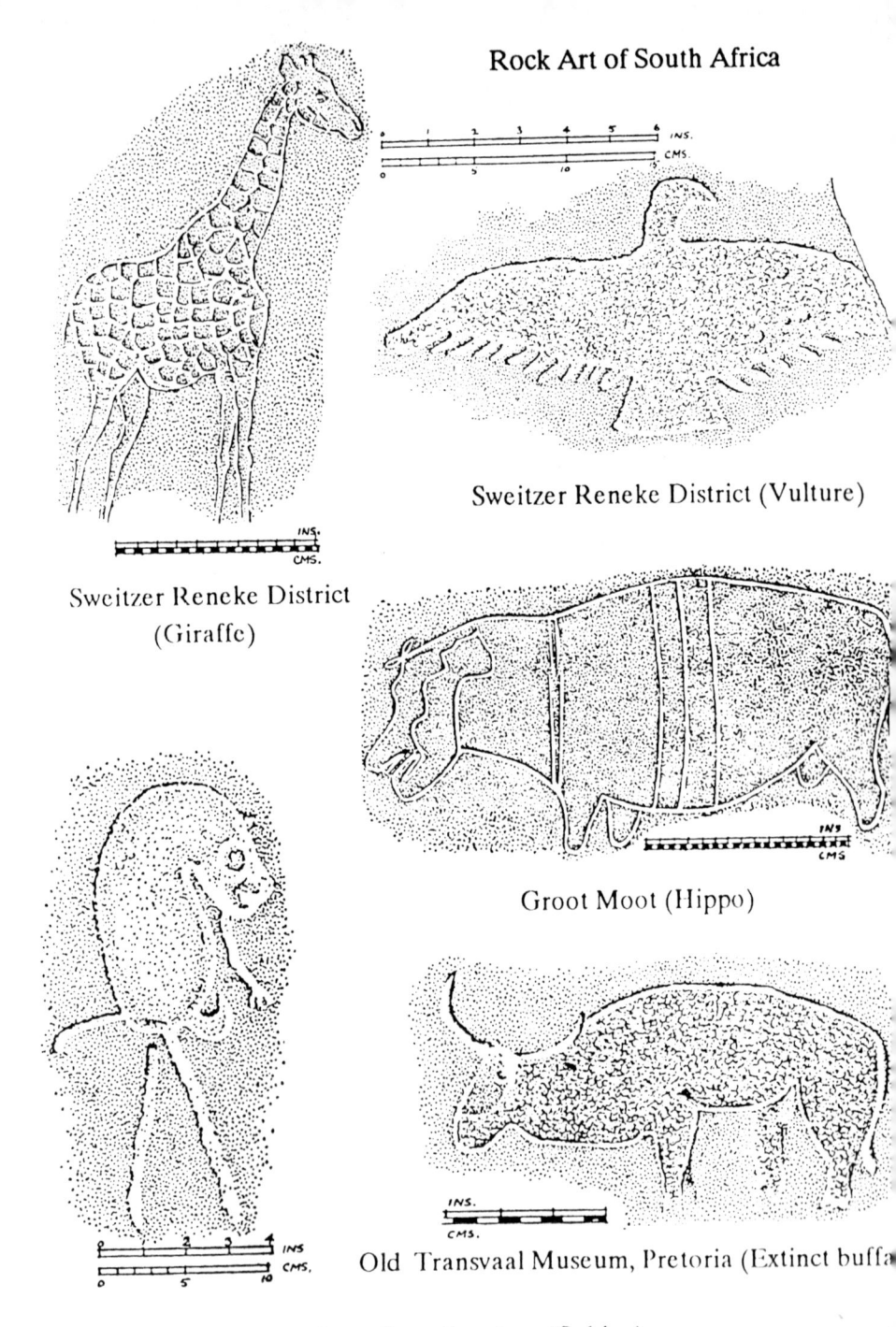

Old Transvaal Museum, Pretoria (Extinct buffalo)

Vryberg District, Northern Cape Province (Sphinx)

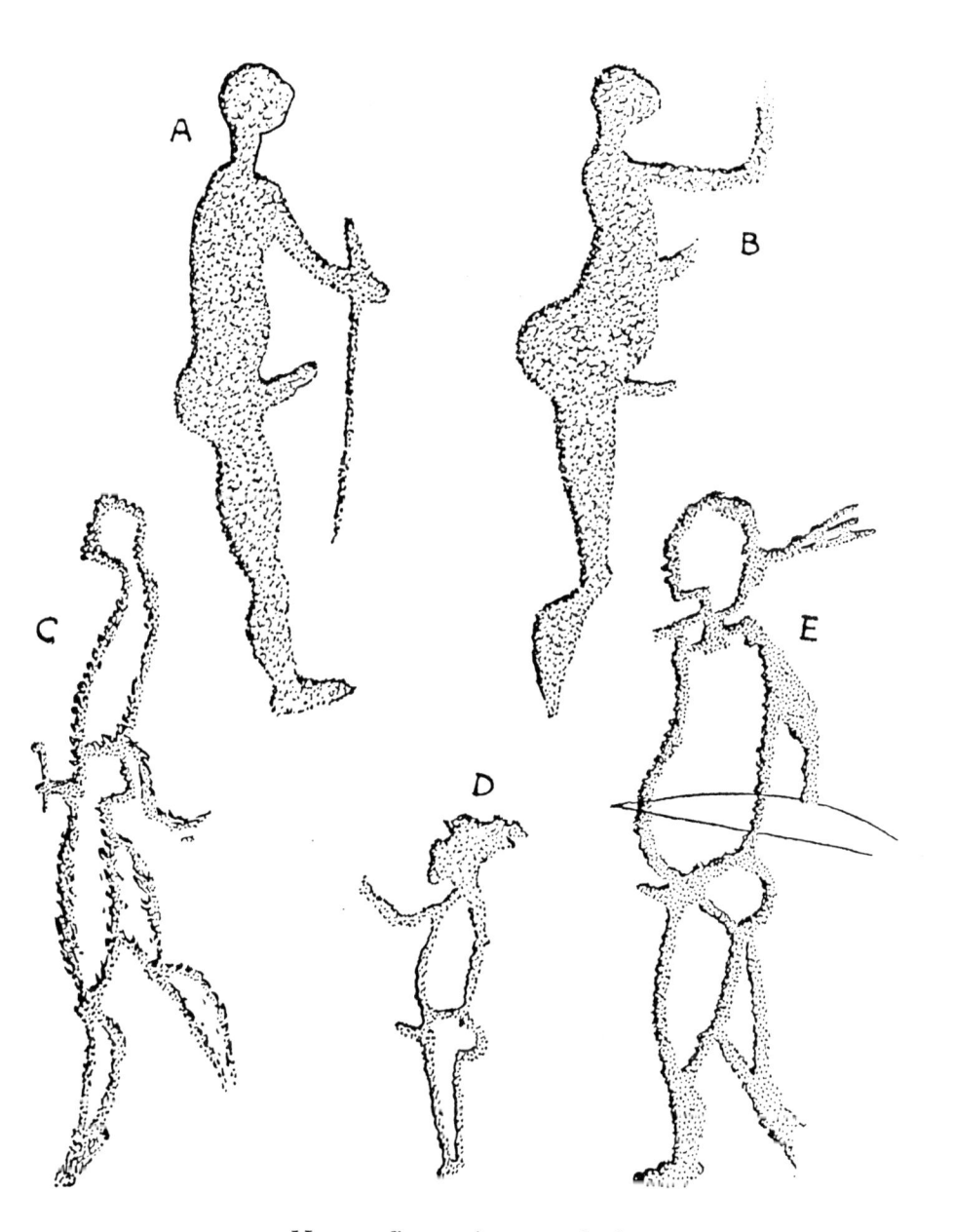

Human figures in petroglyph.

A & B   Kinderdam, Vryburg District, Northern Cape Province.
C & E   Bosworth, near Klerksdorp, Transvaal.
D   Kuruman River, Northern Cape Province.

ROCK ENGRAVINGS

Mtetengwe River near Beit Bridge, Zimbabwe.

The petrograph of a 3 metre giraffe (camelopard) has the two legs for the Sphinx with the square hoof and ten lines for Zoser on the front leg. The lines on the body give the geometrical alignment for the equinox, solstice and 52°. The neck has the lines for Zoser at the top above the Sphinx chin lines. The mane has the geometrical lines with the group directions for Zoser and the Sphinx. The total of the lower section is for the age of initiation. The eye is for Ra and the ears are for the pyramid, Zoser and the Sphinx. The tail is for age and the descent down the pyramid.

The fact that water flows over the petrograph giraffe most wet seasons indicates that the giraffe is a water measure. The other two giraffes are similar. If water does not flow over the giraffe it will be a dry season.

Bumbuzi Rock Shelter, Wankie Area.

The spoor engravings of a buck are shown here with the equinox down the centre and the solstice and 52° on either side. The top of the spoor represents the lifecycle. The division is for the Sphinx. The equinox is for the passing on of knowledge. The larger spoor next to it is the same. The two together are for Zoser (four halves). The double lines next and slightly lower are for the Sphinx and geometrical alignments. The figure near the spoor is bent and is for the Sphinx and the lifecycle, with the short limbs for Zoser.

(a) Melsetter Area.

Here the parallel imbwe lines are for the Sphinx, equinox, solstice and 52°. The large dot has four dots on one side and three on the other for Zoser and the Sphinx. The centre design has four circles on one and two on the other side, with the third joined to the circular line. With this are the dots for the equinox, solstice and 52°. The dots outside and above the circle are in two groups of four and three with the stick of age next to them. The dots for Ra are one big and two small ones and four big and three small which total 10 dots for Zoser, the Sphinx and the geometrical alignments.

(b)

The three sets of parallel lines are for the Sphinx and are on the line for the equinox, solstice and 52°. The joined dots are for the Sphinx and the surrounding ones for Zoser and the geometrical alignments.

(c)

There are three sets of parallel imbwe lines for the Sphinx. Four are the same length for Zoser and give the geometrical alignments. The dots are grouped in two sets of five and seven with two on either side of the large Ra dots for initiation. The joined dots are for the Sphinx and lifecycle. The varying sizes of the dots are moisture evaporation measures.

(d)

The joined dots give the geometrical alignments and the smaller ones are grouped for the Sphinx and Zoser.

(e)

This shows the dots for pre-initiation and the joined sphinx dots for the initiation. The circle is for Ra and the joined dots are for age.

(f)

The Ra dot in the centre with the dots joined to it is for the geometrical alignments, the lifecycle and the Sphinx. Five dots are for Zoser and the sixth has the tail for the Sphinx stick. The circle is for Ra and the 'D' on the end is for the pyramid and lifecycle.

(g)

The big dots are joined to the small ones and represent the geometrical alignments as well as the passing on of knowledge. The four dots at the top are for Zoser. The three below for the Sphinx. The lined design has four lines on one side and the three on the other with the 'D' loops for the lifecycle and the pyramid. The joined imbwe (Shona) dots are moisture measures which must have water connecting as a sign of good rains (compare these with the Kabbalistic alphabet).

(h)

The three lines are for the Sphinx. The arrow represents the geometrical alignments. The other symbols represent Ra and the lifecycle. The three lines and arrows when added together are for the Sphinx when all the objects are added together they make five for Zoser.

(i)

The joined dots are for the Sphinx. The stem represents the lifecycle. The separate Ra dots are for the geometrical alignments. The four dots are for Zoser.

(j)

The square of Zoser has the dots of the Sphinx 4, 2 in the centre. The other 'U' has the dots for Zoser and is divided for the Sphinx. These two designs form the geometrical alignments. The gourd calabash-shaped objects represent the pyramid of life and the stem the Sphinx. The surrounding dots are for the age of initiation and training. There are 10 dashes between the objects for Zoser, the Sphinx and the geometrical alignments. These are also rain measures or gauges. The size of the 'dots' indicates the amount of rain and/or evaporation taking place and predict the fruitfulness of the ensuing year.

Rock Engraving Ingorima Reserve.

The whirls emanating from the Ra dot in the centre of the circle are also shown on Egyptian hieroglyphics and Kabbalistic alphabet. The whirl above them is for the 52°. The top represents the equinox and close to it is the childish meandering similar to the Labyrinth painting at Umtali. The last whirl is for passing the emanating knowledge to the next generation. The dashes are for the Sphinx and Zoser. The other lines are comparable with the painting of Dengeni Cave in the Zaka area.

The engraving is on a vertical rock and could be a map giving directions, because to the north the terrain is flatter and more accessible than the Honda (Hondu) Valley which gives the hot, wet, tropical climate. The old and very young prefer the valley and flatter terrain, while the fleet of foot Bushman would probably travel the mountainous way, act as lookouts and give warning of any trouble, such as slave traders.

Rock Engravings Inyanga Downs.

One whirl is similar to the labyrinth painting of Muromo Farm in the Umtali area and denotes the youthful meandering followed by the serious ascent of the pyramid to learn the science of knowledge and eternal scrolls.

The engraving could be another warning of slave traders, but this time from the east. The traders probably worked their way down overland, then split into two groups, dividing the attention of the lookouts, and surprised the people in the valley.

Chifubwa Stream Rock Shelter.

This depicts an inverted 'U' with a dividing line for the 'people who bend the bow' (Sinaitic script), 'palm of the hand'. The complete engraving shows the inverted 'U' for the lifecycle and the corners are used for the solstice and 52°. The central divider is for the equinox. The parallel lines are for the Sphinx.

There is another clear 'U' on the line of the 52°. The St Andrew's Cross is on the line of the solstice and gives the geometrical alignments. The two lines represent the Sphinx and the four ends are for Zoser. The varying dots are moisture measures. Those joined together must have water joining them as a sign of good rains.

On the bevel edge are two rows of parallel dots. The top row has five for Zoser. The second row carries seven for the Sphinx. Further along the bevel is a hollow representing Ra. All the markers line up for the geometrical alignments. The other engravings are for the science of the universe and knowledge.

Spoor Engravings, Sunga Road Shelter, Wankie District.

Here the clear spoor marks give the equinox down the centre with the solstice and 52° on either side. The two sections represent the Sphinx. To the side of the spoor is a hollow 'pyramid' giving the equinox, solstice and 52°. Below the buck spoor is a 'T' with an inverted 'V' giving the geometrical alignments. The 'T' represents the pharaoh's ankh and the 'V' the pyramid. The three designs line up to the equinox, solstice and 52° and are probably derived from the Egyptian 'A' symbol.

The Samfya, Lake Bangweulu Groves, Zambia.

This gives the geometrical alignments and denotes culture and moisture gauges.

Munwa Stream Luapula Valley, near Johnstone Falls and Kashiba.

The circle of Ra and the dots for the age of initiation are separated by a half circle from the other section of the engravings. This represents the rise and fall of man. The squares forming a snake give the days of the year. There are two 'U's representing the graduation from the four animal feet to the two bird feet. Other engravings give the teachings of Zoser, the pyramid and the Sphinx.

(b)

The ladder of knowledge and the pyramid of Mr of life are shown here. The oval shape represents the stages of man from birth through childhood to the adult years of knowledge, the science of the universe and culture in readiness for the final initiation.

(c)

The circle of Ra has the age of initiation and knowledge on the outer edge. The Law of Zoser is in the centre. The circle forms the geometrical alignments for the equinox, solstice and 52°. These engravings could be compared with the symbols of the pharaohs and their tombs.

Ayrshire Farm Lusaka.

The pyramid of knowledge and the geometrical alignments. The three dots for the Sphinx and the square for Zoser. (Canaanite script 1000 BC for fish.)

(b)

The three fingers of age and the circle of Ra with the dividing line representing the initiation and the passing on of knowledge to the next generation. The three-fingered engraving could be compared with the Sinaitic script 'palm of the hand'. The circle may be from the South Arab script of the Iron Age.

The petrograph of the giraffe at Mtetengwe River near Beit Bridge is virtually a map indicating the distance and direction of other engravings. The tail represents the Inyanga area, the head represents Kasenga, Johnstone Falls, which is south of the headwater of the Nile and Congo Rivers. Lusaka is the shoulder area of the giraffe while Wankie is the chest and heart (spoor). Zimbabwe Ruins forms the central point of the reproductive organs.

When Zimbabwe Ruins is taken as the central point, the

rock engravings of the Inyanga Downs area are on the line of the solstice. The Zimbabwe to Melsetter area is on the line of the 52° as is Zimbabwe to Lusaka. The equinox is on the line of the Wankie area and Zimbabwe to the Munwa Stream near Johnstone Falls.

The equinox and alignments are now approximately 30° out of alignment for the true north, which dates the engravings to the same era as the Zimbabwe Ruins. The measurement of the overall distance is a feat which could only be accomplished with a thorough knowledge of the heavens and navigation, as at sea.

The two smaller giraffes represent South West Africa and the area between the animals represents the Kalahari. The giraffes, therefore, must be a map of the network of the Bowman's culture.

The buck engravings of South Africa represent the feet of the giraffe, which then shows that Africa was on the map when the pharaohs ruled Egypt. The animals must then represent the culture of the Sphinx and Zoser as well as justice, initiation and scientific knowledge of the heavens.

The rock engravings are water level markers for rain and rivers. That is the reason why they are situated in wet areas, where stones could be moved by the force of the water and paintings lost. The rock engravings area would be marked for the trained eye and could be located when necessary. The quern stones are popular because they can be used at the kraal (village) for grinding mealies. They can also be used away from the rivers for local conditions. Rivers can be affected by rains hundreds of miles away. So, widespread rains indicated general expectations of crops, with regard to feast and famine, and areas to avoid because of predicted poor crops.

SOUTH AFRICAN ENGRAVINGS

Bosworth Farm, Klerksdorp (Petroglyph lioness).

This is about 30 cm long and has the geometrical alignments from the baseline of the feet, as has the lioness from Doornkloof, Krugersdorp District.

Doornkloof Krugersdorp District (Rhino).

The rhino has the baseline to the feet for the equinox and gives the solstice to the neck and jaw. The 52° runs from the chin. The eye is for Ra. The square ears are for Zoser and the two horns for the initiation.

Doornhoek, Krugersdorp District (Bontebok).

The bontebok shows the equinox line along the tummy and across the legs. The horns are for the lifecycle and it has the outline of a bird's head for initiation and the heart and feather of justice.

Groot Moot Krugersdorp District (Roan Antelope).

The roan antelope has the baseline alignments. The horns are for the lifecycle. The ears are geometrical. The end of the horns, ear and mouth give the equinox.

Groot Moot (Sable).

The eye is for Ra and the end of life. The baseline gives the alignments. The Groot Moot buck looking over its shoulder also gives the alignments. The eland gives them from the feet and line of the shoulders. The elephant engraving has the feet for the vertical equinox. The Ra eye is for the 52° while the tail gives the lifecycle (elephants have four front toes on each foot and three toes on each hind leg, giving seven a side for Zoser and the Sphinx.)

Groot Moot (Hippo).

The hippo has the baseline of the three feet for the alignments. The three body bands are for the beginning, middle and end. The hippo grunts in four for Zoser and the lines of the engraving are two and three for the Sphinx.

Old Transvaal Museum, Pretoria (an extinct buffalo).

The buffalo has the alignments along the baseline.

Sweitzer Reneke District, South West Transvaal, now the Old Museum.

A bird is depicted here. There are 12 and 7 feathers on each wing for Zoser and the Sphinx. The feathers themselves are for the heart and feather of justice.

On another engraving the giraffe neck design gives the age of initiation and the body the lifespan. The four lines on the face are for Zoser. The eye is for Ra and the 'horns' for initiation.

Sweitzer Reneke District, Africana Museum (Giraffe).

The pecking of a giraffe has the markings on the body for the age of initiation. The neck pattern is in pairs of squares with three at the body join. The hind legs give the equinox on the baseline of the feet. The two legs are closely shown for the Sphinx and initiation. The other two sets of lines are for youth and age.

Also in this museum is the Eland which has been worked in 'delicate pecked technique'. Two legs are attached to the body and the other two are not, to represent the Sphinx. The tail is in the shape of a bird head for the heart and feather of justice.

Vryburg District Northern Cape Province now Old..

Transvaal Museum - the mythical 'Sphinx'.

The Sphinx has the Ra eye and the two legs of initiation. The hand has three fingers for the close of life.

Bosworth Farm, Klerksdorp (hippo).

The petroglyph of a hippo has the Ra eye. The body and tail lines are for Zoser and the Sphinx, the tail shape is similar to that of a flamingoes head.

Bosworth Farm, Klerksdorp, Transvaal (buck).

The buck is about the size of a hand and gives the geometrical alignments from the base of the feet, the lines on the side are seven for the Sphinx. The four legs are attached to the body for Zoser. The horns represent the rise and fall of the lifecycle. The triangular eye is for the geometrical alignments.

In the same village is the engraving of a giraffe. It has ten pairs of patterns on the neck for Zoser and the age of initiation training. The chest represents the heart. The two legs are for the initiation. The bird is for the heart and feather of justice, the neck represents the rise and fall of man. The head gives the geometrical alignments with the jaw, ear, eye and mouth. The objects near it are for the geometrical alignments.

Klipfontein, near Kimberley, Cape Province.

There is a petrograph of a Ra dot and circle with the geometrical lines radiating from it in groups of 2, 3 and 4 for Zoser and the Sphinx. Next to it is a 'sun' with three lots of markers on the inside of the circle. The outside lines are for Zoser, the Sphinx and geometrical alignments. There are 24 lines joined to the circle for the age of initiation and 30 in all for the age of discretion. The rock upon which these 'suns' are worked is triangular and gives the alignments of the sun for the equinox and solstice.

Gestoptefontein near Ottosdal, Transvaal.

The petrograph has a single circle with 8 lines from it. Six are diagonally opposite each other and two are slightly 'out of alignment'. They give the geometrical alignments and represent Zoser and the Sphinx, but with its two side and two narrow arms also forms a Maltese cross. The ends of the cross, however, are missing. A child draws the sun as a circle with radiating lines from the centre, similar to an eclipse. These engravings could therefore pertain to an eclipse of the sun overhead and mark the end of an era. 'U' Chaka killed his only son at the time of the eclipse when he discovered that his girlfriend's child was his son.

Driekopseiland, near Kimberley, Cape Province.

The circle has lines radiating from it. Ten of these lines are not joined to the circle, twelve are joined. These give the geometrical alignments. The other circle has the lines on the inside, which seem to be divided into groups of five and three for Zoser and the Sphinx. A third circle with 25 lines radiating from it gives the geometrical alignments.

The three circles combined make one overall design. The circles and asterisks are derived from Egypt for the equinox, solstice, 'duck foot' Ba and 'O' for On and Amon.

Mossamedes, Angola.

The circle here has 12 lines on the outside. Another smaller circle has fourteen lines radiating from it. A third again has 12 lines radiating from it but also two inner circles. The twelve lines on this latter circle are arranged in groups of four toward one side, five to another side, leaving three roughly for the third side and direction. This circle represents the never ending lifecycle and the passing on of knowledge. Ra is in the centre and the lines are for the geometrical alignment.

It is quite possible that when these two sets of three designs were worked they were in geometrical alignment with the others, which would add to the meaning of the equinox, solstice and 52°. They could also have worked in with the surrounding country.

The circle asterisk engravings show that they were near the tropics where the sun passes overhead. The asterisk is a very early sign for God, Ra, and shows the combination between the Asterisk and O (astrological sun sign.)

Kinderdam, Vryberg District, Northern Province.

The petroglyphs are of humans. One holding a stick forms the geometrical alignments, with the stick to the head and base of the feet.

Kinderdam, Vryberg District, Northern Province.

The Ra nose is shown. The horns are for the bird. The ear relates to the heart and feather of justice. The feet are for the Sphinx. The rounded hips are for the lifecycle and never ending knowledge. This engraving is comparable with Meads Griqualand East, Cape Province and the shortened buck rock painting. The engraving of a foreshortened sphinx animal in the same district shows the foreshortened training of the younger generation and has the end of the chin and tip at the back for the alignments.

Redan Transvaal Petroglyph of a Ra dot.

The two circles are for the never ending knowledge and initiation. The lines from the circle are in pairs and give the geometrical alignments.

Bosworth, near Klerksdorp, Transvaal.

This figure wears the initiation apron at the back and gives the geometrical alignments. The small knobkerrie denotes circumcision. The second figure with a bow wears the Egyptian diadem from the back of the head.

Kuruman River, Northern Cape Province.

Bushman are reputed to have a prominent genital which ties the paintings and engravings into one ethnic group. When the engravings were in their original compass settings, markers of stones, rocks, sticks etc. would be used, similar to the sundial, to give the optic geometrical alignments. Others could be determined by the moon and zodiac (see Silozwane Cave), the signs can be seen at night to work out the position of the sun to see when the shadow could be exact.

Zoekoe (hippo) Valley is the heart of the Great Karoo and has a cave with Hillton-Bushman paintings of abstract red vertical stripes and disjointed legs and arms which suggest the disruption of culture. The Bushman pottery is a whitish colour with indents of science and culture. In contrast the Hottentot (Khoi) pottery is plain yellow.

A cave near Trekboer Kraal has red-backed animals with white heads, necks, underparts and legs. These give the geometrical alignments. The animals face forward, down to the ground and over the shoulder. A recent rare engraving found near Zoetviel shows an animal and figure giving the geometrical alignments with the figure's feet, legs, head, neck and tail. The stone indents are for the alignments and culture of Zoser and the Sphinx.

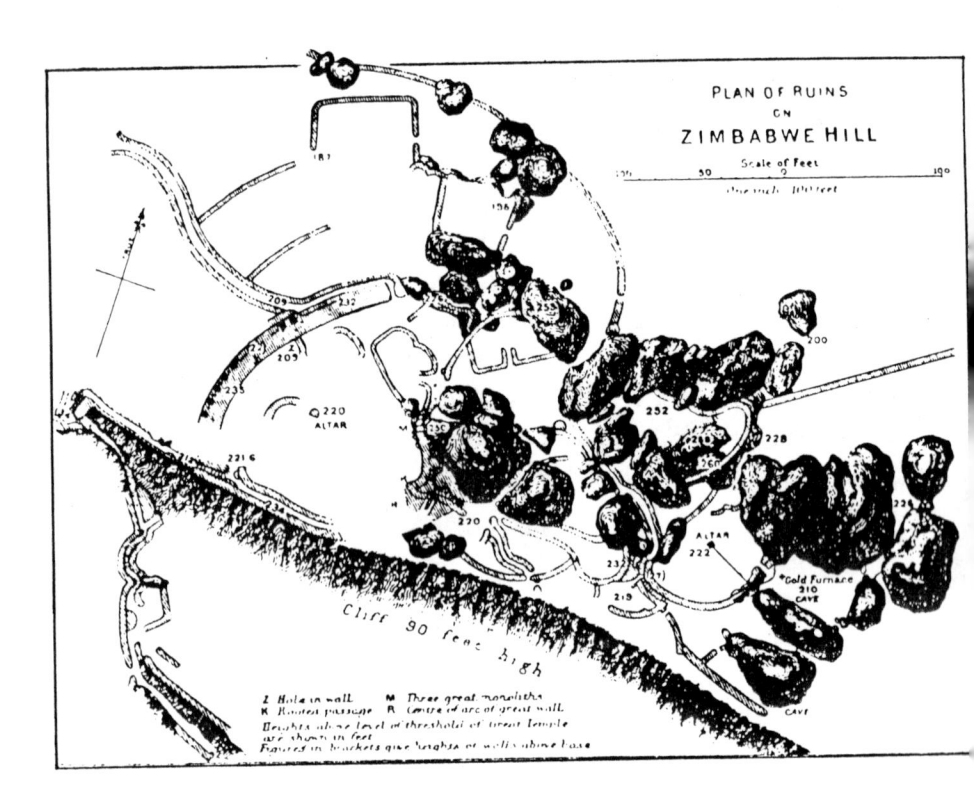

Zimbabwe Ruins

Guide Book.

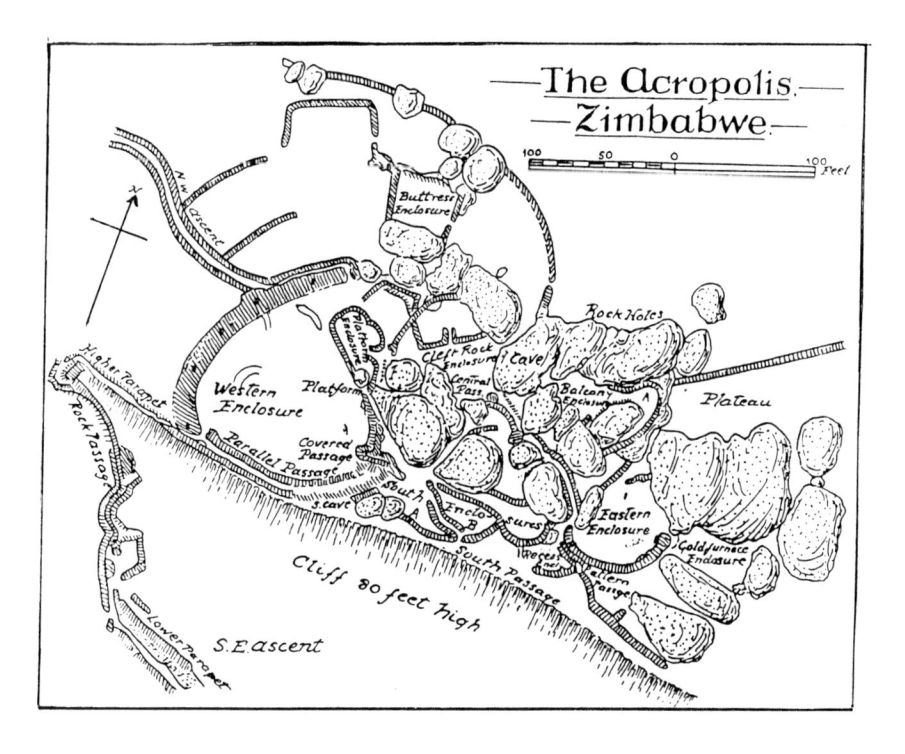

The Acropolis, Zimbabwe

Guide Book.

Elliptical Building from area 14. General view showing wall lines, ground markers in front of obelisk cone and double earth cones on the right.

Elliptical Building stone monolith looking towards obelisk cone.

Guide Book.

Cul-de-sac and in the distance Ba Recess Enclosure wall.

The 'pyramid stone' hari.
Westen Enclosure showing pyramid hari stone and entrance to Covered Passage.

Outside wall of Elliptical Building showing chevron and monoliths.

Elliptical Building and Parallel Passage and author.

View from Acropolis Balcony enclosure looking towards Elliptical Building.

Elliptical Building obelisk cone and columned wall bands.

Photo: U.M. Erasmus

Acropolis outside Western enclosure.

Acropolis Covered Passage and author.

Acropolis Cul-de-sac looking towards Ba Recess enclosure.

On an embankment the maze of excavated earth design. Acropolis in the background.

Photo: U.M. Erasmus

Granite rock road and line of quartz across road.

Line of quartz across the road and mound of stones on each sides.

A

B

Elliptical Building,
Zimbabwe Ruins, Area 12 & 13,
double earth cones.

Photo: U.M. Erasmus

Ruin No 2.
Excavated earth designs with a goyo stone on the platform.

Excavated earth cement designs and equinox pointer.

Phillips Ruins.
Stone built Crocodile and cone where the green Zimbabwe soapstone bird was found.

Excavated earth cement design near covered passage.

Excavated earth cement geometrical design near Western enclosure wall.

ZIMBABWE RUINS 'THE HOUSE OF STONE'

The Elliptical Building is entered by the North Entrance for knowledge. Inside No. 1 is an earth crocodile representing the Sphinx and giving the geometrical alignments. The stones of the crocodile are for Zoser. The west corner loophole is on the line of the equinox. The solstice and 52° are to the stone marker in the centre of the enclosure. Area 2 has the loophole on the outer wall which is on the line of the equinox.

Area 3 has the ground design near the north wall, but at the time of visiting had not been excavated, but probably gives the geometrical alignments and pertains to the earth crocodile which is climbing up the south east wall of Area 3.

The North West Entrance shows the equinox diagonally across the entrance with the solstice to the south west of it. Area 4 has the 52° along the south wall. Area 5, the west wall of the enclosure, is on the line of the 52° and has a foundation stone near it.

The West Entrance to the Elliptical Building has the geometrical alignments for the south east wall. The east end of the entrance wall has the equinox to the west monolith. The solstice is to the centre monolith (two for the Sphinx). The 52° is to the west monolith and the fourth monolith represents Zoser.

Area 6 gives the equinox to the West Entrance corner, where the wall joins the 'cone' ending. The solstice and 52° are to either side of the entrance of Area 7, where a curved marker represents the lifecycle and the triangular corner marker, the pyramid.

Area 8, the Sacred Enclosure, is entered through the gap in the west wall. The steps are for the Sphinx and Zoser. There is a solstice stone foundation line from the Large Cone to the south west.

The Large Obelisk Cone (Gen 11 v4) is ten metres high and 5 metres in diameter at the base for Zoser. It has 52 layers of stone. From the top of the straight side to the top of the cone is for the lifecycle. The straight sides have the layers for the age of initiation. The shape of the Cone is similar to the pharaoh's crown of upper Egypt. The smaller cone has the 24 layers of stone for the age of initiation and is 2 metres high. The steps in front of the larger cone represent the seven steps for Zoser and the stages of man from birth, sit, stand, walk, run, marriage, acme at the apex followed by the descent, use of a stick, two sticks, stand, sit and the end of life.

Area 9 has a double earth cone. The Platform stonework is for the geometrical alignments and culture of the Sphinx and Zoser. One has the equinox to the loophole on the west wall. The Platform represents the lower Egypt crown together with the original red soil, which has been removed, representing the feather of justice. The bird comprises the six remaining layers of the green chlorite schist stone on the east side of the east wall of the Platform. These are of varying lengths giving the geometrical alignments. The solstice and 52° are diagonally across the rows and the equinox is horizontal. The rows are made up of seven for the Sphinx, five for Zoser, twelve for the age of initiation and the lifecycle. Early in the morning, at the time of the equinox, the sun shines directly on the decorated wall section and next to it, and glances off the four bands on the decorated wall. These four bands (Bent claimed that there were five) of green chlorite schist represent the feather and heart of justice, Zoser and the Sphinx and give the geometrical alignments. In some places it will be noted that only single green stones have been used, and not two, dividing the layers into groups for science and culture. The number of stones used gives the days of the year. The earth cement tortoise Sphinx marker is the most important of all as it gives the geometrical alignments all on its own as well as those for the Elliptical Building. Because of its 'shell' and design it also represents Zoser and the Sphinx.

The flat dressed stone has the 24 stones cemented onto it for the equinox, solstice and 52°. The stone divides the stones for Zoser and the Sphinx. It also represents the age of initiation.

There is another separate set of 12 foundation stones for Zoser and the Sphinx.

The Double Amon Ra earth cone between Area 12 and 13 represents the double crown of Egypt. The upper one is for the higher good mind that overcomes evil "Be not overcome with evil, but overcome evil with good." (Romans 12 v21.)

The second Double earth Cone has the equinox from the south side and forms a right angle at the edge of the other Double Cone.

The West Entrance of Area 15 is geometrically designed. The steps are a royal measure high and the two steps are for the Sphinx. The stones are for the age of initiation and Zoser.

The curved wall has a marker in the centre of the fallen stones which lines up with the tree cone south of the stones for the equinox.

The West Passage is 22 metres in length and had two monoliths for the Sphinx which were 4 metres high for Zoser.

Area 10, the north/south wall, has an equinox loophole. The earth crocodile marker beside the south wall is for the Sphinx and gives the geometrical alignments.

The Parallel Passage from Area 8 has the steps descending for Zoser and the Sphinx. They also give the geometrical alignments. All loopholes are aligned for survey and geometrical alignments. The loopholes of this passage run from south to north and are as follows;

The first loophole A1 is on the outside wall and in line with the 52°. The equinox is to the south end of the Chevron Pattern on the outside of the main wall. The inner wall loophole B1 is on line with the solstice. The 52° is to the north end of the Chevron Pattern on the outside of the main wall.

This Chevron Pattern could be likened with the Egyptian serpent of the Pharaoh's headdress. It is 88 metres in length (52, 24, 7 and 5). The distance between the sets is indicated by the number of top layers of stones above the Chevron Pattern and represents the 52°. The equinox is down the centre of the chevron points and the total number of chevrons represent the days of the year. The two bands are for the Sphinx. The square dressed stones dividing the two bands are for Zoser. The 52 monoliths on top of the wall above the Chevron Pattern are placed at measured intervals and extend a metre above the wall, representing the stick of age. The chevron pattern represents the drought season and the time of year to reap and store the crops, which is March and June according to the Egyptian hieroglyphics.

Loophole B2 is on the line of the 52°. Loophole B3 (inner wall) is on the line of the equinox. There is a line of foundation stones between the Parallel Walls of the passage and these mark the equinox. The double row of stones is for the Sphinx and the four across for Zoser. The number of stones is for the lifecycle. The flat stones are approximately 12 metres in extent from A1 (Outer Wall) to the twin holes and outer chevron design.

A3 and A4 loopholes are on line with the equinox. B4 is on line with the 72° for the universal lifespan. The loophole with the stones gives other alignments.

A5 is on the north side of the Outer Wall of the Parallel Passage and does not go right through to the other side of the wall. It is, however, on the line of the equinox.

One of the stones of the North Entrance has a small chip missing from one of the stones which is in line with the loophole on the north side of the Parallel Wall. There are five steps for Zoser, one on one side and seven on the other for the Sphinx. The Outer Parallel Passage represents the stick of age and the descent of the pyramid, which leads to the Chevron Pattern.

The wall gap between the north and North West Entrance has 52 stone 'steps' on either side of the slopes at a 52° angle representing the design of the pyramid. From the base of both walls alignments are taken to the North Entrance and the north outside wall of No. 1 enclosure, as well as to the solitary monolith on the top of the west wall of the Elliptical Building.

The Parallel Sphinx Passage is 73 metres long and thus represents the universal lifespan and age of initiation. The width between the walls varies between one and two metres for the Sphinx and initiation. The outer wall varies in thickness between three and five metres for Zoser and the Sphinx. The Elliptical Building stretches 40 metres in one direction for the universal lifespan and 20 in the other (inner walls) for the age of initiation.

The design of the Elliptical Building represents the child in the womb and the flexed position. Thereafter it pertains to the whole lifecycle of man.

Ridge Ruins No. 1 is approximately 60 metres from the Elliptical Building. The main wall was seven metres high and 62 metres long (52, 10). The wall gives the geometrical alignments and represents the science of the universe, knowledge and culture. When the North Entrance of the Elliptical Building is seen from the vantage point of the No. 1 Ruin it is in line with the main Sphinx Outer Parallel Passage wall and to the north east of the North West Entrance. The high wall of the North Entrance represents upper Egypt's pharaoh's crown. The lower south wall the lower Egypt's crown. This accounts for the platform approximately 1 metre from the top of the wall which had been used to support a soapstone 'feather'.

The Ancient Ascent of the Acropolis (Mr Pyramid) is approximately 72 metres above ground level for the universal lifespan and has its main entrance at the Outspan Ruins. There is a cone on the south side of the construction and an earth marker to the south of the stonework, all of which work in with the geometrical alignments for the science of the universe and culture. The split walling is not a sign of poor workmanship but of very skilled craftsmanship.

The Ancient ascent has markers on the way up, the main one being the section below the Acropolis' Western Enclosure which is about 52 metres above ground level and angled at 52° with the lower wall of scientific knowledge.

The Western Entrance to the enclosure is on the line of the east/west equinox. The steps give the Ra geometrical alignments and are for the age of initiation, culture and science of knowledge.

The south west corner of the enclosure has the wall markers on the south east wall. The equinox is to the first original cone, the solstice is to the second cone and the 52° is to the fifth original cone.

The curved wall join on the east side gives the equinox. There is a design between the ends of the main wall. The original first cone was on the west wall but this section has disintegrated.

Obelisk Cone 1 (originals). The equinox and solstice are to the west end of the curved wall join. The 52° is to the wall end just to the south. All the original Ba cones were positioned from the south west main wall markers described with the enclosure. The first cone being the equinox; the second for age of initiation; the third is on the 30° for age; the fourth on the 40° for Zoser and 40 weeks' pregnancy; ten degrees for quarternary; the fifth for the lifecycle; the sixth the rounding off of the lifecycle with the entrance between six and seven cones for the passing on of knowledge; the 7th cone on the 72° for the lifespan and the Sphinx.

The stones used for the obelisk cones are for the science of the universe, days of the year and culture. The monoliths are for the geometrical alignments, Sphinx, Zoser and feather of justice. The monoliths measured the metres length above the wall and the width represented a finger. The hand measure is across the monolith.

The main wall of the Western Enclosure is 8 metres high, 6 to 7 metres wide and 45 to 46 metres long (45+7=52). The parallel passage wall on the south side is 24 metres long for the age of initiation and, when added to the main wall, gives the expected lifespan. The parallel walls are at an angle of 30° and represent maturity. The red fill-in soil of the enclosure is for the lower Egyptian pharaoh's crown. The granite stone is for upper Egypt's, the triumph of good over evil.

The curved wall gives the geometrical alignments and has the science of the universe. The number of stones used for the construction of the wall represent knowledge and culture, Zoser and the Sphinx.

There is an excavated earth design between the south parallel wall and the curved one. The earth curved wall of the design is for the lifecycle with the hole in the centre for the equinox, Ra, and the passing of knowledge. The crocodile represents the Sphinx, the stones are for Zoser. The double cone is similar to the double cone of the Elliptical Building, but is on a much smaller scale. The hollow bowls and other earth designs give the geometrical alignments.

The Platform Enclosure is reached by a 3 metre passage and winding steps. It is 7 metres above the original floor level for the Sphinx. The indent on the Platform Wall marks the equinox alignments. The solstice is to the north end of the Platform Enclosure's south east wall. The 52° is to the east end of the Balcony. A three metre protruding monolith placed on the wall gave the geometrical alignments and the extra metre gives four for Zoser. Above the boulder is a measure gauge.

There were two metre monoliths protruding above the wall of the Platform Balcony (Bent) which were positioned to give the angles of the solstice, 52° and equinox.

©

"Two shaped stones with even bands of asbestos form substance with a serpentine with veins of chrysolite. The erosion left grooves on the fribos bands. Another irregular polygonal pillar-like stone object of coarse-grained basalt, the smooth faces forming natural points, forms, part of a rough prism. Another fragment of schistose rock is apparently horn blendic. There are also several round blocks of diorite found on the platform."

These stones were placed in position and used as a sundial, equinox 0° 6 am, 10° 7 am, 20° 8 am, 30° 9 am, 52° 10 am, 72° 11 am, 90° midday etc.

The 'Pyramid Stone' Hari (Shona) above the walling represents the Mr and acme and gives the geometrical alignments. This stone marks the highest optic point of the whole construction.

There was also a geometrical set with the disintegrated wall south west of the Balcony.

There is an excavated earth design just west of the Covered Passage and on the line of the 52° from the previous design near the curved wall. This design has two pointers for the geometrical alignment and Sphinx with the dish between the pointers forming a triangle. The inside shape of the dish is of a tortoise shell, representing the science of the universe and culture.

The Covered Passage steps are for the Sphinx and Zoser as well as the geometrical alignments. The north opening also gives the geometrical alignments with the walling.

The 'cul de sac' to the south, between the boulders and wall, has the geometrical alignments at the entrance to the boulders and another to the walling at the entrance.

The steps between the north wall are for the culture and give the geometrical alignments diagonally across the gap.

The Ba Recess Enclosure has the 5 Zoser recesses similar to those between the King's Chamber and Grand Gallery of the Great Pyramid Antechamber which gives the geometrical alignments from the south west corner of the Recess wall. The No. 1 north east recess is on the 60° angle and therefore 30° off the north/south equinox for the age of maturity. No. 2 recess gives the geometrical alignments. The next recesses, 3 and 4, represent the Sphinx and Zoser. No. 4 is on the 52° and No. 5 on the 40°. These line up with the enclosure for the geometrical design. The wall curve is for the lifecycle. The wall opposite is 7 metres high for Zoser. The steps represent the Sphinx, Zoser, lifecycle, pyramid and geometrical alignments.

The Sunken Passage was two metres across and 7 long for the Sphinx. The north opening is on the line of the solstice.

There were probably about 24 roof beams for the age of initiation. The southern end was on the line of the 52°. The walls and roofing gave the science of the universe and knowledge.

The four different floor levels were for Zoser. On the lower floor level soapstone symbols and bowls for science, culture and the geometrical alignments were found. There was also an assortment of geometrical stones used for the alignments. Beside the north end of the east wall is an earth crocodile giving the geometrical alignments and representing Zoser and the Sphinx.

The Dentelle Patterned section, now collapsed, on the north west wall had four patterns for Zoser and the Sphinx, geometrical alignments, initiation and measurements. Where Bent marked the 'altar' is a geometrical set.

The Gold Enclosure: ('Gold furnace' is a misnomer because the heat would cause expansion and contraction which would interfere with the alignments and cause buckling of the masonry) has a set of geometrical alignments beside the boulder on the west side of the enclosure and was roofed with rock chips and earth.

The solstice boulder has been pitted on the north west side. These marks and a quantity of stones found in the cave represent the 52 year cycle, days of the year and science of the universe. The final test of initiation was probably performed here which would account for the gold of knowledge. Where Bent marked the furnace is a set of alignments to the boulder and cave.

The Balcony Enclosure has the solstice along the straight south wall overlooking the Eastern Enclosure. The platform is 13 metres long (10, 3) and 4 metres wide for Zoser and the Sphinx.

The View has the same rounded boulders as markers as the outcrop of rock below them.

The Central Boulder Passage of the Cleft Rock Enclosure has the boulder on the solstice, the last wall the equinox and 52° to the north west end of the small rock. The cave in the Cleft Enclosure represents the lifecycle. The 3 loopholes are for the Sphinx, Zoser and the geometrical alignments. The five metre wall is for Zoser.

The enclosure north of the Cleft Rock Enclosure has the geometrical design from the south west corner.

The exit north of the main Western Enclosure is on the equinox. Then it turns southwest for the 52° and lifecycle as do the steps near the bottom of the Acropolis, representing the descent of the pyramid of life, finally terminating at the point of the equinox. The exit is geometrically designed for the equinox, solstice and 52°.

The Boundary Wall is the outer circle and represents Ra. The sections are for the days of the year. Other groups represent the 52 year lifecycle, Sphinx and Zoser, as well as giving the geometrical alignments.

The Dolly Holes are for the solstice and the Sphinx. When one stands with two feet on the ground the four holes are for Mr. and Zoser. The lifecycle is shown by the curve of the holes which are used for measuring the moisture content of the atmosphere in September just before the rains.

The No. 2 Ruin excavated beside the museum gives the geometrical alignments for the equinox, solstice and 52° as well as the teachings of Zoser, the Sphinx and Ra.

On the west side of the ruin is a straight solstice wall joined to other geometrical walls leading to the equinox loophole for the passing on of knowledge. The stones above it are for Zoser and the Sphinx.

On the platform is a concave 'Goyo' (Shona) hollow stone

with the 'meg' sphere stone placed in the hollow of a 'grinding' stone. This lines up with the two Sphinx stones beside it for the geometrical set. The next section has squared Zoser hollows lining up with the north, with the Ra equinox bowl hollow. The square sides of the shaping give the solstice and 52°. The walling and two sunken hollows to the north of this platform are for the geometrical alignments and work in with walling of the nearby steps.

The path of the ruin is white and next to it a small jutting section with four sphinx stones placed on it. The fifth, for Zoser, is to the north of them. The 'equinox pointer' lines up with the walling next to it for the solstice and 52°. The section to the north of this area has the small stone wall for Zoser, the Sphinx and the initiation. The walls and steps are all for the geometrical alignments. The half circle represents the pyramid and the two lines the Sphinx.

The curved wall north east of this section has the geometrical walls for the centre representing the Mr. Ra and the double section the Sphinx. To the west of it is another small section of a double cone similar, but smaller, and serving the same purpose as the one in the Elliptical Building. The main stone walling aligns the south side of this ruin. The east/west equinox represents the days of the year, the path on the north side the 52 year lifecycle.

There is another design close to the Shangani Memorial, but this had not been excavated at the time of visiting. There is a cone-shaped boulder which has been placed in the solstice position and forms part of the design. This boulder cone was probably used as a marker so that the earth markers would be protected and not lost to the trained eye. The earth markers were probably covered to protect them as they were too valuable to be lost or damaged by those who did not understand their true value.

On an embankment is an excavated area which is a maze of earth designs. The visible Acropolis is probably aligned with the maze.

The Valley of Ruins represents the age of initiation. There seems to be a hollow section in one part, but again this has not been excavated.

Posselt Ruins have 'earth markers' of a crocodile which give the geometrical alignments with the circular markers. The crocodile represents the Sphinx, the circles Ra and the Sphinx, and the Arc markers the Mr. All these markers work in with the walling around them for the scientific knowledge of the universe.

The Phillips Ruins has a stone construction of a crocodile Sphinx. The head and east foot give the solstice and 52°. The stones down the centre back of the crocodile are for the equinox, the age of initiation and Zoser.

From the east foot to the tail is the 52° and the climb up the pyramid. The tail on the east/west indicated the Ba and the passing of knowledge to the next generation. The west 52° foot represents the stick of age.

The step section on the west side of the crocodile's body has 52 stones used for the lifecycle and the five steps for Zoser. There are two recesses on either side of the outer wall steps for the sphinx. The recesses form the optic geometrical alignments for the equinox, solstice and 52° as well as the science of the universe and knowledge.

The walling to the south east of the crocodile has the number of stones for the days of the year and the triangular earth markers for the geometrical alignments in the corner, the ground markers to the west of the wall at ground level give another set of geometrical alignments with the crocodile.

The 7 layered stone obelisk cone just south of the crocodile's head and the number of stones are for the age of initiation. The Zimbabwe monolith was discovered here and protruded a metre above the cone, which was a royal measure high. The most important 'Zimbabwean' soapstone bird brings together the ancient philosophy of Africa, Egypt and the pre-Christian era of the ancient monuments such as Stonehenge.

The green soapstone Sphinx monolith has a crocodile ascending the front of the 'leg' design. The double eye is for Ra. The teeth are for the age of initiation and the length of training. On this side of the monolith are two Sphinx bands and five Zoser chevrons, which also represent the pyramid, the angle of the solstice and the 52°. The ten chevrons are for the quaternary. A youthful figure can be seen under the bird's two claws.

There are four separate indents. One is situated beside the crocodile's head. The second is between its feet. These two indents are one above the other for the north/south direction. A third indent is under the opposite side chevron and forms the east/west with the second indent. The fourth is on the wing of the bird and is north/south with the third indent and the 52° with the second indent. These indents give the chest decoration alignments as head and face optic lines.

Above the crocodile front view are two chevrons and an embossed Ra circle. The circles are geometrically designed for the equinox, solstice and 52°. The front view of the bird represents sex, marriage and initiation. Under the bird's claws are five chevrons and two Ra circles. The geometrical alignments are to be taken from the crocodile's eyes, ears and tail.

The claws of the bird represent Zoser and the legs the

Sphinx and initiation. The chest has the chevron design for the age of discretion (15+15=30), Ma, Ra, Ka, Ba and Mr. One chevron is for the science of Zoser and the other for the culture of the Sphinx. Ba for the 360° and Mr definition. Ba and Mr could start the next chevron or triangle sequence. Mr is made up of Ma Ra for continued knowledge.

The wings of the bird represent the feather and the chest the heart and justice. The equinox square is under the wing for the passing on of knowledge and through to the other side where there are two embossed Ra circles for the geometrical alignments. Below them are five Zoser chevrons. A seated elderly figure can be seen under the bird's claws. The dot indent between the Ra circle forms the equinox and the degrees radiating from it to the legs, wings and equinox hole.

The crocodile has one eye and single foot with five toes on this side of the monolith. The tail represents Ba, Mr and the stick of age. When a crocodile moves its feet, the body bends into a curve so that the tail moves from side to side and does not remain central. This gives three (two feet and tail) on the one side and two on the other. The crocodile's tail has a section of double ridges with the end section of single ridges. The monolith viewed on the left side denotes descent and a profile of the crocodile section of the monolith is shaped like the calf of a human leg. The bird should be positioned to face north.

The Cape Raven (Corvulture albicollis) represents the lost soul and spirit of a loved one, lost during a flood and not found again, whose spirit has been returned and put at rest in the monolith.

The red-eyed dove (Streptopelia semitorquata) is the bird of peace which can have a *'hoarse call of Kraaa'* (Roberts Birds of Southern Africa). It is also associated with the story of Noah and the dove which flew back to the ark with a twig. On the outside of the Phillips Crocodile Enclosure is one of the original plain monoliths still in position and at the same angle as the wall. The monolith gives the equinox, solstice and 52° with the wall close to the monolith. The small shaped enclosure near the monolith has the step enclosure for the geometrical set and scientific knowledge.

The people who constructed the ancient stone buildings in Southern Africa used shapes such as the crocodile for earth designs and cones for obelisks and reference survey points in relation to the sun's shadow and locality.

In Egypt, the builders of the Great Pyramid of Cheops used the Great Sphinx of Chephren as a fixed survey reference point, hence the great accuracy of the Great Pyramid. The Great Sphinx obelisks have unfortunately been removed, but the similarities with methods used in other parts of the ancient world, shows the importance and the spread of ancient cultures.

The Great Pyramid is on the Tropic of Cancer and the Great Zimbabwe Ruins are on the Tropic of Capricorn, the same longitude and latitude. The Sphinx in both cases is on the south east side of the main construction, the features in both cases have been damaged.

All alignments are taken from the 'heart' or diagonally sectioned square (see diagram). Scales have reciprocals to weigh and measure which must balance for the 'heart and feather'. The copper St. Andrew's cross soapstone casting from southern Africa gives the 23.33°. The value, therefore, is in the design of accuracy and not the metal content as outsiders believed.

Modern cathedrals have their transepts on the north/south axis, the altar and presbytery area to the east, and there is often an apse for the positioning of the obelisk. Other positions are the font and the heart of the building, which can be a dome as St. Paul's, a spire as Salisbury Cathedral or a tower as Winchester Cathedral. The nave of the latter has alongside it on the north west wall the foundations of the previous structure of St. Swithin's Saxon Minster, the apse containing the head and feet shape of a Sphinx.

Churches in the southern hemisphere face the opposite direction to those in the northern hemisphere because of the position of the sun and the equator. The 'natural' directional instincts are also reversed as are the oceans and circulatory currents.

Outside the Maund Ruins, on a flat outcrop of rock, is a geometrical design which is in very poor condition. The ruins' rounded entrance wall and steps were all part of the equinox, solstice and 52°.

The South East Ruin is a short distance from the rest of the ruins and constructed with rounded stones more in keeping with the Inyanga area, not the flat stones to be seen on other sections of Zimbabwe.

On an outcrop of granite to the north of the South East Ruin and to the east of the Acropolis is a line of quartz. The Africans will not cross this line unless they take a stone with them. Consequently there is a mound of stones on either side at the end of the line. There is another line beside the road on the way to Kyle Dam, though it is not as clear as the line near Maund Ruins.

During the building of the ruins the Africans wishing to cross the line had to pay a toll of a stone per crossing and this is how the ruins were built.

At the time of the equinox Zimbabwe was 13° west of the 'true north' which adds 858 years to the total i.e. $13 \times 66 = 858$.

This calculation applies to all ruins in Zimbabwe.

In 2000 AD the Elliptical Building and Acropolis will be 40° out from true north which would date the building 40+13=53x66=3498=1498 BC, 4 loopholes x 66 = 264+1498 = 1762 BC for the Elliptical Building and 1498 BC + 366 = 1864 BC for the Acropolis.

The west wall of the Western Enclosure of the Acropolis had seven circular cones on the other side of the entrance. The wall, therefore, denotes the length of time taken for the construction of the Acropolis and represents the days of the year.

The Elliptical Building has alignment loopholes at the base of the parallel walls, four outer walls and four inner walls. There is a half loophole, representing half inside and half outside, and another loophole in the north wall. The loopholes denote the number of degrees at the start of the construction to the culmination of the alignments and, therefore, give the age of each section by the number of loopholes. On the outside of the wall these are for the construction of the Valley Ruins. The four loopholes through the outside wall denote 4x66=264 years to build and the same for the inner walls.

The recesses (Acropolis) and green horizontal stone lines of the Elliptical Building also denote the number of degrees before the section culminated with the alignments. All this is very feasible because the equinox and solstice can be calculated in advance. A day is equal to a degree, one degree of the sun, and one degree equals 66 years. Therefore, seven days from the equinox or solstice equals 462, 66x7, years approximately.

The green scarabs were used by the pharaohs during the Middle Kingdom 2000 BC to 1650 BC and this may explain the use of soapstone markers in the Zimbabwe Ruins. Gold was common to both Africa and Egypt and, I believe, far more significant and durable than iron, which could be replaced economically by wood for agriculture. Metal was retained for religious, scientific and war symbols.

The rock chips of the Gold Enclosure linteled entrance and covered passage support great weight of stone above them and are comparable with Stonehenge, etc.

The position of the letter 'Z' indicates the classification of the construction. Zimbabwe has the letter 'Z' in first position denoting greatness and completion before use. The Chevron Wall on the Elliptical Building and the larger cone represent the 'K' in Hebrew. The inner wall and smaller cone are duplicates.

The 'Ironwood' (euphorbia) was probably introduced into Zimbabwe Ruins after they had passed their usefulness - ironwood is poisonous and could bring about death to those who tampered with it. Those who knew what it signified would no longer use the Ruins. Skeletons were found between the Parallel Walls which appeared to be of a later date, which could have defiled the area and the whole construction. Earth designs, mastabas and burial areas must not upset the geometrical alignments, science and culture. The ironwood would therefore mark the end of an era and was placed in a position for all to see. The Ruins were then allowed to become overgrown and 'lost'.

When an area was selected for building and stone was required, a fire was made near a cleft in the kopje, as this would provide the rounded 'cone' stones. The fire would heat the granite and the rock would peel uniformly from the inside because the outside of the kopje would remain cool and would not, therefore, expand. Each time a fire was made it burrowed further into the rock. This method saved a lot of time and labour and did not require water. The labour could be used to trim and transport the stones to the building site. Transportation occurred by placing a circular grass cushion on the head, on which the stone was placed.

Some of the caves were worked until they collapsed, resulting in rock formations such as those on the top of the Acropolis at Zimbabwe, while other workings remained as caves. Some of these were transformed into art galleries while others, such as the one near Kyle Dam, were not. It is interesting to note that stones from the same granite kopje were used for the construction of the dam wall, but in this case the stone was blasted from the top.

Peeling the rock from the top would have been dangerous, arduous and slow, but the exfoliate peeling done by the elements would be used whenever possible if suitable sizes and shapes were available.

The granite stones used for the construction of the ruins reflect the colour of the sun's rays, white for knowledge with the black shadow of the sun's rays for age. The early morning rays are yellow for knowledge and the science of the universe. This is why the ruins were not roofed over and green grass and leaves represented the heart and feather, even more so after a drought, when the rains were poor but the trees would still come into leaf.

During the New Kingdom (1570-1070 BC) in Egypt, huge temples were constructed out of living rock, probably assisted by the firing of wood to heat the rock and cause peeling, so that the Bowman learnt the art of producing stones for the construction of the ruins of Zimbabwe.

Diagram 1.

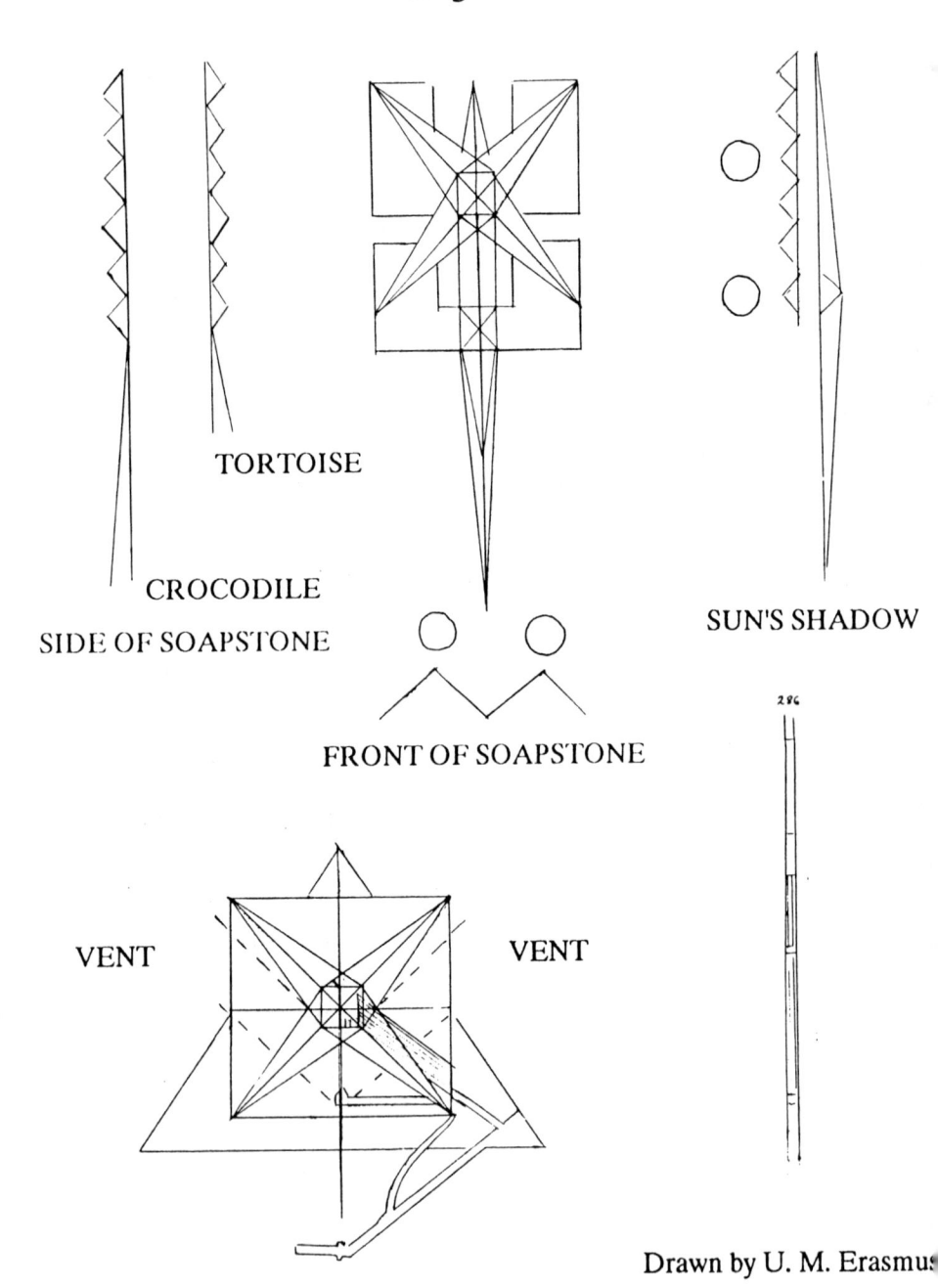

TORTOISE

CROCODILE

SIDE OF SOAPSTONE

FRONT OF SOAPSTONE

SUN'S SHADOW

VENT **VENT**

The Great Pyramid and Vertical Sphinx

Drawn by U. M. Erasmus

Diagram 2

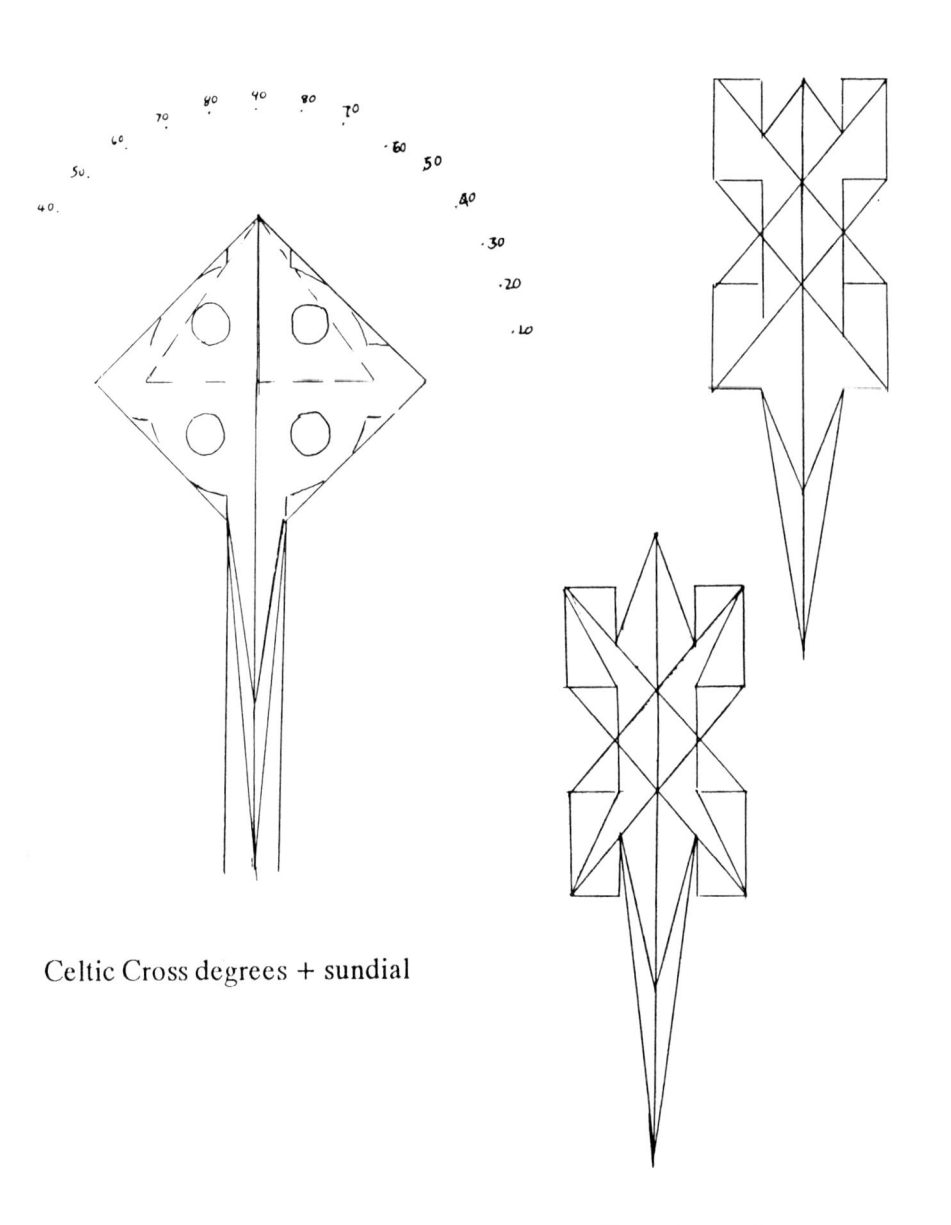

Celtic Cross degrees + sundial

crocodile and tortoise

Drawn by U. M. Erasmus

Diagram 3.

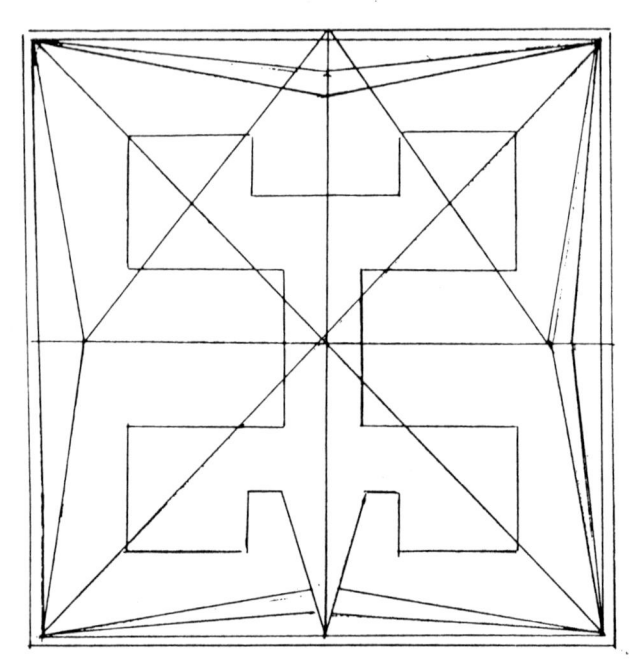

Capstone outside square.

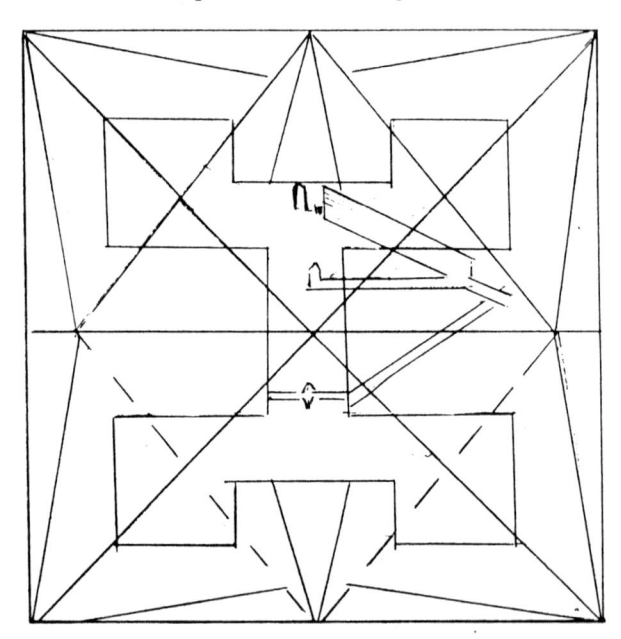

Great Pyramid + Sphinx   **Drawn by U.M. Erasmus**

ornaments

Smiling zebra

Headless animal

Headless turtle

Footless ornament

Zebra (side and front)

Squared headless ornament

Pregnant animal

Drawn by U M Erasmus

Soapstone

Fragment of bowl with procession of bulls

Fragment of bowl with hunting scene

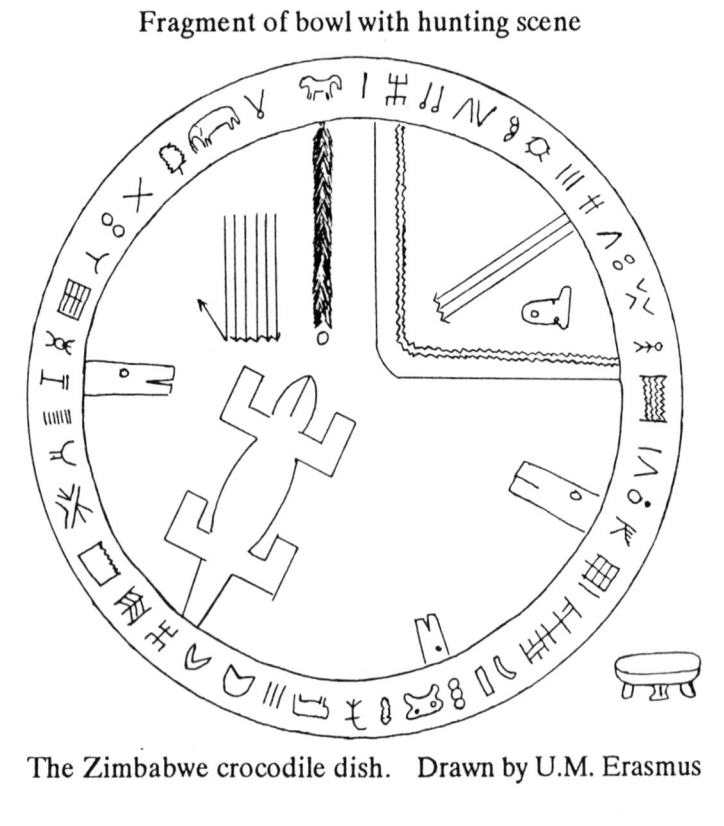

The Zimbabwe crocodile dish.   Drawn by U.M. Erasmus

Guide Book.

Ivory lions

Wooden Zimbabwe dish

Zimbabwe soapstone figurine

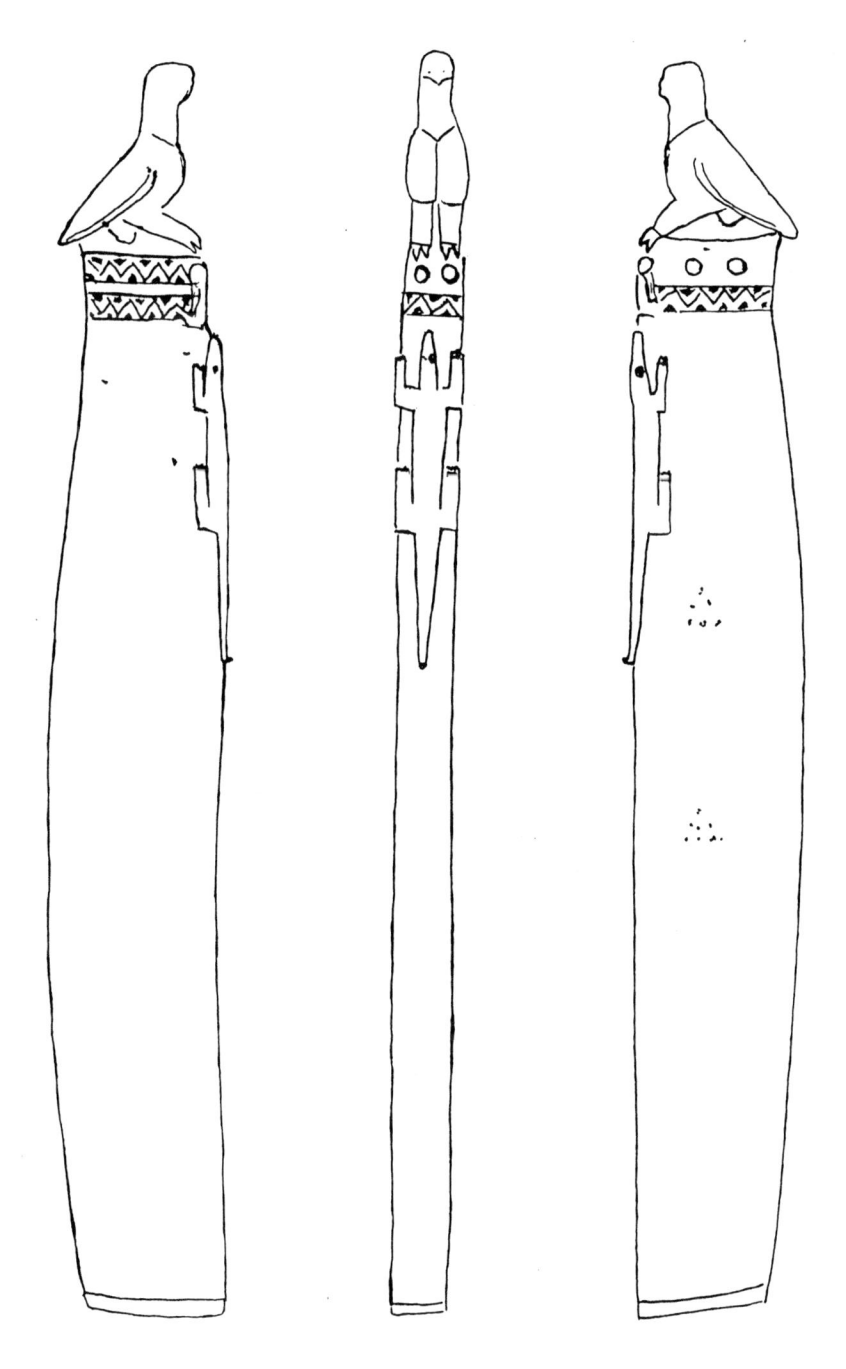

Zimbabwe, Green Soapstone Bird

Drawn by U.M. Erasmus

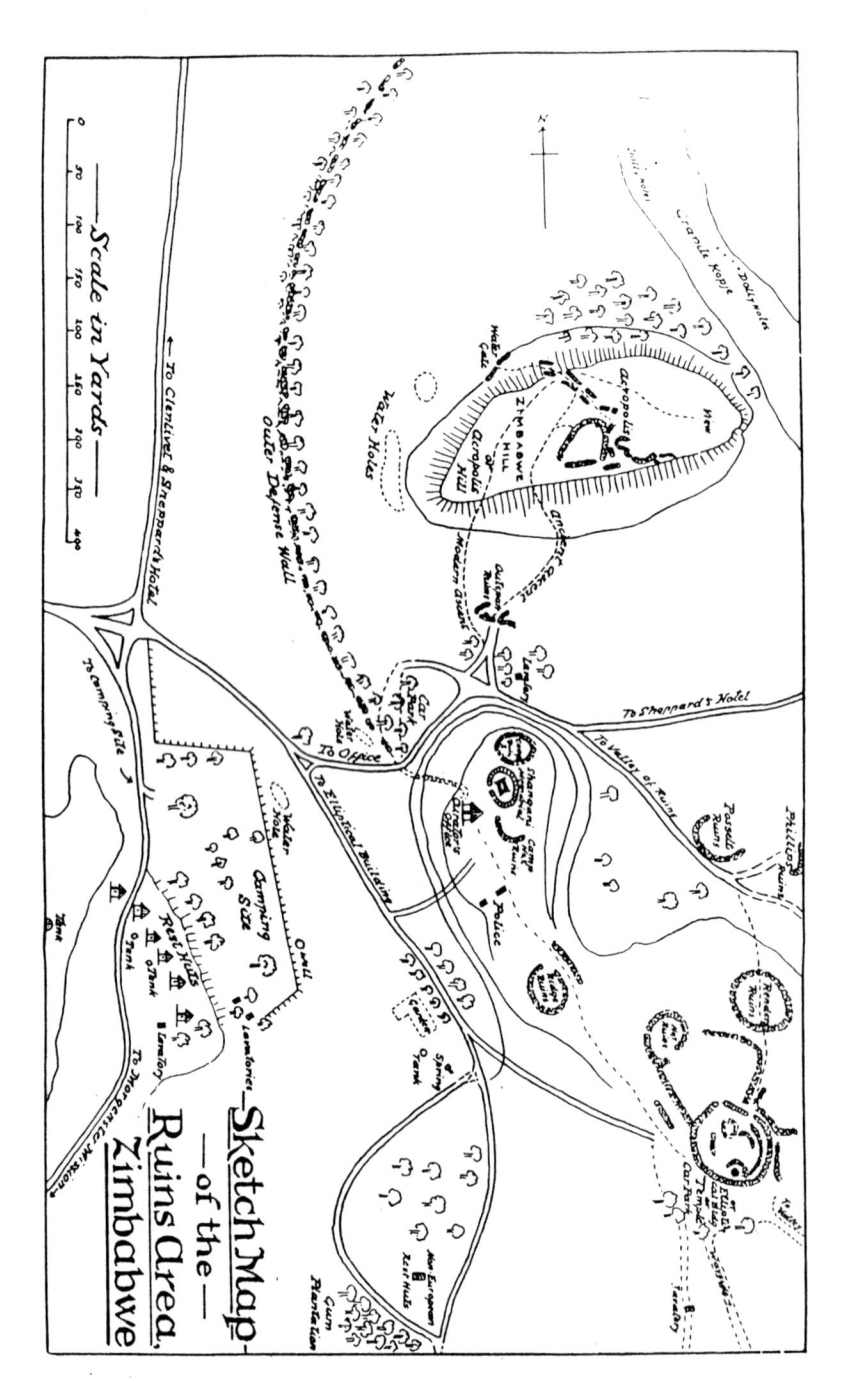

Zimbabwe Ruins

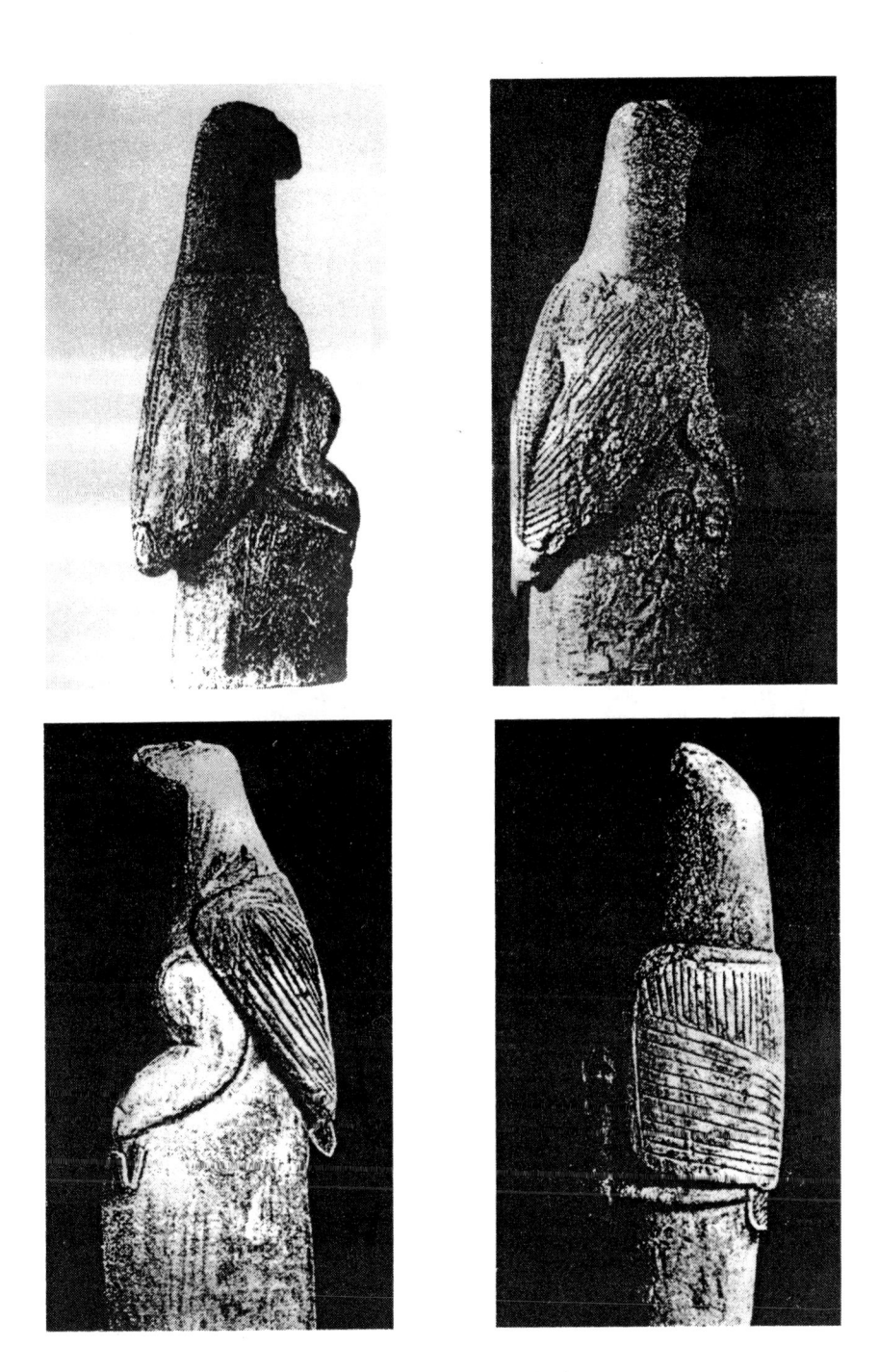

Soapstone birds, Zimbabwe

Guide Book.

Mr R. N. Hall, first curator of Zimbabwe Ruins.

Soapstone bowls of the Zimbabwe culture

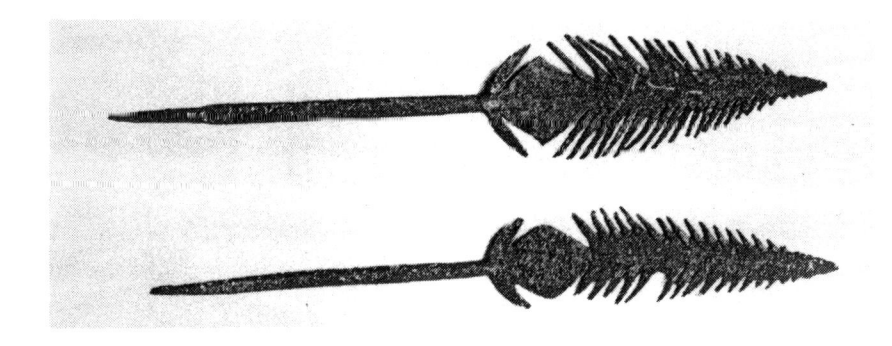

Bronze spearheads

Guide Book.

Ivory figurine, Vlei Ruin

Guide Book.

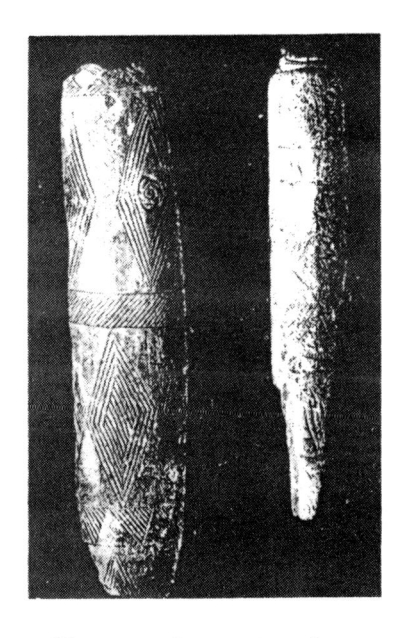

Decorated soapstone beams

Collection of shaped stones.

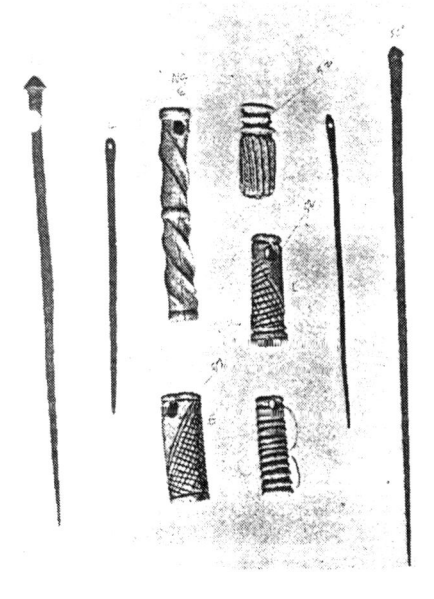

Iron pins, needles and
ivory objects.

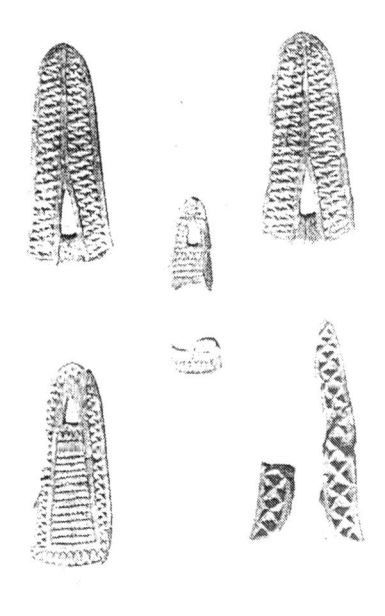

Ivory disks.

SYMBOLS

The symbols used for the building of the Zimbabwe Ruins are simple but exact and are made of stone, ivory, metal, pottery and wood. The wood was sometimes covered with gold for preservation. (Exodus 25 v10-11).

The 'fixed' Ba ground markers were made of an earth cement, which consisted of carefully selected earth mixed with water, then moulded and dried in the sun and, if necessary, fired to give it long-lasting properties. Mud and plaster were also used in the pyramids.

Fixed ground markers were necessary, because they could be constructed at the exact time of the equinox and solstice to ensure that the alignments were exact at the time the stone construction was undertaken, just as surveyors use theodolites and make points of reference. Once the work was completed these markers were covered over and preserved for future ground plans and as reference for repairs, Mr and the passing of knowledge.

The Zimbabwe crocodile dish (goyo) with the working symbols, angles and bearings round the rim has a space between the first and last symbol. These symbols are used in an anticlockwise direction, astrologers work the same way and this is used as a guide to the correct way up of the dish.

The centre has a double chevron line from the centre of the rim for the equinox. There are five arrows for Zoser with the head giving the 52°. The two lines with the arrows represent the Sphinx. The angled shank arrows and the line of the arrow head give the solstice. The similar headed crocodile gives the east/west equinox and both have the Ra eye.

The crocodile represents the Sphinx with his legs and tail.

The head represents the rise to the top of the pyramid and the descent to the tail for the fall of man. The feet give the geometrical alignments for the equinox, solstice and 52°. The small crocodile head represents the winter solstice and 52°.

The divided section has the chevron for the days of the year, with the three arrows diagonally across for the solstice and the Sphinx. The arrow heads are for the 52°, denoting age. The animal represents the Sphinx and the half circle for the pyramid with the dot of Ra in the centre.

Around the rim of the dish is an animal with an arched tail, depicted for the pyramid and legs of the Sphinx. The dot and 'V' are for the sun. The dividing line is for the passing on of knowledge. The elephant (God) has the trunk of age, the feather of justice, the 'X' of the solstice and 72°. The two dots are for Ra and the inverted 'Y' is for the sun's shadow, followed by an iron symbol and the squares of the Sphinx and Zoser. The next symbol has the base of the pyramid with the dot of Ra in the centre and the Sphinx section towards the centre of the dish. Then there is a geometrical cross and lines of knowledge followed by another symbol and geometrical lines which in turn are followed by the dot and pyramid. The chevron of knowledge and geometrical alignments are next. The double trident is an iron God of war. The next three symbols are for the pyramid, followed by another Sphinx and so on around the dish. The wavy line symbols are 'imbwe' for the earth cement designs and the figure 8, the triumph of the upper mind over the lower and eternity.

The wooden Zimbabwe dish has a single crocodile in the centre with the nose of the pyramid and eye of Ra. The tail is for initiation, the legs and feet for the Sphinx and Zoser and the body markings for scientific knowledge. The rim of the dish has the 52 chevrons in one set, the turtle above the crocodile's nose and the animal opposite at the crocodile's tail, marks the equinox. The sun marks the solstice and the legs and feet of the crocodile give the geometrical alignment. The symbols at the side of the dish represent the dot of Ra and the geometrical alignments with the pointer and lower twist. The goyo (quern) for measuring the moisture content of the atmosphere is clearly shown.

The stand of the dish has the centre cone with outside stands for the geometrical set and represents the three for the Sphinx, two for knowledge and one for God. The chevron is for Zoser with the total number of chevrons for the age of initiation.

The circular stones with the lines on the rim give the geometrical alignments for the equinox, solstice and the 52°. The dots are for the Sphinx and Zoser with the Ra circle in the centre and the equinox hole for the passing on of knowledge. The dots represent the years between the age of initiation and the apex of the pyramid.

The circular stone without the hole in the centre has the lines around the rim. Four in the one set, eight in the other and joined lines. All these have their meanings.

The decorated rosette soapstone, which is grey in colour, has two grooves for the equinox and solstice with the dots for the 52 year lifecycle, the Sphinx, Zoser, the days of the year and the science of the universe and knowledge. The holes give the equinox at midday. The dividing lines are for the shadow of the sun, the solstice and equinox.

The joined set of three stones has the diagonal lines for the equinox and solstice with the total number for the 52°. The three sets are for the Sphinx with the dividing grooves for Zoser.

The flat game stones have the seven Sphinx (4+2+1) hollows one way and the five Zoser the other. The square is also for Zoser, with the oval at the other side for the equinox and Mr, passing on of knowledge. The number of hollows are for the years between the age of initiation and the age of retirement.

The septangular block is for the equinox, solstice and 52°. From one side the four sides for Zoser can be observed and from the other side, there are three for the Sphinx.

The symbols vary in size and shape. The thimble size object has two rows of dots for the Sphinx and initiation, with the 52 year lifecycle shown by the total number of dots. The angle of the side is for the solstice, with the Ra equinox hole at the top. The rows at the top of the thimble are for the age of initiation. Another plain thimble has the equinox hole and sloping sides for the pyramid and lifecycle. The 'L' shape gives the geometrical alignments for the equinox, the top of the upright and foot, the solstice and 52°.

The cylinder-shaped symbol has the five Zoser sets of three rows of dots for the Sphinx. The total number of dots is for the days of the year. Another cylinder has a set of seven chevrons and below a set of five cubed lines. The seven chevrons represent the Sphinx (4, 2, 1) and the days of the year. The set of five is for Zoser and the lifecycle.

The buffalo-shaped horns on a grey soapstone bowl give the equinox down the 'stand'. The solstice and 52° are from the 'stand' to the horns. The 'stand' represents the stick of age and the horns the rise and fall of man.

The grey soapstone dish of horned animals shows the horns of initiation, the tail for the Sphinx and age, the eye of Ra and the mouth for the pyramid.

On the large grey soapstone dish the diagonal lines around the outside are divided into sets for the 52 year lifecycle, the age of initiation and the days of the year. The bands are for Zoser and the Sphinx. The animals in the centre of the dish represent the Sphinx and knowledge.

The grey Zimbabwe soapstone bowl comprises animals, man, bird and zebra for the child who crawls. The eye of Ra and the ears to listen with, for Zoser. The man of knowledge and the stick of age held aloft. The birds' feathers of justice and the tail feathers are all for Zoser. The pyramid is denoted by the shape of the tail sections of the bird. The zebra has the lines of the lifecycle and initiation and the tail itself denotes the stick.

The soapstone figure has the head denoting hear all, see all, say nothing; the Ra eyes and ears, the lips and the lifecycle. The bust represents Ma, Ra, Ka, Ba and Mr, the Sphinx and the geometrical alignments. The cubed pattern has 8 across and 7 down, 7x8=56. Others are 8+6=14+56=70; 70+2=72 for Zoser and the universal lifecycle 6x8=48+4=52; 70+52x3=366 the days of the year. The third design has the two legs and feet with the 5 Zoser toes and the dot of Ra at the centre top.

One side of the figurine has the cubed design 6x6=36. The horizontal lines below are 10 deep and a short line and there are seven shallower lines 36+10+6=52 or 36+10+7-1=52. The other side shows a cubed design of seven across and six down 6x7=42. Below this are 13 horizontal lines 42-13=29 and the square enclosing the cubes gives 30 for the age of maturity. The arms give the geometrical alignments and represent the Sphinx. The hands have five fingers for Zoser.

The north/south is taken from the Pole Star in the constellation of Ursa Minor (the bear) and the pointers of the Southern Cross. The equinox and solstice are worked out by the sun and the length of the day and night. The days of the year are divided by four to give the equinox and solstice. The degrees are worked out by the number of days to or from the last equinox or solstice.

Working in an anticlockwise direction, as the astrologers do, seven days to the next equinox equals 7 = 3 1/3 by the angle of the sun's rays or 91-7=84 days ÷ 7 = 12 weeks after the equinox is the solstice.

The full moon phases from the time of the equinox give the 52° less four days, or two full moon phases plus a week and four days for the solstice gives the 52°. This explains the 'fertility' symbols which have been found and the methods of calculating the angles and degrees without scientific instruments but simply by using the sun and moon.

The zebra hari ornament has the red background for youth with the black lines of age and knowledge on the top which are the same as the bottom bands of the pyramids. The 52 lines on the side are for the lifecycle. The circles down the centre of the back represent the equinox and the passing on of knowledge. The front view has the circles and dots for Ra, with the five diagonal lines on one side for Zoser. The seven on the other side are for the Sphinx (4, 2, 1). They also serve as the solstice with the centre vertical for the equinox.

The iron axe has the handle for the equinox and the curved blade represents the lifecycle. The ends of the curve give the solstice and 52° when a short straight bar is set into the earth. Because of its uneven length the curve side gives the direction of the wind and consequently the iron axe works on the same principle as a weathercock.

The 'gong' is made in the shape of two Upper Egypt crowns and is joined at the top by a curved handle for the lifecycle and the passing on of knowledge from one generation to the next. Similar gongs are still used in the northern part of Africa. The gongs found on the Acropolis may have been rung at specific times instead of the drums to coincide with the sun shadows on the 'sundial' stones.

The 'gong' Ba stick has the ring of Ra with the ends of the staff forming the solstice and 52°, the staff being the equinox. The gong stick is placed in the ground so that the sun shadow falls on the outside of the 'gong' for the solstice and through the top loop and narrow section for the equinox. It should be noted that the joining curve at the top of the double gong is uneven to allow for the distance and positioning of the equator, because the sun is not directly overhead at the time of the equinox.

The 'V' symbol, also shown on the crocodile dish, can be used for the shadow of the sun.

The iron cross has the vertical equinox ends bent over to prevent the loss of the rings, which are on the shaft. The top ring is double, one inside the other for Ra, and the lower one is single, for the continual lifecycle. The cross represents the north/south, east/west equinox. The 52° is from the flattened section of the shaft to the end of the equinox arm. The solstice is from the ends of the equinox arm and shaft. The cross is placed vertically in the ground and the crossbar sun shadow timepiece is measured morning and afternoon. The main stem gives the midday equinox.

The bronze spearhead is the symbol of war and has the 'feathers' of justice in reverse, protecting a square of Zoser and the two ends of the Sphinx and initiation.

The iron battleaxe and arrows are also symbols of war. The straight bar has the ends at the angle of 52° and the sides at the top and bottom for the solstice. The length of the bar is half a metre and represents a royal measure and the age of initiation. The cross has the equinox through the centre and the solstice across the corner of the ends to its opposite counterpart and also acts as a hand measure (Egyptian hieroglyphics).

The copper St. Andrew's cross is a hand measure for the equinox, solstice and 52° (Egyptian hieroglyphics) for the Sphinx and geometrical alignments, the value was not the metal but what it signified.

The bronze symbols comprising a circular Ra disc with a cross on the top of the whirl and a half disc above which represents the 52°, Zoser, the Sphinx and the science of the universe with the cross for the equinox and solstice and geometrical alignments.

The bronze bracelet has the centre forming the geometrical alignments. The top and bottom represent the pyramid and lifecycle. The two curved lines on either side represent the Sphinx and Zoser (2, 4). The five whirls are for Zoser and the seven are for the Sphinx. The side of the bracelet has in the pattern the geometrical alignments and represents the Sphinx and Zoser, the days of the year and the science of the universe and knowledge.

The bronze bell also has the Ra dots included in the design as well as the bird for the feather of justice, Sphinx and Zoser.

The gold circlet has the twist for the days of the year with the embossed chevron for the pyramid, Ma, Ra, Ka, Ba, Mr, equinox, 52° and the lifecycle. On one side of the divider are five well-spaced twists for Zoser and the other side shows seven for the Sphinx. The divider itself is for the solstice and the age of initiation.

The ivory cone obelisk tower and the Upper Egypt Pharaoh's crown are similar in shape. The dots are for the days of the year and the bands represent the Sphinx. At the top of the cone is the eye for the equinox. Across the bands on the body of the cone are the solstice and 52°. The cone represents the pyramid and lifecycle.

The Zero (Shona) stone washers, found in a variety of sizes, were used as plumbline spacers for the inclined layers of stone. The incline is clearly shown on the Conical Tower. The different gradients were required for the various plumbline alignments which kept the walls evenly inclined. (The pyramids also had inclined layers.)

The black beads have a set of five for Zoser with the dots joined together for youth and guidance. The two central beads represent the solstice and initiation. The white of the dots is for geometrical knowledge. The red represents youth and the blue is for the universe and initiation. The diagonal lines are for the solstice and the geometrical alignments, including the Sphinx and Zoser. The set of seven similar beads is for the Sphinx and age, four for youth, two for initiation and the one with the stick for age. The total number of dots represents the days of the year, the age of initiation and the science of knowledge.

The black beads with the white dots and blue centre around the top and bottom are for the age of initiation. The white dots with the red centre are for the Sphinx and Zoser. All the dots together are for the lifecycle. The black bead with the parallel white wavy lines has two sets visible at one time for the age of initiation. The lines are divided into four and two for Zoser and the Sphinx.

Of the soapstone monoliths with the decorated sides and plain section, one has the diamonds for the geometrical alignment of the equinox/solstice and 52°. It carries the number of lines for Zoser. The Ra dots are in the centre of the diamond. The curved lines are for the lifecycle and ten for Zoser. The bands of diagonal lines are for the 52 year lifecycle and solstice. Below this is another diamond with one side for Zoser. The other lines in the centre are for the age of initiation. The next band has the chevron pattern for the solstice and 52°, while the lines in between are for Zoser. The next diamond has been broken.

The next monolith has the diamond lines for the solstice and 52° with the multi-lines for the teachings of Zoser and the Sphinx. The chevrons represent the pyramid and science of knowledge.

The third monolith has the horizontal band of lines for Zoser and underneath is a trellis pattern for the lifecycle, age of initiation and the expected lifespan. The following section is similar to a diamond cross, giving the solstice along the lines and the equinox through the points. The fill-in lines represent the Sphinx and Zoser. The lower chevron pattern has ten down and five across for Zoser.

Found in a prominent position on the Platform section of the Acropolis was a two and a half metre (broken) soapstone monolith which would only have had two metres protruding above the baseline. The first symbol is the tortoise with two Zoser feet at the top and three underneath the body of the Sphinx and the Ra head. Below the tortoise is a band of four diamonds for Zoser followed by a diamond with a Ra dot in the centre. Next is a chevron line, a second diamond with dot, another chevron line and a third diamond with a dot. Continuing on the other section of the monolith is a triangle for the pyramid. Then a diamond followed by a dividing line and the solstice diagonal line with another dividing line. A pair of back-to-back lines are for the Sphinx and four for Zoser. This is followed by a band of diagonal lines, five going one way for Zoser and seven going the opposite way for the Sphinx. Underneath these is another diamond for the geometrical alignments. Then follows a chevron of diagonal fill-in lines for the Sphinx, the equinox and solstice. Below this is another diamond with a double outline for the Sphinx and the inner lines of the square for Zoser. The next diamond is similar. However, the third has the diamond outline with the Zoser centre. The diagonal lines are for the solstice, 52°, Sphinx and Zoser.

The soapstone monolith with the surmounted bird has a plain undecorated main beam. One has the headless bird with a double row of dots down the centre back (crocodile of two by two) to the top section of the circle on the upper wing for the lifecycle. There is a double row of five dots from the bottom of the lower wing to the edge of the lower wing. The double row of dots has seven (14) for the Sphinx which also give the age of initiation and lifecycle. The two circles below the bird are also diagonal and if a line is taken from the top and joined at right angles to the lower two this forms an 'L' for the solstice. The paired Ra circles form the equinox and 52°, the Sphinx and knowledge. The bird has the wing feathers of justice and the four for Zoser.

Another bird shows the circle along the lower wing edge. The seven smaller ones are for the Sphinx and the five larger circles are for Zoser. The pattern below the wing denotes the pyramid, lifecycle, solstice and 52. There are 24 feathers on each side 12+12=24. The tail feathers are geometrically aligned.

The turtle bird monolith with the upside-down cow/bull below its feet represents the Sphinx. Between the legs and horn is the square of Zoser and the rise and fall of man. The turtle bird has the five claws for Zoser on each foot. The back has the diagonal lines of justice, solstice and initiation. The turtle head of the bird has the Ra eye and mouth for the lifecycle. The line down the centre front is for the equinox and knowledge. Another turtle bird has the five Zoser claws and the wing is marked with the 52 diagonal solstice lines. The vertical lines are for the equinox. These twelve lines represent seven for the Sphinx and five for Zoser. The eye is for Ra and the mouth for the lifecycle. The eye and the wing line up for the equinox and the wing and chin for the solstice. The third turtle bird has the five Zoser claws on one foot and the four Sphinx on the other. The curved lines under the feet give the geometrical alignments and the circular mark near it represents the lifecycle and gives the geometrical alignments. Another turtle bird has the Sphinx's feet resting on a double chevron representing the pyramid, solstice and 52°. The claws are for Zoser. The next bird has the tail feathers for culture and the lifecycle. The outline of the wing gives the geometrical alignment. The number of feather lines gives the age of initiation, Zoser and the Sphinx. The legs are for the initiation, Sphinx and Zoser. The line under the claws is for the lifecycle and geometrical alignments. The head gives the geometrical alignment for the equinox. From the side view using the neck, body and leg the solstice and 52° can be found. The head shape is of a turtle with an open mouth which incorporates the animal part of the Sphinx.

Turtles put their heads above water when they come up to breathe air and hear all, see all and say nothing. The turtle bird could have been used singularly or in groups for the Sphinx, Zoser, geometrical alignments and the science of the universe and knowledge.

The symbols found are invariably damaged in some way, either the design has been damaged or its pedestal, which in itself gives accurate measurements and has a specific meaning, even when it is plain. Consequently, any part of a symbol that has been broken or damaged renders it useless and is therefore discarded as imperfect. Had the famous 'Zimbabwe bird' not been damaged it would probably not have fallen into the hands of outsiders.

The American Zuni Pueblo Indians have a black basalt bird inlaid with turquoise, which is similar to the Zimbabwe birds. They are associated with the journey made 'to the place of emergence'. Some North American Indians' peace pipes are made of stone and are similar in shape to the ground markers found in Zimbabwe, which probably also mark the area of silence (peace). The 'thunder bird' of the North American Indians seems to have a similar meaning to the Zimbabwe birds.

Fragments of a Chinese celadon porcelain bowl of the Sung period (960-1279) which were useful for the scientific, geometrical and culture association were found. The blue and white willow pattern has the days of the year on the outside rim. The squares are seven and five with the dots for initiation. The leaves on the trees are for the lifecycle, the trellis gives the equinox, solstice and 52°. A genuine pattern has birds With fish tails for the Sphinx. The story and rhyme has the following meaning:-

Two pigeons flying high - initiation, justice and marriage. Chinese vessel sailing by - science of the heavens and navigation. Weeping willow hanging o'er - rise and fall of man. Bridge of three men, not of four - Sphinx and Zoser.

Between 1279 and 1368 the Mongols controlled China from Peking to the Mediterranean countries. The most famous Yuan emperor was Kublai Khan. There are still Turkish-speaking moslems in Kashaga, Chinese Turkestan. Sinkiang borders Russia and is not far from Afghanistan and the Gobi Desert nomads. Marco Polo (1256-1323) journeyed overland to India, China and other eastern countries during Kublai Khan's rule.

The blue and white Ming bowl (1368-1644) found at Dhlo

Dhlo near Bulawayo in Zimbabwe also has the wavy line on the rim for Zoser, the loophole between the flowers for Ra and the lifecycle. The pattern represents culture and science as well as giving the geometrical alignments.

It is possible that Kang Yin, a lieutenant of Pan Ch'ao, whose expedition penetrated the Persian Gulf in 97 AD, traded with Africa until the rise of Islam and junks were superceded by the dhow in the Indian Ocean. The Y'ang dynasty started in China in 618 AD Kang T'ang Zanj.

The camel is the symbol of Allah and Islam (Surah VII 'The Heights' verse 73). The stone camels must therefore be Islamic and date back to the Kublai Khan dynasty and the occupation of China by Islam.

The Gobi Desert camels were probably introduced into Africa, after the Thera catastrophe, which left North Africa with desert conditions where neither man nor domestic animals or crops could survive. The camel then became the symbol of life, communication and transport, enabling Islam to take over North Africa.

KHAMI RUINS

The Khami Ruins near Bulawayo are named after the river which skirts the ruins and later joins the Zambezi River. There could be a connection with the Egyptians Khamsim hot wind which blows south or south-east from March to May for a period of 50 days, because Khami is close to the Kalahari desert and has similar conditions.

The chequer pattern of Khami gives November to February (Egyptian hieroglyphics) which is the warm growing season. The number of patterns for the science of the universe, culture, Zoser, the Sphinx and optic geometrical alignments.

The Monolith First Ruin has the pattern section for the age of initiation and the steps up to the ruin are for Zoser, the Sphinx and the ascent of man as he climbs up the Mr of life.

The Passage Ruin has the east/west entrance with the circular obelisk cone marker for the geometrical design at the entrance, which is on the west side. The Passage is 15 metres long with the marker at the 12 metre point for the Sphinx and Zoser giving the geometrical alignments with the nearby walling. The geometrically aligned passage divides the enclosure. The pattern section is for the age of initiation and the Sphinx. There is a geometrical set from the south end of the outside wall and next to it a boulder. This boulder represents man's rise and fall in life. The shorter outer parallel wall is for the Sphinx and gives the geometrical alignments with the cone at the north end. The stones represent Zoser, the Sphinx and the age of initiation. Inside the enclosure the boulder, main walling, the walling and rock in the vicinity give the geometrical alignments including the 10, 30, 40 and 72 degrees.

The north east opening for the outside main wall has a

section for the rise and fall of man. The boulder and triangular section next to it represent the pyramid and Mr as well as the geometrical alignments. The squared wall near the north main wall is for Zoser and gives the geometrical alignments. The main side wall is 2-3 metres high and 12 metres long. The two patterned lines of double layered stones are for the Sphinx, Zoser and scientific knowledge.

The Precipice Ruin has the main outside wall built on the line of the 72° for the close of life and universal evolution. The chequered pattern gives the days of the year while the boulder at the base of the wall marks the science of the universe and knowledge. The length of the wall is 66 2/3 metres, the number of years to the degree. The height of the wall is seven metres for the Sphinx and Zoser. The wall is the longest retaining wall of its type in Zimbabwe. The breach areas in the wall were probably for the Sphinx and Zoser. The third one was for the descent and therefore three metres for the stick of age.

The three gaps in the wall denote death, probably at the precipice on the east side of the ruin, or the west precipice facing the chequered pattern. This would, therefore, have been an area of death. Bulawayo therefore gets its name 'the place of killing' from Khami.

The two-tier wall represents the pharaoh's double crown. The upper wall and 'crown' of good is broken, leaving the lower crown of evil and mind so that all could see why the wall was deliberately damaged and broken, evil prevailed over good.

The squared entrance at the north west end of the main wall gives the west (death) access to the walled courtyard which is 16x18 metres (2,3,4,7 by 1,2,3,5,7) which represents 16+18=34 the age of discretion. There are 5 metres of free-standing wall for Zoser. Then it continues north in a curve for the lifecycle and ends at the boulder. The unnamed wall and boulder section has the pattern section for scientific knowledge, Zoser and the Sphinx.

The Vlei Ruin had a small decorated section for Zoser and the Sphinx on the south side of the main wall. To the south west of the main enclosure is an outcrop of granite and an equinox line of quartz. The central small enclosure has three boulders for the beginning, middle and end. The wall on the west side is only 1/2 metre high. Inside this area some animal bones were found for the Sphinx, pottery for the science of the universe and geometrical alignments. The ivory figurine found here has the eye of the equinox at the base of the post for the passing on of knowledge to the next generation. The figure is perched on the top of the post in a flexed burial position. This area marks the end of an era. The face gives the geometrical alignments. The toes are for Zoser. One hand is under the chin but the other lower arm and hand are facing down, representing the decline of man and the use of a stick. By using the eyes, nose and mouth, the face gives the geometrical alignments.

The platform area measures 30 metres for the age of responsibility in one direction and 60 for the age of decline in the other. The walling joins the south side walling at right angles. The two metres above the platform represent Zoser. The loophole is for the equinox and the passing on of knowledge to the next generation.

The Multi-cone Ruin No. 4 is on an outcrop of granite rock and has four and five stone terraced circles for Zoser and the Sphinx. At the summit of the rock is a circular earthen construction measuring six metres in diameter and a metre high and half a metre thick giving $6 + ½ + ½ = 7$ and $6 - ½ - ½ = 5$ for Zoser and the Sphinx. The numerous small stick imprints are for the science of the universe and culture.

Hill Ruin No. 3 has a decorated wall which is 23 metres long for the age of initiation and three metres for the Sphinx. The herringbone represents the 52 year lifecycle. The dolerite and chequered patterns are for the science of the universe, Zoser and the Sphinx. The entrance gives the geometrical alignments with the walling to the north for the equinox, solstice and 52°.

The Ankh Crux Ruin is about 24 metres in diameter. The hard way up was the original ascent and the easy way down was for age. The niches beside the steps were for the geometrical alignments. There is a loophole on the west wall and the north loophole is for the equinox, Zoser and the Sphinx. Taking account of the shape and height, it also gives the geometrical alignments with the corner. The terraced walling is for Zoser and the Sphinx with the dagga (earth cement) covered steps for the ascent of man through life. The post is for the stick of age. There is a circular construction in earth cement near the top of the enclosure which, in conjunction with the nearby walling, gives the geometrical alignments. There are said to be two further earth constructions on the Crux Ruin but they were not, as yet, visible when I visited it.

On the south side of the summit is a flat-topped granite stone carrying the Egyptian ankh crux, mandare or Maltese cross. It is made up of twelve stones on the two arms for Zoser and the Sphinx while the two together give the age of initiation. The other two arms are made up of ten stones for Zoser. The total number of stones represents the number of years in the lifecycle. The arms give the equinox and diagonally across them the solstice. The boulder has a crack along the line of the equinox and has a triangular shape at one end for the pyramid and the rise and fall of man. This triangular shape and the crux form the 10,

30, 40 and 70 degrees.

The crux lines up with the other markers of the enclosure for the geometrical alignments, based on the original positioning of the crux.

The main wall and boulder of Hill Ruin A, form the solstice to the west, the equinox is between the boulders and the wall forms the 52°. The platform measures 30 x 16 metres (10,4,2) and the wall is two metres high for the Sphinx and initiation.

The Hill Ruin has a 10 by 20 metres levelled area for Zoser and the age of responsibility. The wall surrounding platform B is 2½ and 1½ metres high. It is decorated with dolerite among the granite stones for scientific knowledge and the geometrical alignments. The diamond patterned granite stone found near the north end of the wall was the main marker. Of the diamonds one does not have a dot, the second has a dot at the lower point, the third has a dot at the side and the fourth carries a dot in the centre. These dots are for Ra and the geometrical alignments. They represent man's rise in life. The four diamonds are for Zoser and the three dots for the Sphinx.

The equinox runs from the corner of the wall near the boulder to the west side of Ba 2. The solstice is to the other side of Ba 2. The 52° is to the west side of Area Ba 1. Area B is 30 metres. The angled wall Bb on the west side of the path is on the line of the solstice. The 52° is to the corner of Ba and the equinox was to the 'diamond' stone. The dolerite stones mark the 10, 30, 40, 52 and 72 degrees. At the entrance between area B and C is another equinox with the 'diamond' stone.

The niche on the wall of area C gives the equinox to the boulder obelisk cone and the straight section of the Alcove. An ivory elephant tusk found in the Alcove was for the geometrical alignment and lifecycle.

The entrance to the Lower Section of the Passage is on the line of the 30° for the age of maturity.

On the floor in the Middle Section are some holes which line up with the geometrical design. The earthenware cone found in the middle section for the optic alignments indicating the 10, 30, 40, 52 and 72 degrees as well as the solstice. The middle section itself is on the line of the equinox and is 4 metres for the Sphinx. The five holes are for Zoser. The niches on the solstice side of the section are on line with the solstice and mark the 10, 30, 40 and 72 degrees. The equinox and 52° are on the north west corner.

The south east corner of the Passage gives the equinox and also to the boulder at the top near the steps. The solstice and 52° are to either corner of the Passage's south west wall. The Alcove where the elephant's tusk was found represents knowledge Mr, the lifecycle and man's climb to the top. The Upper Section has the niches on the west side of the Passage wall. These mark the 20, 30, 40, 52 and 72 degrees and the solstice.

Cd1 has a 10 metre diameter and has a ½ metre high dividing wall from the south wall. This divider has square and circular holes on the top. The squares line up with the square niches and the circles with the rounded goyo dishes at the base of the niches. The ivory lions were found in a niche north of the divider wall. They were probably arranged to give the geometrical alignments with the corners of the niche.

The set of steps on the west side of Cd1 has four steps up and two down; to the west is a flat square area for Zoser. These steps represent Zoser, the ascent of Mr, the pyramid of life, the Sphinx and initiation. The iron and bronze weapons were found outside against the west side wall.

The steps in Cd1 are for Zoser and the Sphinx as well as the geometrical alignments. The loophole is for the equinox and the passing on of knowledge from one generation to the next. The pattern is for scientific knowledge.

Just north of Cd2 is a chequered pattern wall giving the equinox diagonally across the corner and the outer geometrical alignments which give the 10, 20, 30, 40, 52° from the pattern. The pattern itself represents scientific knowledge.

Cb3 is 10 metres in diameter for Zoser and the dividing wall is for the Sphinx. There is another marker on the north side of Cd3 which is triangular and gives the solstice along the west side, the equinox along the east of the lifecycle curve Cb3. On the south side of the main west entrance wall the line of the 52° also represents the lifecycle. The recess has five Ba niches for Zoser and the standard degrees.

The various levels at Khami give the correct alignment with each other. The decorated sections are for the days of the year, science of the universe and culture. Unfortunately, much of the patterned walling has fallen and it is difficult to define what the walls represent. There are three decorated terraced walls on the north side of the Main West Entrance for the Sphinx. The other side of the terrace is for Zoser. The fact that the Main Entrance is on the west side and that the western decorated section can only be seen from the outside denotes death.

The Khami Ruins are about 20° out of alignment for the true north which would date them at about 20+13=33x66=2178 or 178 BC.

The fire which damaged the passage area was probably a deliberate act, performed when the lifespan of the ruins had expired and the optic alignments were no longer accurate or, alternatively, the ancient philosophy became debased. The posts of the Lower Section were probably positioned by the sun to give the equinox, solstice and 52°. The distance from the entrance to the boulder represents Zoser and the Sphinx. The Passage was the key to the whole area and therefore had to be destroyed by fire to ensure that it could not be used again. The splitting and breaking of the boulders shows how the exfoliate peeling was done to obtain the stone needed for construction. The fire may have been hastened by the abuse of the people who turned Khami into a killing ground.

The lowing of a bull is also associated with Khami. A crocodile when cross makes a lowing noise, possibly the result of crocodiles fighting over prey which may have consisted of humans who met their death at the Precipice Ruin. This would explain the quantity of copper bangles found on the banks of the Khami river.

The bull and crocodile were both treated with reverence in Egypt, India and Zimbabwe, probably because they represented good over evil. They probably pertain to 2000-4000BC and the worship of the Golden Calf.

Some ivory disc pendant symbols with a diamond shaped hole at one end were found at the ruins. This marks the area for the optic geometrical alignments with the divider bars for the equinox, solstice and 52°. The pair of symbols has the chevron design, which gives the days of the year in the centre panel and the lifecycle round the edge. The four separate Sphinx chevrons under the pyramid hole and the ten at the base are for Zoser.

The other pair of symbols has the total number of chevrons for the days of the year, using both sides. The double row of dividers down the centre is for the Sphinx and Zoser. The angled rows of chevrons are for the age of initiation.

The third disc has the diamond for the geometrical alignment and Zoser. It is also divided into two sections for the Sphinx. The total number of diamonds is for the age of initiation and the lifecycle. The five represents Zoser and the pair the Sphinx.

The earlier mentioned Sphinx ivory lions have the eye of Ra, the ears of Zoser, the mouth of the lifecycle (hear all, see all, say nothing) and the legs of the Sphinx. The body design gives the number of days in the year. The diamonds represent the optic geometrical alignments through the points and by the angle of the lines. There are ten diamonds for Zoser, four toes for the Sphinx and they stand for the climb up the pyramid. The space between the stand and the lion's body represents the equinox and the passing on of knowledge to the next generation. The lions are also geometrically aligned to give the solstice, 52° and equinox by the angle of the head, side and front views.

By turning them three quarters to view the back, all four legs can be seen. Turned sideways only two are shown for initiation. In the three quarter front position three can be viewed for the descent down the pyramid.

The ivory cylinders all have the equinox hole at the top so that knowledge can be passed to the next generation. One of them has four twists in the lower half followed by a band and a set of two initiated twists which lead to the equinox and the third band above it. The three bands are for the sphinx. The twists give the geometrical points for the equinox, solstice and 52°.

Another cylinder has the perpendicular lines for Zoser and the three horizontal ones for the Sphinx. These lines and the hole give the geometrical alignments. A further cylinder has the two lines of initiation at the base, with the diagonal lines for the pyramid and 52° angle. The trellis design gives the days of the year. The horizontal lines are for the age of initiation and the vertical ones for Zoser. The top band is for the stick and the descent down the pyramid. Another symbol has the single band at the top and base. The hole gives the solstice and 52°. The two diagonal lines are for the Sphinx and solstice. The trellis represents the days of the year. A different cylinder has horizontal lines from the side. A tenth band and hole give the solstice and the eleventh the 52°.

The decorated obelisk Cone Beaker has chevrons for the days of the year and bands for the Sphinx. The chevrons show the angle of the solstice and 52° and represent the pyramid. The big horizontal and perpendicular bands are for the equinox.

The metal pins have the 52° and pyramid heads. The flat top gives the equinox. The solstice is to the opposite edge of the head of the pin. The length of the pin is used for measuring.

The needle has the 'head' for the solstice and 52 year cycle. The hole represents the equinox. In later years these needles were used for sewing and this accounts for the preference for the round eye instead of the crewel needle eye. *'It is easier for a camel to go through the eye of a needle, than for a rich man to enter the Kingdom of God'* (Mark 10 v25).

The weapons found at Khami Hill No. 1 (see earlier in this chapter). The axe head is geometrically designed with the copper circular insertion representing Ra. The niche is for Zoser and the blade represents the pyramid. The shank has the binding for the days of the year and the woven design is for the science of the universe and the age of initiation.

Another axe has an iron head and wooden handle covered in copper. The axe is geometrically designed to give the equinox, solstice and 52° aligned with the blade. The corded section represents the climb to the top of the pyramid and the initiation.

The spears have the geometrical alignments between the blade and the shank, with the teachings of Zoser, the age of initiation and the science of the universe on the bands.

These weapons would have served as a warning to all who saw them, as they were really 'iron war gods' and evil prevailed where they were positioned.

The following earthenware was displayed in the Harare Museum.

An earthenware pot ornament on a stand with the red background representing youth. It has three rows of chevrons for the Sphinx and pyramid. The squared trellis design is for Zoser and the science of the universe. The chevrons are ten for Zoser, the initiation, age and 52 year lifecycle. Three rows also give the optic geometrical design from the stand of the ornament. The neck is for Ra.

The headless turtle represents the Sphinx with the feet for the baby who crawls and the two-legged bird of initiation. The red is for youth while the black lines represent age. These colours were also used on the pyramids. The chevrons represent the pyramids. The neck is for the geometrical design of the equinox, solstice and 52°. The top of the neck represents Ra and the obelisk.

The zebra has 52 lines representing the lifecycle and the pyramid. The neck lines are for the Sphinx and geometrical alignments for the equinox and solstice. The front represents Ra and the two feet, initiation. The ridge down the back is for the equinox and passing on of knowledge before descending the pyramid of old age.

The headless animal with the geometrically designed diamond on the chest has the solstice and 52° on the white background. The lower section of the design represents the solstice followed by the 52°. The top line of the white represents the pyramid. The neck is for Ra. The chevron on the back is for the pyramid and Sphinx with the tail for the stick of age. The four feet represent the crawling stage. The front view of the bird is for initiation, which is followed by the descent of the pyramid and the passing on of knowledge.

The footless ornament has the plain band for youth at the base. The silver pyramids are for the 52 year lifecycle and the diamonds for initiation and geometrical alignment. The cone represents the equinox and Ra. The head of the chicken, when facing forwards, shows two sets of two chevrons for the initiation and the ascent of the pyramid. The mouth then denotes the passing on of knowledge and the chin the descent of the pyramid. The ornament itself represents the heart and feather of justice and is probably connected with the last rites of sacrifice. The 'incomplete' ornament represents man cut down in the prime of life at the Precipice Ruin.

The smiling zebra has the five Zoser lines on the side of the body and the geometrical cone on its back. The ridges down the rear are for the descent down the pyramid. The face indicates one is taking life easy after completing the working life cycle. The smiling mouth represents the rise of the next generation, taking the place of the retired or deceased one.

The squared headless ornament has the square for Zoser with the two bands of chevrons for the Sphinx and pyramid. The squares give the geometrical alignments. The neck is for Ra.

The Greek gods were Apollo, crow, God of music; Bacchus, goat, God of wine and revelry; Diana, cat, Goddess of the moon and hunt; Mercury, Hermes the bird messenger of the gods, science and treachery; Juno, cow, queen of the gods, guardian spirit of each woman; Venus, fish, Goddess of beauty.

The pregnant animal represents the birth of the new generation and the passing on of knowledge to the next. The red lines are for youth. The cone is geometrically designed and represents Ra. The mane is for the lifecycle and the horns are for the initiation. The down-facing head represents the stepping down of one generation to make way for the next and the teaching of the youth in the art of culture and science. Heidrun was a female goat who furnished meat for slain heroes.

The egg-shaped symbol has the five Zoser markers at the base. Then the red bands of youth are shown. Above these are four markers, the first one for Ra, the second for the geometrical design, the third for the lifecycle and the pyramid and the last for Zoser. The markers are also for the Sphinx. The surface of the egg is for the science of the universe.

The small earthenware figure has the arms in the shape of a cross for the equinox position. The position of the solstice can be found along the arm and body line. The 52° is positioned between the stand and the hands. The dots down the centre represent Zoser. The figure of Astarte, found at Taanack and dated to the 9th century BC, is similarly shaped but the dots form a cross and the legs are divided.

A decorated stone has a chevron motif IYYJ on it which is comparable with the Sinaitic script for water, the palm of the hand and ox-goad and a Taurus motif ŏ , the Khami ruins being next to the river.

Another stone has a square with one central dividing line and two diagonal lines which show the solstice and equinox.

A third has the diamonds with the Ra dot in the centre and three diagonal lines on the one side, 5, 5 and 7 on the other for Zoser and the Sphinx. The next diamond has the Ra dot with 2, 5, 3, lines on the side.

The herringbone pattern dates back to the Canaanite script 'k'. The stones have four hollows one way and eight the other (4+8=12). The square sides are for the equinox and the pointed end is for the geometrical alignments. These stones were querns for the measurement of the air's moisture content and predicting the climatic expectations as to the arrival of the rains, and a game board in the dry winter season. The earthenware vase has the two Sphinx bands and the design for Zoser and culture.

The soapstone carving of a figure has two rows of chevrons for Zoser and the Sphinx. There are 13 hollows across and 6 down which equal 78. These are followed by a row of 5 chevrons and another of four between horizontal lines. The next group has two big Ra circles on the left hand side and the rest are small circles. Eight across and three down equals 24 dots or circles. Then there are nine dots across and 6 rows down which equal 54. Following these are six dots and 6 rows down equalling 36. In all there are 78-54=24; 54-24=30; 36-24=12; 24+30+12=66. At the side of the soapstone there is a row of five chevrons for Zoser followed by a row of four 'V'. Below these is a row of 7 diamonds across and 4 rows giving a total of 28 diamonds. Between the horizontal lines is a band of 4 full and 2 half diamonds. The diamond pattern is repeated lower down but this time without the horizontal lines on either side. Then there are chevrons which in turn are followed by a 'V' and inverted 'V's. Six in the first row and seven in the second. The last group consists of eight diamonds across and five down giving a total of 40 in the group 40-28=12. The earthenware vase has two Sphinx bands and the design for Zoser and culture.

Guide Book.

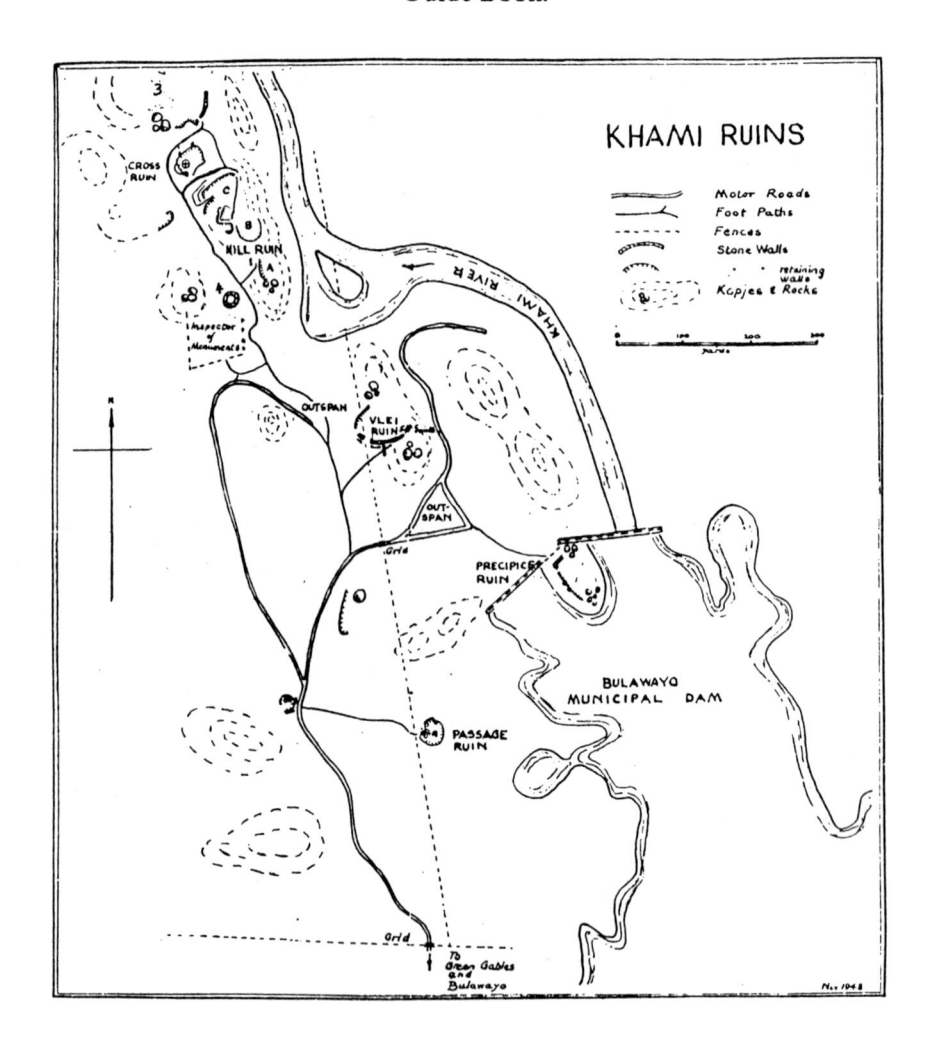

Khami Ruins

Guide Book.

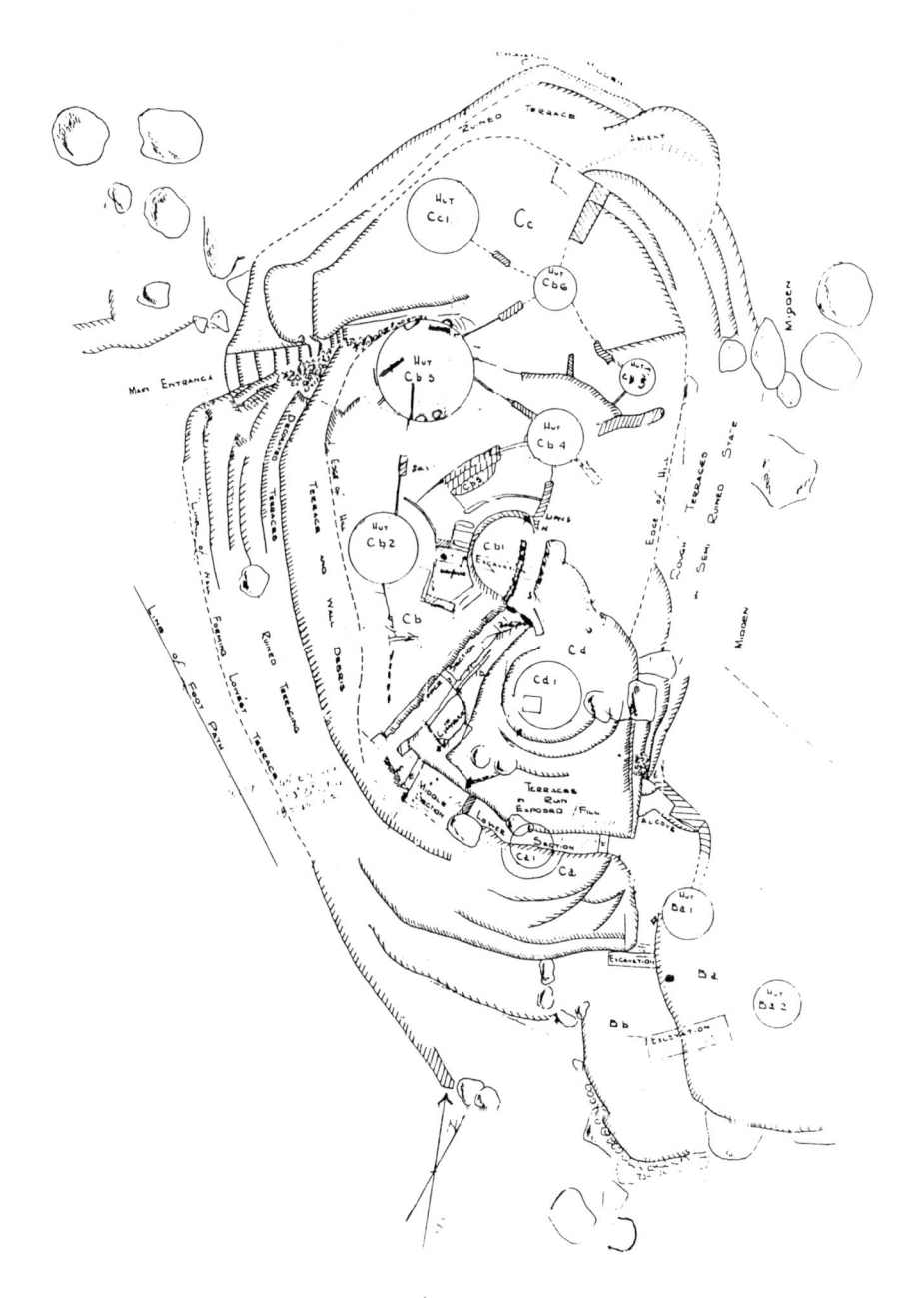

Hill Ruin Khami   Plan Platform B and C

Guide Book.

Earthenware pot

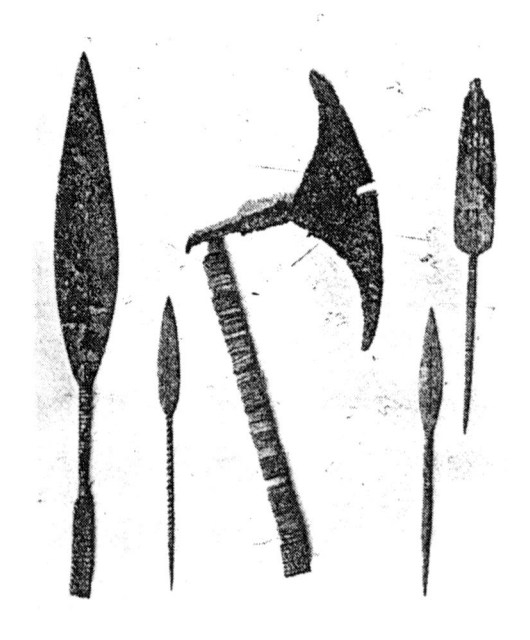

Weapons found at Khami Hill No 1

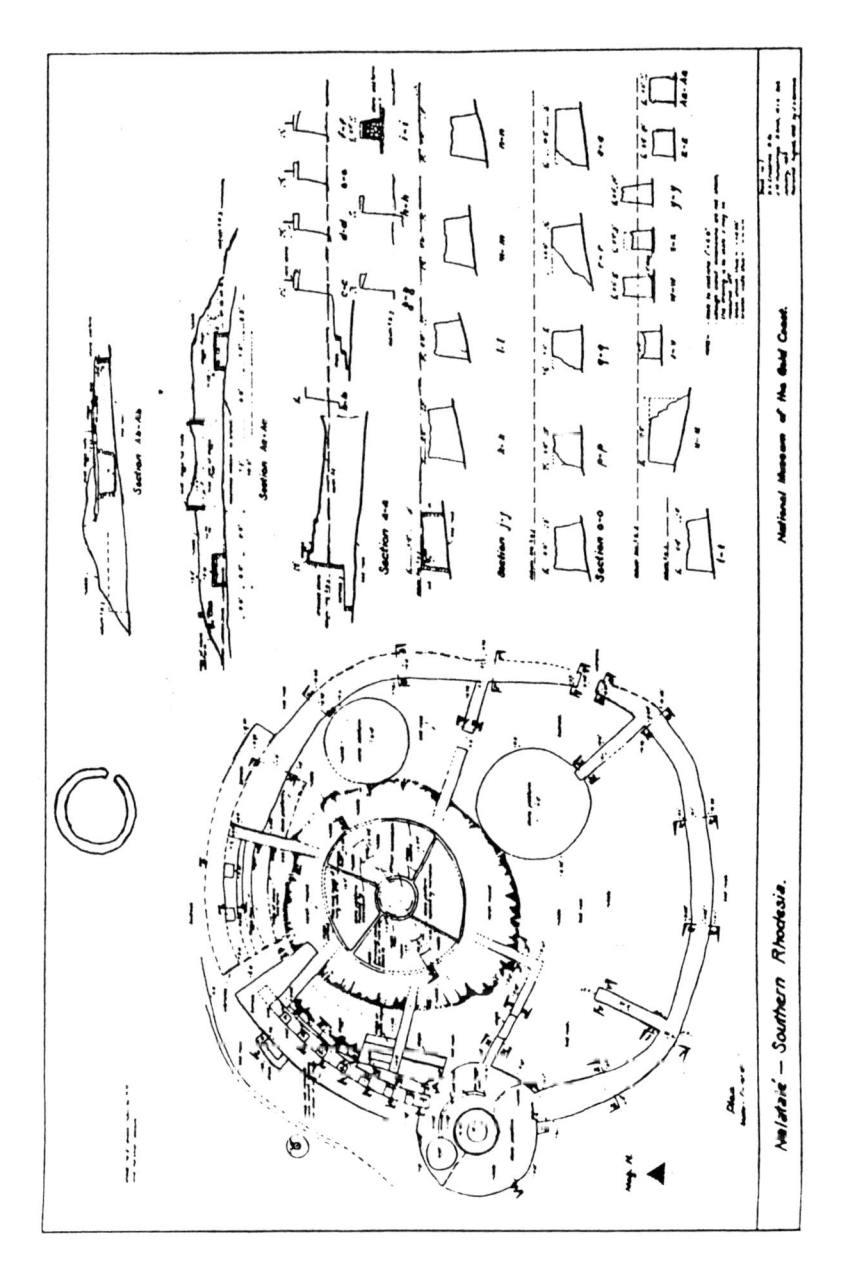

Nalatale Ruins showing wheel-shaped walls

Nalatale Ruins

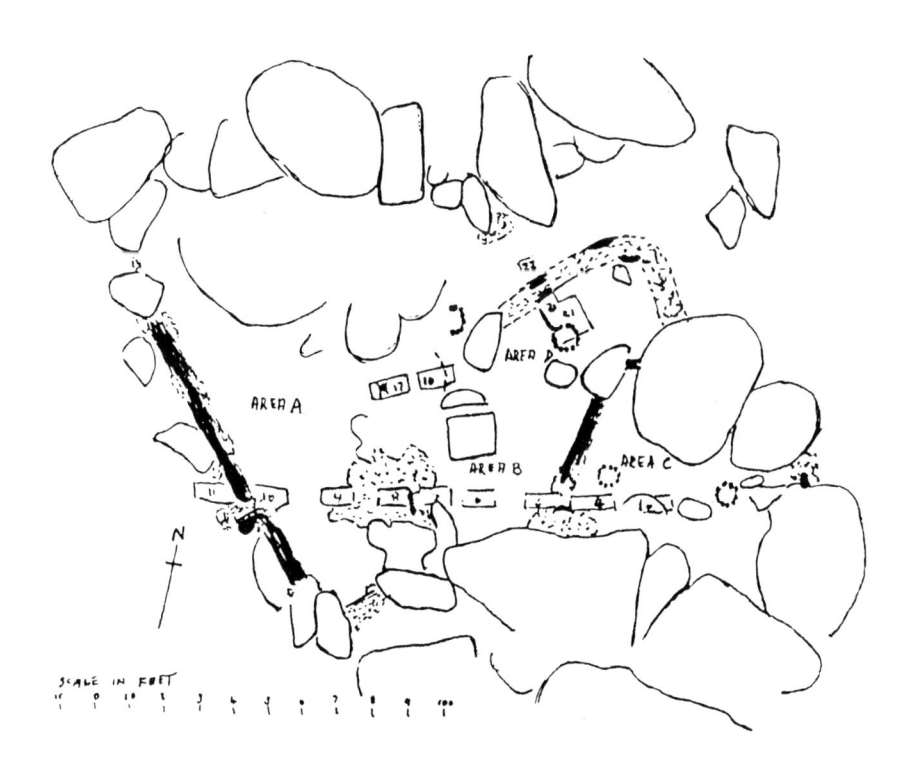

Excavation at Harleigh Farm Rusape. Plan of Ruin No 1.
1958-62 origionally drawn by P. O. Robins and Anthony Whitty.

Nyahokwe

MONOLITH
GOYO
GOYO
MONOLITH
GOYO
U - SHAPE
EXIT

Drawn by U. M. Erasmus

Ancient axe

Joined stones
Zimbabwe

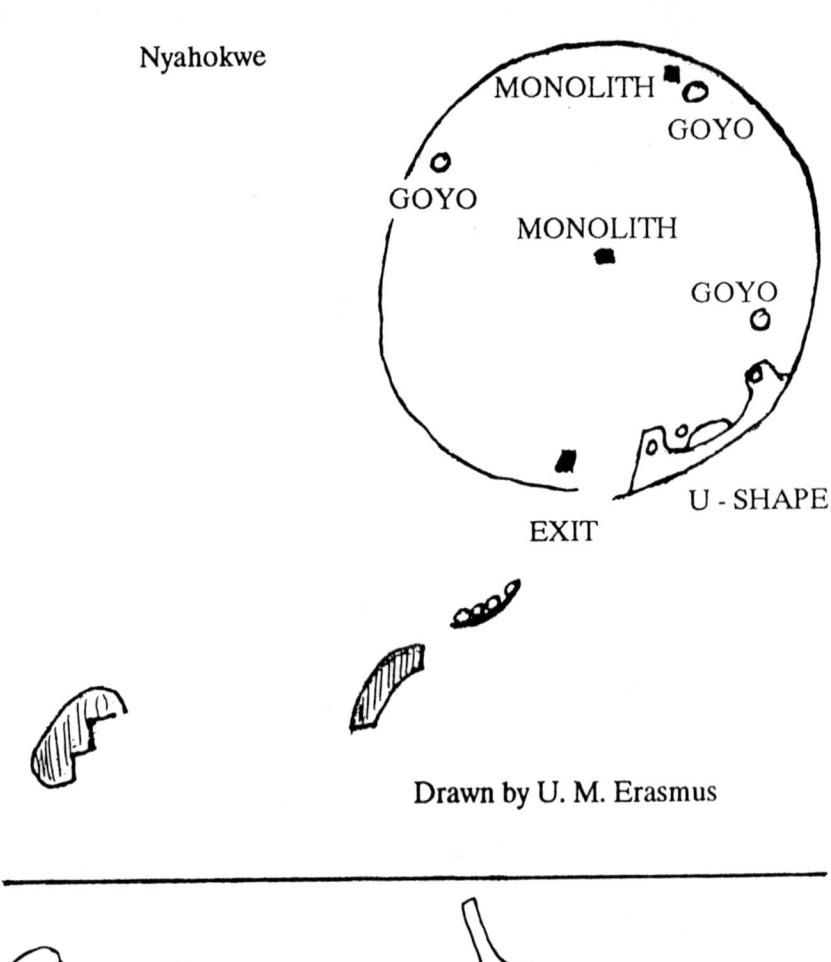

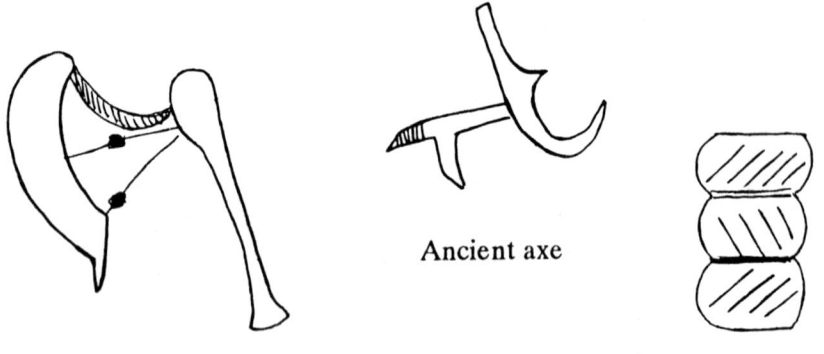

Axe made with iron head, wooden handle,
covered in copper.

Drawn by U.M. Erasmus

Sketch by U. M. Erasmus

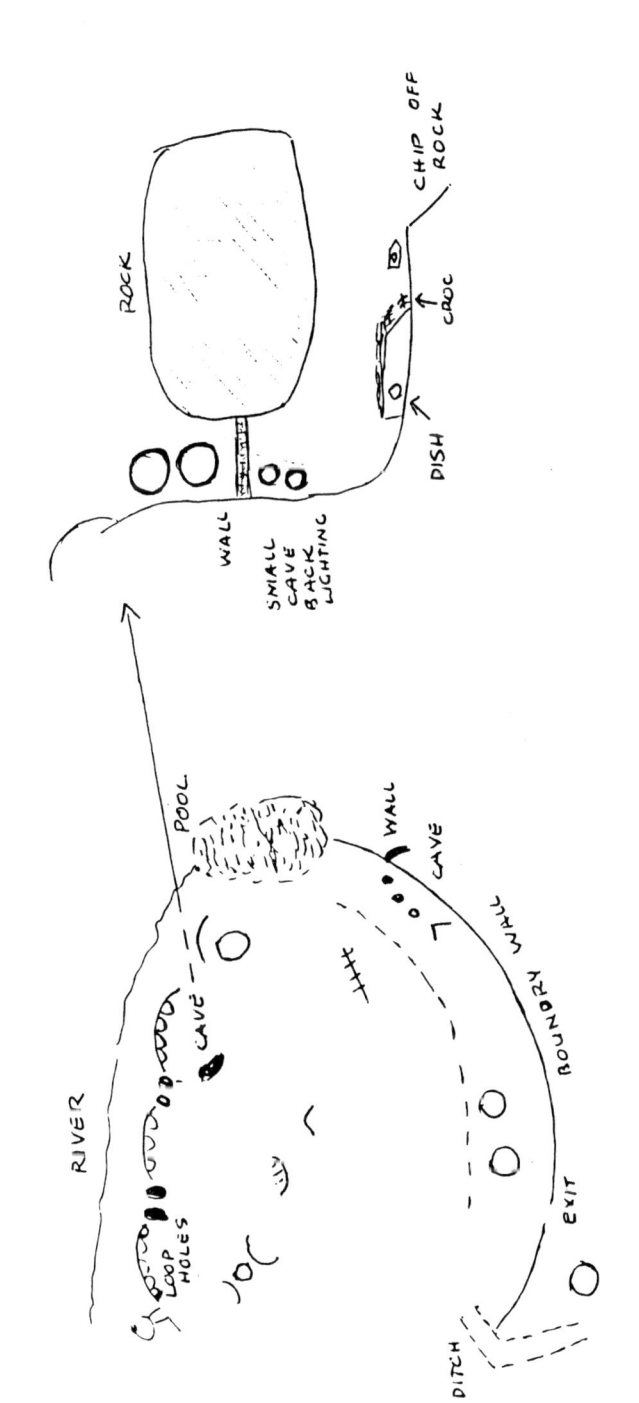

Ruin 2, Denonia Farm

B

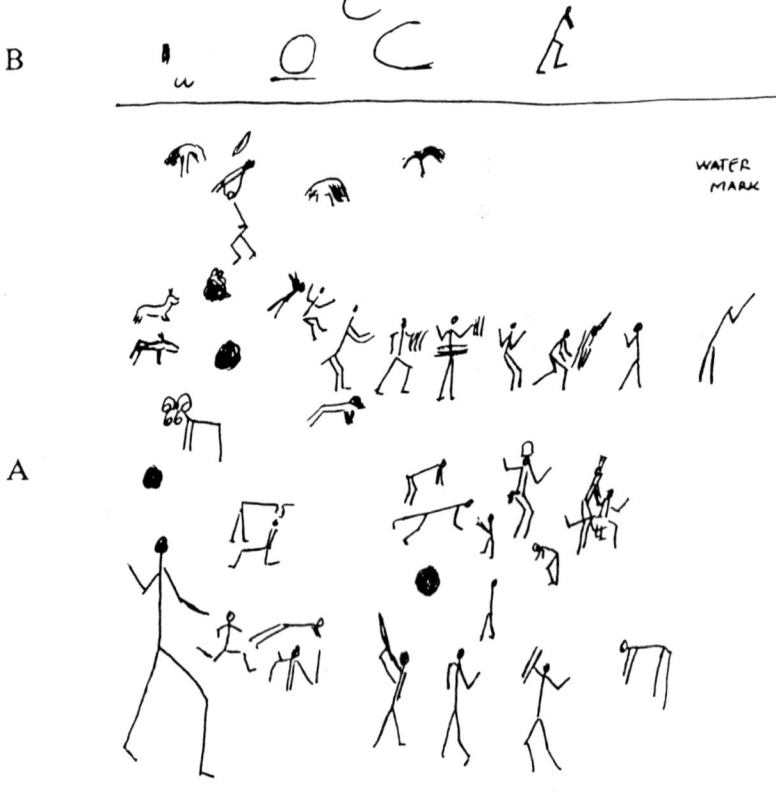

WATER MARK

A

Harleigh Farm, first ruin.   First Ruin.

Drawn by U M Erasmus

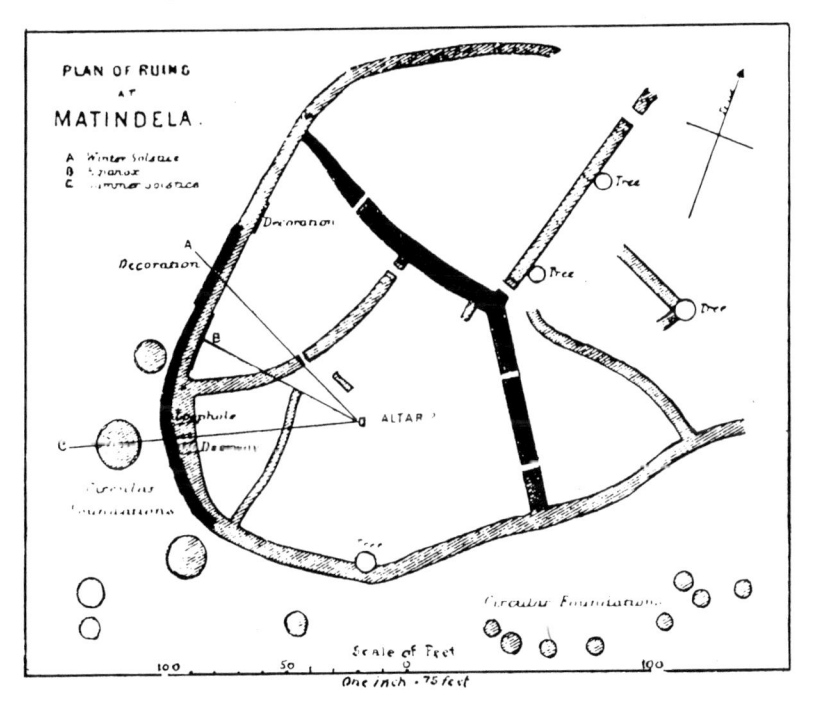

Matindela Ruins

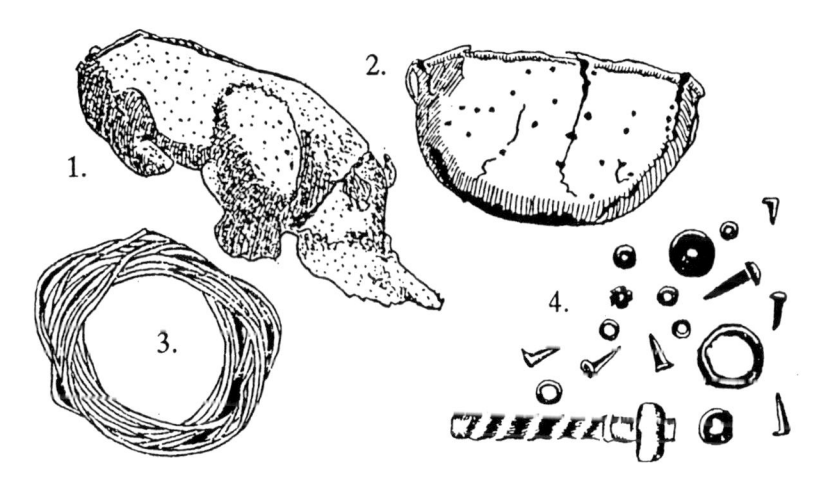

Gold items from MAPUNGUBWE, LIMPOPO VALLEY.
1. Rhinoceros of beaten gold.
2. Bowl of beaten gold.
3. Wound wire.
4. Sheating for 'sceptre'.
5. Ornament, gold beads + 'tacks'.   (Not to scale.)

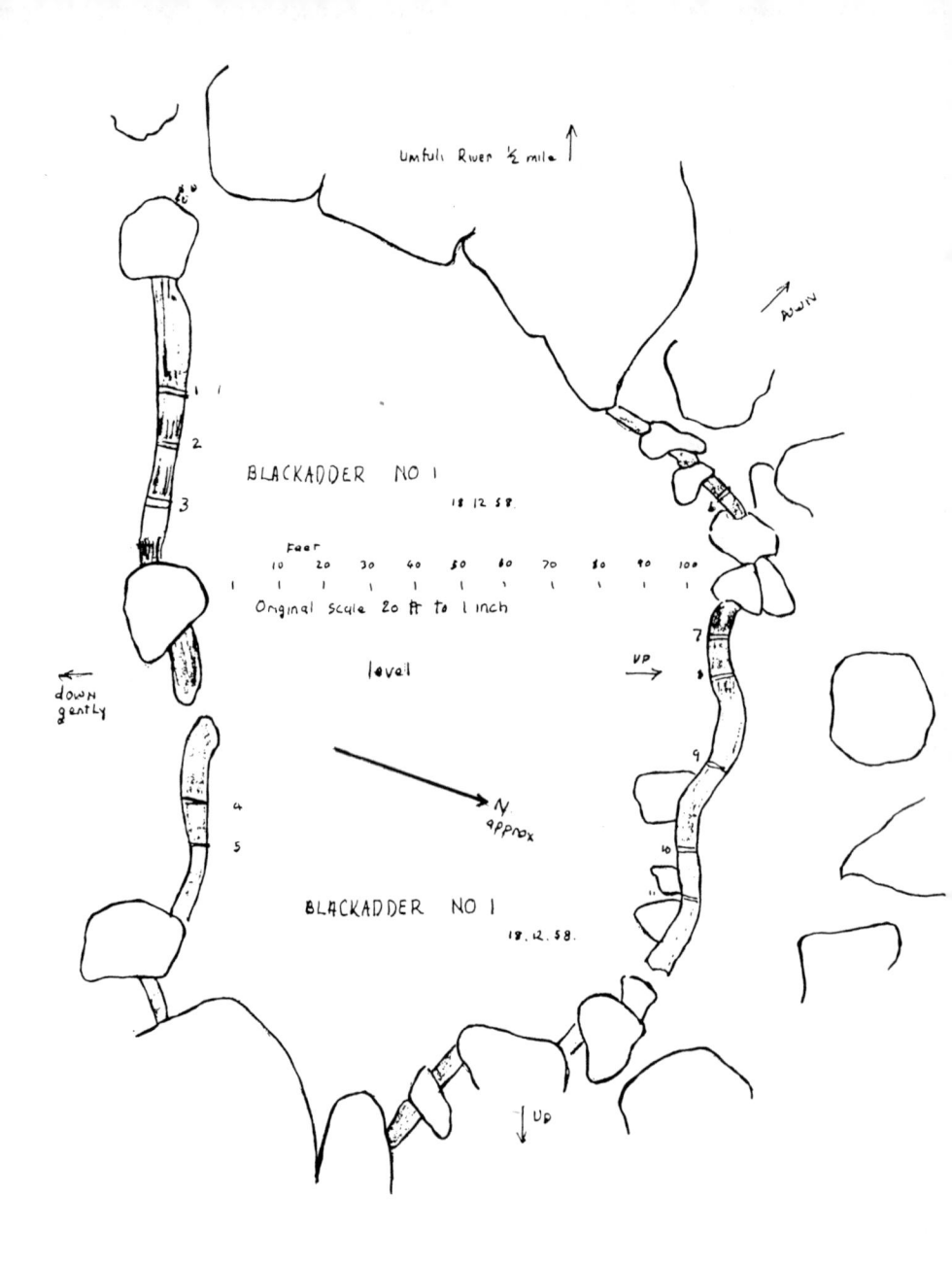

Blackadder Ruin. Surveyed and originally drawn by Anthony Whitty.

Entrance no 1

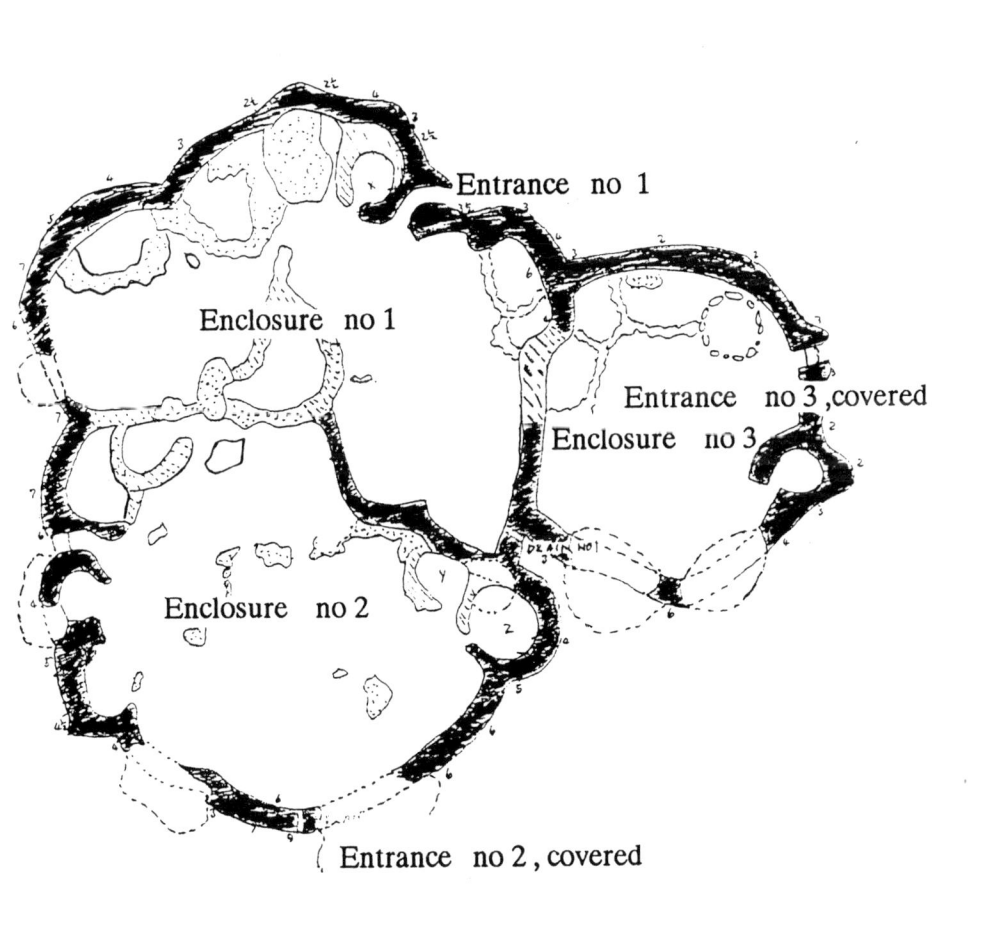

Enclosure no 1

Entrance no 3, covered

Enclosure no 3

Enclosure no 2

Entrance no 2, covered

Legend: Ruin of Inyanga Downs

Surveyed and originally drawn by Anthony Whitty.
A.R.I.B.A   BA.   Dipl   MIA (SR)   1953-54

Legend: Ruin of Inyanga Downs

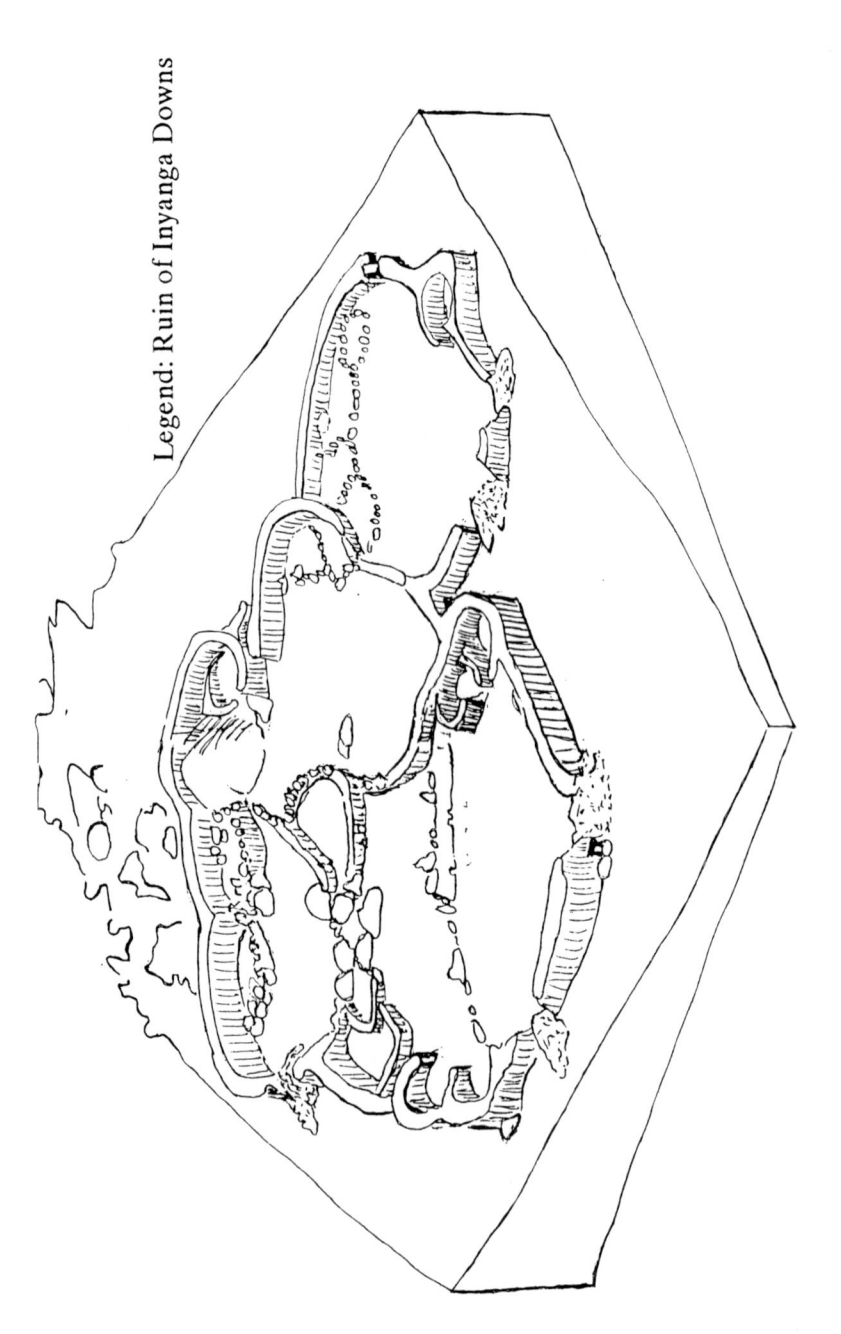

Surveyed and originally drawn by Anthony Whitty.　A.R.I.B.A　BA　Dipl.　MIA (SR)
ISOMATIC PROJECTION　　　1953 - 54

DHLO DHLO

The Main Solstice Entrance to the Dhlo Dhlo Ruins has the decorated south wall with four chequer pattern lines on the lower portion for Zoser. The design above has a short line at the bottom. The second is a little longer and the two top rows are of equal length for the Sphinx and scientific knowledge.

On the north side of the steps is another wall with the herringbone in one space. The square stone is followed by another set of three herringbones, a square and then four herringbones. Then follows a horizontal line of stones and above it a row of diagonal cord or rope stones. At the top of the wall are three rows of chevron patterns.

The next pattern wall has two rows of chevron patterns then one of diagonal stones, cord or rope pattern. The top design of the chevron pattern is for the lifecycle. All patterns together are for the Sphinx, Zoser, equinox, solstice, days of the year and the science of the universe.

The set of steps between the first and second wall pattern sets are for the initiation and knowledge. At the top of the steps is an earthen cement construction for the lifecycle, which lines up with the stones and markers nearby for the equinox and solstice.

Turning to the south there is a set of boulders, two chips and other stone markers for the optic geometrical alignments. To the west is a parallel stone wall for the Sphinx which curves for the lifecycle and the geometrical alignments. It also gives the science of the universe.

Continuing round below the bank the main wall marks the summer solstice area of the ruin. The first circular wall construction is joined on the east side to the main wall and forms the equinox and geometrical alignments on the south side of the circle. The solstice is formed with the mound to the west of the circle. The equinox is between the two circles.

The second Enclosure is joined to the main outside wall. The wall joining the main wall gives the geometrical alignments on the south side and on the north side the solstice. There is a mound in the centre of the wall curve which represents the pyramid of knowledge and Ra.

The wall on the south west side gives the geometrical alignments. The curve is for the lifecycle and the straight section the solstice. On the granite outcrop is a decorated wall of three rows of chequer patterns and a horizontal line of stones which marks the solstice and gives the geometrical alignments with the markers and boulders near it. It also represents scientific knowledge.

There is a Rock Chip to the north of the decorated wall, which has a straight and a curved side of the geometrical alignments and lifecycle. It is mounted on the granite rock with stones representing the Sphinx and Zoser. To the east of the Rock Chip is a circular earthen construction which works in with the stone circles to the east of it for the geometrical alignments. On the east side, and high point, of the ruin is a group of boulders, some walling and rock chips, giving the geometrical alignments. The circular earthen construction forms the geometrical alignments with the walling next to it on the north side and the solstice on the south. The concave stones between the boulders also give the alignments.

Within the remaining wall on a boulder of this enclosure is a rock painting of a single figure. It has the dot of Ra for the head, the equinox for a body and the legs of the Sphinx. The solstice and 52° are over the figure's head. There is also an inverted 'V' for the pyramid.

The grey soapstone found in the ruins has the centre of the 4, 4 chevrons, 8 x 4 patterns 32; ½; 4; ½ diamonds; 4 x 7 = 28 patterns; 3,4 chevrons; 9 x 5 = 45 patterns. The left side has 4, 4 chevrons; 14 x 6 = 84 patterns; 5, 4 chevrons followed to one side by two Ra circles with the design of 8 x 9 = 72 for the lifespan and 5 x 7 = 35 for the Sphinx underneath. This soapstone probably denoted tribal or domestic statistics.

NALATALE

The Nalatale Ruins are on the top of a rock kopje, necessitating a climb up the 'pyramid'. The ruin has two entrances, one is through the north east wall and the other through the southwest wall which is near the steepest climb for the young initiates and represents the steep climb of knowledge and study. The south west entrance is very plain and gives the equinox between the wall endings on the outside of the main enclosure wall. There are ten rows of plain walling topped by a chequered wall pattern which gives the 52° and solstice, and another section of chequered pattern to the north west of the main outside wall gives the days of the year.

To the south of the southwest entrance is a section of six herringbone patterns. There are seven herringbones in each group and four groups, 6 + 4 = 10; 6 x 7 = 42 + 10 = 52. The outside wall pattern gives the geometrical alignments for the south west entrance.

On entering the southwest entrance there is a circle of earth cement which gives the geometrical alignments from the south wall join with the other wall endings. There is a stone on the ground to the east of the earth circle giving the alignments with the end of the wall to the east for the equinox. The solstice is to the circular construction dividing the main outer wall. The 52° is to the wall corner.

The circular obelisk construction dividing the main enclosure wall has a two-metre high stone outer wall, filled with earth. There is an earth circle on the construction with a hollowed-out centre. The north side of the circle has a half metre earthen half circle which has a hole in it big enough to take a pole for measuring the shadow of the sun. From the south east wall join the optic geometrical alignments are formed with the earth and stone marker combined for the equinox, solstice and 52°.

The combination of earth and stone markers is very interesting because it is uncommon to have both used for a single alignment. Usually there is a set of stone or earth markers used independently.

In the centre of the ruin is an earth cement obelisk circle with divided walls giving the alignments independently but also in conjunction with each other, because earth had been brought in to cover older constructions which were no longer in use. This earth circle was about four metres above the original rock level.

If a line is taken from the south square obelisk on the top of the main outside wall to the end of the step wall, it forms the equinox on the east/west line. The north equinox is to the north square on the same section of the wall. The squares on top of the wall give the 10, 30, 40, 60, 80 degrees as well as the solstice. The 20 and 52 degree markers are on the north wall. From the 52, 60 degree and solstice marker the 40° is to the wall join, the end and the 20° the squared corner. There is a parapet wall on the inside of the square obelisk cone wall.

The north east exit is on the line of the 72°, indicating that it is for the descent down the pyramid and close of life. There are steps descending from the enclosure. The west exit wall continues to a circular construction with a hollowed-out centre, similar to the one dividing the main wall of the enclosure. There is another stone circular construction to the north of the main enclosure and the alignments are taken between the two constructions and the joining wall.

In front of the main wall of the ruin is a circular construction for Ra one metre high and 2 metres across and one metre in diameter. The stones used are for the science of the universe and knowledge. On top and in the filled-in centre is a crocodile for the Sphinx with the stone trimmings for Zoser and the geometrical alignments.

The main wall of the enclosure has a low wall which is about a metre high with three separate patterns on it, the bottom one is a plain band of dark stones. The second row has two layers of chequered pattern which is very indistinct in places and seems to merge into the walling. The top row is of diagonal cord or rope pattern stones for the solstice and 52°.

Between the front and second wall is an earth terrace which is retained by the walling. The set back wall has the first decorated row above the terrace showing the herringbone pattern for the solstice and 52°. The herringbone stones are in pairs diagonally above the others and are for the Sphinx. The spacer is for Zoser. One side of the pattern gives the number of herringbones for the age of initiation. After the three row gap, denoting the end of ordinary walling and a set of herringbone designs for Zoser, there are two horizontal stones replacing the herringbone design. The next patterned row consists of plain horizontal schist which is darker than the ordinary stone used and shows up against the background of the other stones.

The chequer pattern above the schist has six rows 2 + 4, representing the days of the final initiation period. The chequered pattern is similar to the hairstyle of the Nubian and Sudanese.

The following pattern is again a herringbone with a number of patterns representing the lifespan. This herringbone is similar to the pharaoh's beard. The following row consists of plain dark schist stones.

The top row of chevrons is for the lifecycle and equinox. These chevrons extend only as far as the first five squares surmounted on the top of the main wall and represent Zoser. Four of these have monoliths protruding a metre above the squares for the Sphinx. There are seven squares in all on top of the wall representing the Sphinx.

The squares have five layers of stone in the front for Zoser and seven on the inside for the Sphinx. This is because the top of the wall slopes towards the inside of the enclosure and has been covered with red earth cement to show that it has been completed. The slope gives the angle of the solstice. To the top of the square is the 52° while the side gives the equinox.

The outside of the main wall gives the science of the universe and knowledge and incorporates the pharaoh's double crown of Upper and Lower Egypt. The division is shown by the terracing. The trees and monoliths represent the feather and the squares the back of the Lower Egypt's crown.

The curved wall on the west main wall gives the equinox with the 'cone' to the north of it. The solstice is to the main decorated wall. The 52° is along the wall of the circle. There is another set from the corner of the main circle wall. The 52° is to the cone. The equinox is to the square jutting section of the main wall. The solstice is to the second square obelisk cone on the top of the wall and the change of pattern.

The corner of the main wall and the circular obelisk cone outside the main enclosure form a right angle at the wall between them. From this point the 10, 30, 40 and 52 degrees are in line with the squared cones on the top of the wall. The solstice is to the jutting squared section of the lower walling, which also gives the geometrical alignments.

The monoliths and squared obelisk cones on the top of the

north west wall show that the construction of the ruin was started seven degrees or 462 years before it was actually used. The square cones on the top of the north wall denote that the ruin was used for two degrees (two sets of optical alignments). There may have been a third squared cone on the wall which would signify that the ruin was used for three degrees or completed a degree ahead of time.

The alignments are approximately 10 degrees out from true north which would make the ruin $10 + 13 = 23 \times 66 = 1518$ years when finished $+ 462 = 1980$ years old.

VAN NIEKERK RUINS

The Inyanga district is mountainous and attracts the clouds and rain. It is also close to the main routes for those who entered and left from the north or south. The terracing is on the lower accessible slopes on the sheltered side of the mountain. The art of terracing was probably learnt at the time of agriculture of the Nile in about 4000 BC. It cleared the land of stone to give more land for crops and retained the moisture, thus promoting growth and preventing erosion.

Moses taught agriculture and put the ox to the plough while his wife taught the value of wheat and barley (Exodus 9 v31 and 32 mention flax, barley, wheat and rye. In Egypt the straw was used for brickmaking, Exodus 5 v7).

Site 1 of the Van Niekerk ruins is on top of the small kopje with an entrance giving the equinox. The loophole on either side of the entrance gives the solstice and 52°.

The loopholes on the outside wall are for the passing on of knowledge and the 52°. The second solstice is between the boulder and the walling on the east side of the main entrance.

On the other side, the south side of the kopje, is an obelisk cone on the ground close to the other low wall markers, these give the optical angles for the equinox, solstice, 52° and the science of the universe.

Site A (between 1 and 2). This enclosure has roughly built walls which do not seem to have been much higher than they are today. There are stones placed in a line on the east side and a stone foundation marker for the geometrical set, lifecycle, Zoser and the Sphinx, there is another set of stones set into the ground for the equinox. The parallel walls are for the Sphinx and they line up with the southern end of the covered entrance to the north. The vault has an equinox entrance on the north side. The tunnel entrance is on the line of the solstice, then it turns to give the 52° and opens into the equinox. The wall at the side joining the entrance gives the lifecycle. The stone marker at the end of the wall is also a marker for the geometrical alignments.

There is a flat triangular stone on the west side of the enclosure and north of the Sphinx wall. On one side of the stone is the equinox, on the other the solstice, and the third side is for the 52°.

The cone outside the enclosure and just north of the entrance to the tunnel gives the geometrical set for the equinox, solstice and the 52°. By their shape and number the cones represent Ra, Zoser and the Sphinx.

Site B has a low stone wall with a dressed triangular stone fixed onto the east end for the equinox, solstice and 52°. The concave guyo stones were for the equinox. The Ra goyo stone has a meg sphere in the centre. Close to this goyo and sphere was another sphere and these two gave the equinox, solstice and 52°. On a second visit to this enclosure the line of concave stones had been removed.

Site 2 has the 52° marked by a big Zoser boulder built into the wall as building blocks. The loophole and vault give the geometrical design. The linteled equinox entrance and loophole slot leading into the enclosure give another set.

Site 3 appears to be just terracing and of little interest.

Site 4 enclosure has the equinox entrance with the solstice loophole slot in the side of the entrance wall. The curved wall is for the geometrical design and represents the lifecycle. The 'Y' wall is for the solstice and the passing on of knowledge. There is a set of squared stones stacked at the north end of the 'Y' arm and these are for Zoser. The 'drain' on the north wall is for the

52°. The single marker forms the geometrical design with the walling of 'Y' and main wall of the enclosure. The Sphinx is represented by the double walling on the south side.

The parallel walling and passage linking the enclosure represent the Sphinx. The paths are made from large stones filled in with rubble, which the terracing does not have. They are clearly distinguished and so prevent the terracing cutting across the parallel walls.

Site 5 has the Sphinx connecting walls and the solstice entrance turning roughly at right angles to the south for the equinox. The lifecycle is shown by the curved section just north of the entrance. The vault represents Ra and the stone, scientific knowledge. The loophole is for the passing on of knowledge. The opening is on the line of the equinox (east/west).

Just south of the vault is a curved line for the lifecycle and pyramid. There is a squared section in the centre for Zoser. The walling with the main walling and enclosure markers give the geometrical alignments.

Site 6 has the solstice entrance with the equinox curve joining it in the enclosure. The grooves are for Zoser and initiation. The raised circular stone slabs represent Ra, and the number of supports, Zoser, the Sphinx and the age of initiation. They also give the geometrical alignments. The curved ground marker represents the lifecycle - as one descends the pyramid of life, knowledge is passed on to the next generation. This explains the loophole on the east side of the enclosure. The vault area represents the scientific knowledge and the number of stones used for the walling and vault, the days of the year. The large stones represent the geometrical alignments.

North of Site 6 is another vault construction, again giving the geometrical designs with the wall indents of Site 6. The platform across the southern side and inside the vault marks the solstice, and the curved side the lifespan. The loophole above the platform on the south wall is for the equinox and Zoser. The stones give the days of the year and the age of initiation.

Site 7 shows the southwest entrance for the solstice with the slot hole in the entrance wall for the 52° and equinox. The loophole on the northeast side and the northwest entrance are for the solstice, the wall shaping is for the geometrical alignments and scientific knowledge.

Site 8 has been constructed with big boulders requiring a lot of strength to lever into position. The number of blocks represent scientific knowledge, the days of the year and age of initiation, as well as giving the geometrical alignments. The entrance is on the south equinox and the loophole is on the 52° for the lifecycle. The central area has four circular markers. Two are joined by stones and one is joined to the south wall for age. The fourth is on its own. These markers represent the Sphinx. The small embankment to the enclosure represents the climb up the pyramid. This enclosure stands out among all the other enclosures because of the size of the boulders used and will be preserved for many years.

Site 9 has the south 52° entrance which curves into the equinox and ends with the solstice. The wall shaping, both inside and out, is for the geometrical alignments. The vault is for the science of the universe and Ra.

Site 10 gives the east side entrance on line with the 52°. The slot is for the equinox and solstice. The curved marker represents the lifecycle and geometrical alignments as well as scientific knowledge. The one circular Ra marker has one half raised and represents the Sphinx, because of the two halves, and the supports on one side are for Zoser. The circular edge represents the lifecycle and the raised side is for the climb up the pyramid. The dividing line is on the line of the solstice.

Site 11. The west entrance is on the line of the equinox. The entrance area with the corner and entrance walling is for the geometrical alignments. The loophole is on the line of the equinox. The dividing construction of the enclosure represents the Sphinx. The vault represents Ra and the science of the universe and knowledge. The loophole is for Zoser.

Site 12 has the parallel walls leading up to the enclosure for the Sphinx. The entrance is on the 52° and, together with the other alignments on the inside of the entrance, gives the solstice and equinox. The vault is for the science of the universe and knowledge, as well as Ra.

Site 13. Here the main entrance gives the 52°, equinox and solstice. The grooves represent Zoser and initiation. The central cone is for the science of the universe. The top section has an outer rim of alternate spaces for the Sphinx and Zoser, over which is a layer of stones for the age of initiation. Then the inner stones are added to them for the 52 year lifecycle. This cone is not cylindrical on the east side but is squared off to show the Sphinx. The feet and arch between the legs are for the pyramid. The total number of stones represents the days of the year. Ra is represented by the circular upper section. The walling and ground marks give the geometrical design.

The main entrance walls of site 14 are tapered towards the centre of the enclosure to give the solstice and 52°. The south squared wall end gives the equinox. The walls and ground markers are for the geometrical alignments and the circular markers represent scientific knowledge. The vault is for the science of the universe while the Sphinx is represented by the parallel walls.

Site 15. The entrance is on the line of the equinox with the wall end for the equinox and 52°. The loophole is on the line of 52° for the passing on of knowledge from one generation to the next. The vault entrance turns from the 52° to the solstice. The north wall ends on the solstice with the main enclosure wall marker on the north side of the enclosure. This marker represents Zoser and the lifecycle. The vault itself represents the science of the universe and Ra, with the double image construction for the Sphinx.

Site 16. The south east entrance is on the line of the equinox and the north entrance on the 52°. The parapet represents the climb up the pyramid and the science of the universe. There are ten circular markers for Zoser and three double ones for the Sphinx. The outside and inner walls represent Ra. The inner enclosure has the entrance on the north wall for the equinox with the inner design for the solstice and 52°. The inner exit is on the south west wall in line with the 52°. The boulders are geometrically positioned to give the alignments for the equinox, solstice and 52° with the other markers. These are, however, too complicated to explain within the context of this book.

The Van Niekerk Ruins have been divided into two groups. The northern group consists of enclosures 4, 5, 6, 9 and 10. The southern section consists of enclosures 7, 11, 12, 13, 14, 15 and 16. Number eight serves as the dividing line between the two groups.

The second set has groups of four 2, 4, 5 and 6. Number 4 does not have a vault. The next group is 7, 8, 11 and 12. Again number 8 does not have a vault. The third group is formed by 13, 14, 15 and 16. Vault number 16 has been replaced by the inner enclosure.

The enclosures have also been paired in connection with or

without the parallel walls. The Sphinx enclosures are numbered A, 5, 6b, 7, 9, 11, 13 and 15. The others are 1, b, 4, 6, 8, 10, 12, 14 and 16. The differences consist of the vaults and the entrances. The parallel walls bring each group up to 10 for Zoser. The two groups together give the total for the age of training and initiation.

The parallel walls themselves represent the Sphinx. They are similar to the causeway of the river Nile and to the pyramids and give the optical geometrical alignments of the equinox, solstice and 52°. The enclosures all work in with each other through the outside wall of the enclosure and the wall indents, each of which again gives the geometrical aligments.

Inyanga has the July to October period as the wet season. This can be seen from the layout of the terracing and enclosures. This period, however, is the dry season for the rest of the country. The Egyptians show this period by long lines followed by a circle with a Ra dot and a half circle (half moon).

The vaults were built along the lines of the underground dwellings in North Africa which were cool during the day and warm during the cold nights (Hebrew belonging to Eber the great grandson of Shem, 2255 BC - 1 Samuel 14 v11).

The Van Niekerk Ruins are about 20° out from the true north which would date them around 20+13=33x66 = 2178 or 178 BC.

NYAHOKWE

The Nyahokwe Ruins of the Ziwa people have a vault enclosure near the base of the mountain which shows the optic geometrical alignments with the tunnel walls and enclosure.

The vault enclosure to the east of the path has the equinox entrance. The enclosure walling gives the solstice and 52°. There is an equinox stone marker on the south side of the enclosure which lines up with the solstice entrance. The 52° is to the circular area south east of the entrance.

The bottom stone of the three tiered stones represents youth, birth and equinox to the initiation and solstice. The second, middle, stone represents the solstice to the equinox, north/south and passing on of knowledge. The third, top, stone represents the 52°, lifecycle and solstice for the decline of life. The three tiered stones therefore represent the pyramid, rise and fall of life, the Sphinx and geometrical alignments.

The vault on the east side of the previous enclosure has an obelisk cone on the north side above the vault, which lines up with the geometrical tunnel to the north of the vault.

The vault has a tortoise earth shape in the centre. This gives the geometrical alignments and represents the Sphinx, Zoser and the pyramid. The vault is for Ra and should be preserved for all time as proof of the value of the vaults as geometrical and cultural constructions. When ascending the mountain there are five Zoser terraces beside the path. A triangular monolith represents the pyramid and gives the solstice, equinox and 52°. The square monolith represents Zoser. On the lower wall beneath the path one of the stones has a St. Andrew's cross marker. This shows the solstice, equinox and 52°. There is a loophole in one of the 'back' walls for the passing on of knowledge when the apex has been reached. The vault enclosure is a little higher up the mountain. The walling and tunnel give the geometrical alignments. The tunnel itself represents the Sphinx; the vault Ra, the days of the year and the science of the universe.

After another climb up the path one finds a rock obelisk chip which has been let into the earth edgeways. This stone lines up with the single rock visible on a granite outcrop and the two markers for the solstice. Because there is only one way up and down the chip represents the rise and fall of man and the ascent and descent of the pyramid. The two obelisk markers represent the sphinx.

The single stone obelisk marker on the granite outcrop curves to give the equinox on the east side and the 52° on the south side. The solstice can be found with the rock chip to the west of the marker.

Ascending the mountain to another granite outcrop there is a circular construction placed on the rock, with a set of Zoser upright stones for the geometrical alignments and scientific knowledge. The upright stones line up for the solstice, equinox and 52°. To the east of this construction are some concave markers for the science of the universe, the 52 year lifecycle, Zoser and the Sphinx. This shows that since the concaves were made no marked exfoliation of the rock has taken place

Continuing up the path the next point of interest is a 20 metre diameter Ra circle representing the age of initiation. The square stone obelisk monolith in the centre represents Zoser, and these are ten metres clear on all sides. It also gives the geometrical alignments with the markers round the circular walling. These are for scientific knowledge.

The 'U' shape on the south east side of the Ra circle enclosure has concave stones placed on the 'arms' of the 'U'. These line up with the walls on the 'U' for the equinox, solstice and 52°. The raised slab forms a low platform which represents Zoser and gives the geometrical alignments with the 'U' and the ground markers beside, on the west side of the raised platform. The platform also has its own complete set of geometrical alignments with the 52° representing the lifecycle.

The vault enclosure on the east side of the initiation, Ra, circles has a Zoser square niche on the outside of the south wall which faces towards the 'U'. The vault has a loophole on either side of the inner enclosure. These represent the Sphinx, Ra and Zoser by their number, shape and positioning. They also give the geometrical alignments. The niches are also an indication as to how long it took to construct the Nyahokwe Ruins.

In the south east corner of the entrance is a set of markers on the ground. The east stone is upright. The concave stone on the south wall side has the Ra sphere and the third stone is next to the tunnel entrance. These markers give the geometrical alignments. The tunnel curve represents the lifecycle, Sphinx and geometrical alignments. The tunnel starts with the equinox then turns for the solstice and 52°, which are also shown by the positioning of the concave stones and the light holes along the tunnel roof. The dressed stones on the roof represent the geometrical alignments and scientific knowledge. The four markers over the entrance are dressed and concave, and they probably had spheres. The centre one is for the stick and the start of the decline of life and the passing on of knowledge. The last one is for the lifecycle. The side of the vault is on the line of the east/west equinox and represents the science of the universe.

North of the vault enclosure is a cone for scientific knowledge. Built into the wall on the west side the concave Ra stones give the geometrical alignments along the edge. The sphere is missing from the concave saucer. There is a dressed triangular (pyramid) stone north of the concave stone, which gives the geometrical alignments.

Just below, the Nyahokwe mountain cliff face is a circular enclosure with the entrance on the south side. Facing the enclosure are two cones on either side of the inner entrance. With the main walling, these form the optic geometrical alignments for the solstice, equinox and 52°. On the south side of the main wall are five Zoser niches giving the equinox, solstice and 52°. The loophole niches on the west wall north of them are for the solstice and equinox, the inner wall has its north end for the 52°. After this it continues south and turns for the solstice and equinox. The inner wall represents the Sphinx and knowledge. The main entrance into the central enclosure is on the line of the equinox. The other outer main wall entrance is on the solstice.

Turning to the west from the entrance is a raised platform 'seat' which has the equinox along one side and the solstice along the other. The 'backrest' has one square upright stone for Zoser and three curved upright stones for the Sphinx and the climb in life up the pyramid. The 52° is shown between the stones.

North of the 'seat' is a cone for the science of the universe with the number of stones for the days of the year. The Zoser monolith is on the west side of the cone.

The raised platform in front of the seat cone represents Zoser with the front broadside upright stones above supporting the stone slab, the end-on upright stone is for the geometrical alignments. The two broadside uprights north of the end-on stone represent the Sphinx and knowledge to stand on two feet. The raised platform once had earthenware pottery round the edge for the science of the universe, the Sphinx, Zoser and the pyramid.

The broken pieces were found on the ground at the base of the platform which worked in with the markers around it for the geometrical alignments.

There is another raised platform south of the central one and this has the upright stone markers for culture, Zoser and the Sphinx, and then branches off to the east side for the solstice. The angle between the ends gives the 52° for the lifecycle. On the edge of the platform is a row of small concave stones. The one marking the solstice is a much shallower concave than the rest of the group. The bigger stones stop on the 52°. The upright and concave stones represent Zoser, Ra, the Sphinx and age of initiation.

The third platform is near the main entrance and works in with the geometrical alignments. It represents the Sphinx, Zoser and the pyramid.

To the west of the platform is an inverted 'L' shaped stone marker with the 52° lining up with the boulder on the north side of the enclosure, which has a circle of stones next to it. The inverted 'L' has the equinox on the perpendicular side, the solstice on the north east and the 52° diagonally across the corner.

The vault close to the east wall has a stone slab on the east side giving the 52° and solstice. From the stone slab the equinox is to the concave stones on the top of the west wall. There is also a chip off the boulder on the east side of the enclosure for the geometrical alignments. Below this boulder is a sheltered area which once had an earthenware obelisk marker for the scientific knowledge, but only the shards remain to show where they once stood.

There are a number of 'earth' markers for the geometrical alignments. These work in with the main markers. The concave stones are for the geometrical alignments as well as scientific knowledge and culture. However, the spheres which were placed there have been removed. There is a line of concave stones between the 'seat' and the vault. These and the upright stones set into the ground are for the alignments and culture.

The Nyahokwe Ruin near the summit of the mountain is built on waste land and is out of the way of intruders and fortune hunters. It is designed in such a way that it can be used indefinitely. The optic alignments are taken from the niches and loopholes to the cone and mountain for the north bearing and from the cone to the loophole and niches for the south bearings. The boulder and other markers are also included in the alignments. It is, therefore, possible that this site has been used for 12,000 years, which would date the ruin as possibly one of the oldest constructions in the world, the stone walls being maintained and markers preserved or covered with soil. The concave stones and earthenware were used in the interim period because they were moveable and easy to position.

Other circular constructions, such as Stonehenge, used the same principle of a central marker for the alignments, therefore, it is only possible to date them from the entrance marker, cones and natural surroundings because of the precision work involved. The large monoliths weathered or fell, giving them a limited lifespan.

There are two sets of individual constructions in the Nyahokwe group which represent the quartenary system. Zoser also taught silence as a golden rule and only after so many years, probably at the time of the initiation, were they permitted to make decisions (honour thy father and mother). Female animals were not killed because the soul passes from the animal on four legs (crawl) to the upright stance (bird) and back to the animal (stick) (Ecclesiastes 3, Exodus 20).

At the Nyahokwe Museum is an iron half moon shaped symbol with a curved handle. When this symbol is placed point down, it gives the geometrical alignments with the indents. The equinox is from the point of the handle, the solstice to the indents, the lifecycle the outer curved edge of the half moon and the whirl of the handle represents the equinox and the passing on of knowledge to the next generation.

The half moon gnomon is used to tell the time. A quern goyo stone is filled with water. The metal half moon is balanced on the inside rim with the whirl on the outside. If the metal has been magnetised it will automatically swing to magnetic north. The metal gnomon could have been magnetised by placing it inside a coil of copper wire during an electrical storm. In Africa, electric storms can be quite severe with the lightning concentrating in some areas where the metal underground acts as a conductor. The copper coil and iron gnomon could be placed on a granite kopje where the lightning could disperse with the help of rainwater. The Chinese used to spin a metal spoon on a copper dial which would always come to rest on the magnetic north.

The earthenware Mbiva Ba vase has a hole in the side for the geometrical alignments with the rim and the base. The dots are for the days of the year and the scientific knowledge, the two obelisks are for the Sphinx. The vase represents the pyramid and the climb up the side of the equinox. The Zuni Pueblo American Indians have similarly designed vases.

A photograph on display in the museum shows another site with a 'Beehive' Shona 'Chipfuko' construction. This has the solstice and 52 degrees shown on the side of the chipfuko pyramid with the equinox arch for the lifecycle. The chipfuko has two steep sides form the base to the top. On one side a more gradual slope is followed by another steep one to join with the other side for the initiation. After acme has been reached the almost vertical descent of the pyramid/chipfuko begins. This construction was used at the time of the equinox when the sun's rays shone down the sides of the construction.

The lower covered 'Mapfwa' construction has the circular hollow below the ground level representing Ra. It also gives the geometrical alignments and is used at the time of the equinox. The arch represents the lifecycle and the roofstones are for measuring the angle of the sun. The arrangement of the stones themselves represents Zoser.

The Sphinx 'Chorongo' has two protruding legs like the Egyptian Sphinx, but the legs are more splayed to give the equinox and geometrical alignments with the hollow underneath the oval and to the equinox holes behind the legs. The claws represent Zoser. The legs are for the initiation. The hollow under the oval represents Ra, but the sphere is missing from the saucer. The oval top represents the continuous circle of knowledge from one generation to the next. The sides of the oval represent the climb up the pyramid to initiation. The symbol on the oval represents the tortoise with the geometrical eyes and head, the arms and legs of the Sphinx and the circle of Ra with the heart and feather under the body.

The Chipfuko, and low Mapfwe covered construction and the Sphinx are used in conjunction with each other at sunrise, midday and sunset.

Another photograph showing an excavated area has brought to light a set of four upright stones which give the geometrical alignments for the equinox, solstice and 52° and are also used as a Mutaro sundial.

A skull with a pot over the face was found here. If the body had been of the Islamic faith it would have been punishment for one who flaunted his knowledge (Surah XLVII v27), in which case the skeleton would have faced the Kiblah (Surah II v50). However, the skeleton was placed in a flexed position, therefore the pot represents the science of the universe and was African.

CHAWOMERA

The Chawomera Mountain Ruin has a 400 metre vertical drop from the summit to the river on the south side of the ruin. Consequently, there are no markers on the outside of the south wall as they would be pointless and dangerous for those who ventured too close to the drop, which represents death.

Inside the enclosure marking the solstice are some low walled circular enclosures which adjoin the main wall on the south and east sides. The main entrance on the rounded north east corner has a low wall for the lifecycle. The two sections represent the Sphinx; all these line up for the geometrical alignment.

The second entrance has a metre long entrance passage at the base of the north wall. There is a stone marker in the shape of an inverted 'L' which has a set of its own alignments. The ends of the wall are for the equinox and, diagonally across the entrance, incorporating the inverted 'L', are the solstice and 52°.

The south west corner of the enclosure wall has a triangular shape representing the pyramid and giving the alignments for the solstice and 52°.

The outside number 2 enclosure has a half circle of single upright stones. The number of stones used represents the lifecycle and the age of initiation. The similar stones are for Zoser. The stones are placed to give the solstice, equinox and 52° across the ends of the enclosure.

The third enclosure has a low wall about half a metre away from the west wall and towards the centre of the main enclosure. The wall has the solstice north end, followed by the equinox and 52° lifecycle. This wall represents the stick of age and the descent down the pyramid. The third enclosure represents the complete lifecycle with the west entrance for the close of life. The south east exit of the main enclosure is between the third and fourth enclosure. Together with the north west exit it forms the 52°. The winter solstice is with the west wall marker which is the higher section of the wall. There are a number of stones at the base of the wall forming markers.

Numbers 4 and 5 enclosures give the optic geometrical alignments between them and also represent scientific knowledge and culture.

The north west exit has the loopholes on the north side for Zoser and the Sphinx and, being on the north, it represents the passing of knowledge.

The parapet represent the Sphinx and covers the same area as the low walled enclosure, showing the area covered by the sun at the time of the solstice.

Below the summit to the north west are two deep vaults. One has the entrance approach on the line of the solstice. The tunnel entrance is on the line of the equinox, then turns for the 52° and ends with the equinox. The concave stones and light holes on top of the Sphinx tunnel mark the turning point and the passing on of knowledge. The apex is for the north/south equinox. The four metre high vault is for Zoser and the science of the universe. The two metre high equinox entrance is from the Sphinx tunnel, which is two metres high. The vault and enclosure wall represents Ra and gives the geometrical alignments.

The second four metre vault has a cone marker on the west side and indents for the geometrical alignments and scientific knowledge. Joining the vault walling on the south side is a circle of stones. The entrance gives the geometrical alignments and the number of entrance stones used in the circle is for the age of initiation and lifecycle.

HARLEIGH

The First Ruin is hidden on a kopje among the rocks of the Harleigh Farm and has the main wall on the line of the solstice. Metal symbols were found on the north side of the entrance wall. The main entrance has the equinox from the south west corner to the north corner. The 52° is across the entrance and lines up with the copper found at section 10. The ivory found just outside the entrance (section 11) is in line with other ivory found at sections 5 and 7 which are on the line of the 52° for the lifecycle.

The south west wall between the boulders is on line with the equinox. The small wall between areas A and B is on the line of the solstice and lines up with Section 17.

The dolerite hammer stone revealed in section 7 gave the optic geometrical alignments.

Section 5 revealed a rectangular slab of sandstone and a dolerite sphere with two flattened surfaces. The remains of the elephant tusk on the west side of B, C, entrance, was for the lifecycle; and the metal symbol, similar to a knife blade, the geometrical alignments.

The two niches on the east side of the 52° dividing wall marks the equinox and 10° with the south one. The second marker shows the 20 and 30 degrees.

From the arc ground marker of section 16, the equinox is to the west wall of area D and the south side of the curved half circle to the north of it. The 52° is to the west side of the arc marker and the north wall of area C. The solstice is to the circular stone of area D.

Area 16 revealed an all-metal symbol, with an eye (wedget) at one end. The eye section shows the solstice and, by using the side of the eye and the outside of the outer edge, it gave the equinox and 52°. This metal symbol is similar to one found at Lobengula's grave near Bulawayo.

Section 17 reveals an earth structure of curved walls with a quarter 'dish' in the corner for the geometrical alignments. From the circular marker of area D the walling shows the ascent in life and the final closing of life. At the age of approximately 95 the chief, whose skeleton was found within the walling of the north east area of the ruin, was in a flexed position, with the hand under the chin and the legs in a kneeling position. The chief climbed the Mr pyramid of life and descended it into the grave.

The red soil represented youth; the yellow, initiation and knowledge. The ash and white beads are of geometrical significance and verify the position of the skeleton. Some nondescript beads represented the heart and feather. The minute gold pellet stands for royalty and the rolls of copper wire measure the lifecycle. Other rolls were found in the areas pertaining to the 52° and lifecycle. The coloured beads and earth reflect the standard of knowledge and culture attained.

Iron is for the solstice and war; copper the equinox; ivory the lifecycle and knowledge; gold is for royalty (chief).

The rock painting on a boulder near the First Ruin depicts the science of the universe. The blades of grass (Sinaitic Script, blossom) give the days of the year and the trees (Canaanite script 1000 BC); the dots are for Ra, the pyramid and geometrical alignments. The animals represent the Sphinx. The curled horns of one of the animals are similar to the Egyptian whirl (pharaoh's crown) and are for Zoser. The figure near the top of the painting has passed his knowledge on to the next generation. Below, two figures can be seen wearing the square Zoser 'hat' performing circumcision and another with a rounded 'hat' for the climb up the pyramid. Near the base of the painting are trophies of armbands.

The lone figure walking in deep contemplation towards the main picture pertains to the seriousness of the initiation, the silence of Zoser and the skill of the Sphinx in walking upright. This could be the chief's epitaph.

Between Ruin One on Harleigh Farm and Ruin Two of Denonia Farm is a stream. Personal observation revealed that near the boundary fence of the Second Ruin are some boulders, with next to them a circular construction. The west side has been built up to the level of the east side to make a level platform. The circular marker to the south is made up of a chipped boulder and gives the equinox and 52° between the chip and the south corner of the chipped boulder. The chip, circular platform and boulder give another set of alignments. The number of layers of stone used around the edge represent the lifecycle, Zoser and the Sphinx.

On the south side of the boulder is a one metre wall and a cone obelisk which are five metres apart, giving the geometrical set with the boulder cone nearby to represent science and culture.

On the south east side of the boulder is a triangular stone slab mounted on a stone foundation of knowledge. The equinox is with the foundation stones and the triangular stone. The solstice is along the south side of the triangular stone, while the 52° is along the third side.

The high outcrop of rock has a cone obelisk on the top represents the pyramid of knowledge. The rock and cone give the geometrical alignments between them, and line up with the lower cone for the 52° which is also aligned with the triangular stone and chip boulder. Together they form a grand triangle for the equinox, solstice and 52°. On the north side of the Balancing Rock is a circular cone and a line of stones set into the ground, joining it to the main loophole wall to give the equinox, solstice and 52°, the parallel lines of culture and the circular cone base Ra.

The main north east wall of the enclosure has loopholes. By the direction and angle of the slope these give the equinox, solstice and 52° and represent the ascent of life. The groupings of 3, 5, 2 loopholes are for Zoser and the Sphinx. The linteled entrances are on the line of the equinox for the passing on of knowledge. The east entrance is for the ascent of the pyramid and initiation. The exit on the west side of the enclosure is for the descent of the pyramid, as the ground has a gentler gradient for those who are ageing.

The entrance on the south east side has the loophole wall on the north east side of the walling and a boulder on the south side. There is a rock chip marker on the outside of the entrance which lines up with the boulder for the optic geometrical alignments. The cave just inside the entrance has the west side on the line of the solstice. The stone 'U' on the ground is for the equinox and 52°. The number of stones also represents culture and science.

The two metre high wall on top of the big boulder has four stones for Zoser. The layers of stone are for the Sphinx. With the boulder to the south, the ends of the wall give the equinox and solstice, while the wall itself shows the remaining alignments.

To the south of the outside of the Inner Enclosure wall is another cave with a small wall under the boulder. Small boulders can also be found under the rock of the cave and together give the equinox, solstice and 52°.

The stone wall just south of the cave and near the rock pool is on line with the solstice and includes, because of its height, the science of the universe and culture; length, width and number of stones give the geometrical alignments.

On the outside of the main wall are two circular cone obelisk bases which line up with the Balancing Rock, and the high cone to the north, and to the east the south cave wall.

The cone obelisk to the west of the covered entrance of the main inner section, and the south end of the ditch give the geometrical alignments to the entrance. The ditch is equivalent to the two parallel walls and is for the Sphinx and equinox.

The open entrance on the west side of the Balancing Rock entrance has the steps for culture and the alignments for the solstice. Inside the Balancing Rock enclosure near the entrance is a stone chip and a circular cone base which form the geometrical alignments.

Under the Balancing Rock is some stone walling. The north section is for the equinox, solstice, 52° and lifecycle. The number of stone layers are for the Sphinx and Zoser. The walling above the Balancing Rock gives the geometrical alignments and the science of the universe. This high walling lines up with other markers which can be seen from this vantage point.

South of the Balancing Rock is a circular marker with three remaining jutting stones. These represent culture, Zoser and the Sphinx. The boulder beside the jutting cones gives the geometrical alignments within the area of these stones.

The small shelter south of the jutting stones and boulder has the equinox along the west side of the walling and the solstice along the north wall. The curved hand-high wall across the corner is for the lifecycle, the stone construction is only about one metre high and deep. The small boulders on either side of the entrance are a weathered colour but those inside are unweathered, which could have resulted from excavation or a recent construction. There is another set of geometrical alignments from the boulder to the marker stone near the hand-high shaping corner wall.

Under the Balancing Rock is the main cave. The south entrance has a concave quern stone with two long parallel and one short side for the equinox, north, south, east and west. The third and fourth sides are for the solstice and 52°. The chip off the rock on the south east side beside the entrance and the boulder inside the cave give the optic geometrical alignments.

Against the west wall, just north of the quern stone, is a long table built with small flat stones, one metre in length and height and half a metre wide, covered with earth cement. There is an extra wall on the south west side, in line with the solstice. The 52° is from the south of this extra wall to the south east corner of the table. An earthen crocodile is climbing up the south west corner of the table. On the table stands a fixed cement dish, similar in design to one excavated near the Covered Passage of the Western Enclosure of the Acropolis at Zimbabwe. This cone dish gives the optic alignments with the two obelisk cones on the top of the north wall of the cave.

These cones are circular. One is constructed with small flat stones, similar to those of the table, and represents Zoser and the Sphinx. The other cone is covered with white earth cement and represent knowledge. These cones can also be seen from outside. (A small cave has been created by clearing away the earth from under the boulder.) Near the cones is a low white-coloured cement wall, two metres long and half a metre high and a hand wide. The wall is slightly curved (similar to one found at Khami Cd1). This smaller cave allows high back lighting for the cones on the top of the wall inside the main cave.

The passage descends to the corner of the cave where another metre high curved wall gives the alignments with the table and the north east exit, where two metre diameter cones are standing next to each other, nearly touching. The south cone is an earth colour for lower Egypt, the other one is white/blue, the colour of Upper Egypt, mind and universe. It may also have some connection with the stars. These cones line up with the stone entrance for the equinox, solstice and 52°. and also with the ground circular line of stones nearby on the outside of the cave. This in turn lines up with other markers and the rock entrance.

When I first visited the cave there was a wall between the exit and the cones. This was built with small stones and was two metres high. There was enough space above the wall to allow light to reach the cones on top of the wall. As explained earlier these cones are also aided by back light from the adjoining cave. The wall represents the Sphinx in height, and the number of stones the days of the year and science of the universe. The stone could have been used for other constructions. The cave is well guarded by bees who live among the cracks in the rock.

DIANA'S VOW

Diana's Vow Farm near Rusape has a small ruin which is disintegrating. However, it is still possible to find markers. The linteled entrance to the ruin is for the equinox and the passing on of knowledge from one generation to the next.

The boulder on the west side is north and south for the equinox. The boulder to the north east is for the solstice. The pitted rock high up on the west equinox boulder is for the 52 year lifecycle and the descent of the pyramid.

Another set of optical alignments is north/south with the boulder and cone marker to the north. This cone and the tunnel give the solstice alignments and the equinox with the cone and boulder ending.

The tunnel has its own set with the entrance on the equinox. It then turns for the solstice and 52°. The roof holes are for the change of direction and equinox. The tunnel itself represents the Sphinx.

Another geometrical set is with the cone base placed on the flat rock at the entrance to the cave. This forms the equinox, solstice and 52°. One must crawl to enter the cave and until the step in the middle is reached. This is for the Sphinx. Then one emerges from the cave in the upright stance.

The rock painting is on the boulder in the alcove adjoining and below the ruin. It shows the youth in training for their initiation and knowledge to balance on two feet.

At the base of the painting are lines for Zoser, while the animals represent the Sphinx. On the right hand side, next to a very dark ascending snake, is a figure dressed similarly to those seen on the walls of the Egyptian pyramids, where the Jews were portrayed with a cloth over one shoulder. The Warozvi tribe near Fort Victoria wear a cloth in the same manner and the Bushman use a skin.

Above the buffalo are some skin bags as initiation symbols and gourd of knowledge. The animal skins represent the Sphinx. The lines dividing the painting are for the teachings of Zoser and the Sphinx. The section just above the lines shows a bird for the feather and heart of justice. The figure resting on the ground has the heart and feather in each hand and balances on one foot and elbow, again similar to the Bushman's sleeping position.

The main figure of the painting is balanced on one foot and elbow, the body decorated with the science of the universe and knowledge. The dots are for the days of the year and the groups are for the age of initiation, the lifecycle, Zoser and the Sphinx. The dots are white on a yellow body for the initiation and knowledge, the eyes are for Ra, the two lines down the nose and the animal head are for the Sphinx and Zoser. The angle of the resting leg is for the pyramid and lifecycle. There is a chicken on two legs on the knee of the Sphinx which represents initiation. The dots on the calf are for Zoser. The smaller figure with the stick represents old age. The genitals and flowing urine represent the lifecycle.

GOMO KADZAMA

The Gomo Kadzama Ruin near the Odzani Dam road has a vault construction with the entrance for the solstice, equinox and 52°, the south equinox entrance lines up with the perpendicular rocks on the stone kopje to the south of the vault. The vault itself is in poor condition. There appears to be some shaping in the vault, which was probably for the optic alignments. The square area was for Zoser on which a stone with traces of false gold was placed as a marker. The walling round the enclosure appears to have represented scientific knowledge as well as the geometrical alignments.

On an outcrop of rock are some earth markers, one of which has the solstice marked out with stones on one side of the rim of the circle and ends with the stone on the inside of the rim. This lines up with the outer stone markers for the geometrical design. These stones are for Zoser and their position indicates the Sphinx and the age of knowledge. Some of the natural rock has not been covered over with earth so this is also used for the geometrical alignments.

Another circle has an oblong stone with two perpendicular grooves on the longer side. These give the solstice and 52° to the corner of the stone. The solstice is across corners and the equinox is along the shorter sides.

For a third circle stones and 'earth' markers were used in the centre. These circles are all in line with each other for the equinox, solstice and 52°. Had these circular constructions been used as a kraal, they would not have weathered so well or been in such a good state of preservation. It is also possible that the circles were placed there in fairly recent times by those who were undergoing training and would, perhaps, have worked on the reconstruction of the vault, but were prevented from doing more by the lack of privacy and fear of interference by outsiders. The circles represent Ra, the double rim the Sphinx and the stones, Zoser.

There is a concave stone which lines up with the stones near it to give the geometrical design. Another flat stone has the sides for the equinox, solstice and the 52° with the loose stones on the top of the second design.

Gomo Kadzama kopje ruin has a linteled entrance on the line of the equinox, with the solstice across the entrance and from the north linteled covered entrance. The 52° is to the boulder on the north side of the entrance. A second design is on the north east side of the kopje. The line of stones north and south are for Zoser. The equinox runs from the southern end while the solstice and 52° can be seen with the 'fallen' stone, which gives the alignments at either end, and with the smaller stones just beyond the fallen stone. The solstice is with the squared Zoser stone on the west side of the equinox stones. The third side of the stone has not been squared and represents the pyramid and knowledge.

The Gomo Kadzama kopje commands an excellent view. To the south can be seen the perpendicular stones of the kopje beside the vault ruin. To the west the perpendicular boulder kopje, which is on the line of the solstice, can be viewed.

To the north east on the line of the solstice and 52° another hill kopje, with an outcrop of rock surmounting the grass slopes, can be seen. It will be found that there are ruins in line with the Gomo Kadzama and that this ruin is positioned so that one can view the line of direction leading to the next ruin of the construction.

MURAHWA'S HILL, UMTALI

Murahwa's Hill has a steep ascent to the top for the pyramid. Pot shards found here were originally markers, but have long since lost their significance and positions.

Ascending the kopje there is a rock chip forming a tunnel which is on the line of the solstice, the north side of the east boulder is lime green. Diagonally across the tunnel the equinox is shown, while the sides give the 52° for the lifecycle.

On the summit of the kopje are four concave oblongs for Zoser, one on the line of the equinox and the Sphinx. They represent birth, initiation, the lifecycle and death. There is another set of three on the line of the solstice, also representing the Sphinx.

Another group further on are for Zoser and are on the line of the equinox.

Lower down the kopje is a group of 24 concave oblongs for the age of initiation. They give the optic alignments, solstice and 52° and also the geometrical alignments. The incomplete concaves represent those still to be initiated. There is a circular group for Ra and the lifecycle. There are ten concave oblongs on the equinox for Zoser and two on the line of the solstice for the Sphinx. The concaves are for the measurement of moisture in the air.

The caves on the south west side of the kopje have a rock chipped like a tortoise which represent Zoser, the Sphinx and the science of the universe. The tortoise is looking out over the valley below. The concave where the chip originated has a few painted objects depicted on it for the geometrical alignments. There are more art paintings on the cave rock face which have suffered at the hands of vandals and infamous signatures of the vain. However, I did see the remains of two buck, a thorn tree bow and stakes or arrows.

*****

The following items were on display at the Umtali Museum. On Tilbury Farm, Umtali, a stand was found with a bird on the left, a tortoise in the centre and a crocodile on the right. The bird and crocodile symbols are the same as on the soapstone monolith of the Zimbabwe bird. The crocodile is for the child who crawls and has seven lines for the Sphinx on the one and five for Zoser on the other side. The lines are at 52°. The equinox and solstice are on its back.

The tortoise has the circle of Ra for the eyes and the geometrical alignments, and because of its shell it represents the stages of man and Zoser.

The bird is for the heart and feather of justice, initiation and walking on two feet. The fourth side is blank for when man reached the decline and close of life.

The soapstone carvings at Partridge Hill, Vumba, have the equinox hole, the cubes of Zoser and the diamond of initiation, which also gives the geometrical alignments. The lines are for the age of initiation and the curved top for the rise and fall of man. The lower section has been broken off and forms an inverted 'V'.

On Eastlands Farm, Umtali, a carved oblong was found with a man on the front wearing a 'hat' for Upper Egypt and knowledge. The double image chevron on the top represents the lifecycle and pyramid. The square face is for Zoser, the eyes for Ra. The nose and mouth lines are for the age of initiation and three lines at the side of the face for age. The body lines are in a loose chevron for the age of initiation and give the equinox and youth. The apex is for the peak of life, the solstice for the decline. The circular feet are for the Ra and the space between the Sphinx legs is for the pyramid.

The 'washing stones' squares are for Zoser and the age of initiation, the angles for the geometrical alignments, Zoser and the Sphinx.

The tortoise turtle, represents the curve of the lifecycle, culture and scientific knowledge.

The figures represent the stages of man in regard to the Sphinx and knowledge. The figure positioned on all fours is for the crawl of a child. Two feet indicate initiation, then bent with old age. The faces are flat and represent geometrical alignments. The eyes are for Ra.

MISCELLANEOUS

Nughaza Ruin

The Nughaza Ruin (based on the Rhodesian Herald 04.09.1969) has a ten-metre diameter circle which is divided into four quarters which are on the line of the equinox. The north east central quarter corner has the 20° to the south corner, the 52° is to the smooth earth cement daga 'step' at the entrance opening and the solstice is to the north east end of the wall. From the south corner the 10, 20, 30 and 40 degrees vary with the pottery, bracelet and markers which were found there.

The north west quarter of the construction has the equinox corner with the 52° to the south west end of the entrance gap. There are other geometrical alignments to the post holes and slots which give their own set of alignments.

The south east quarter of the construction from the inner curve corner has the equinox north and south with the 52 and 40 degrees to either side of the curved daga step. The 30° is to the corner of the outer wall. If the true north is correctly positioned on the plan, the construction is more recent 13 x 66 = 858 or 1142 AD but if 20° out then 178BC.

The Circular Ruin near the Lundi river gives the geometrical alignments from the south east entrance to the east wall shaping for the equinox, the solstice is to the angle of the north side entrance wall, the 52° is to the north entrance. The patterned area is between the entrance on the east side of the enclosure and is for the science of the universe and culture. The Circular Ruin is about 20° out of alignment which is about 20+13=33x66=2178 or 178 BC.

The Little Zimbabwe Ruin has the equinox from the two

cones to the main entrance walls on the south side of the ruin, the solstice is to the main east wall and the 52° is to the north entrance. There is another set from the south west main wall entrance joining another set from the inner circular enclosure wall. This ruin is about the same age as the Circular Ruin.

Matindela Ruin has the main wall opening between the equinox and 30°, the west main wall has alternate inside and outside decorated sections. The dentille pattern is for Zoser and the herringbone is for the age of initiation and knowledge. Aligning the southern end on the equinox, the 52° is to the southern end of the second inside decorated section and the 72° is to the northern inner section representing the lifecycle.

The 1st cone has the equinox to the end of the outer pattern wall, the solstice to the design change and the 52° to the north section of the second inner pattern. The second cone has the equinox and solstice to either side of the first cone, the 52° is to the loophole. The third cone has the solstice to the second cone, the 52° is to the patterned section of the main wall and the equinox is to where the points join.

The two south cones have the 52° along the side, the equinox and solstice are to either side of cone three. The fourth cone has the equinox and solstice to either side of the third cone and the 52° is to the tree corner.

The south group of four cones forms the geometrical alignments between them. The south east group of four between them form the geometrical alignments.

There are 14 cones in all, eight small and three medium size and there are three single larger cones, which are on the west side of the patterned section of the main wall. The cone sets are for Zoser and the Sphinx and the baobab tree represents the feather of justice.

Inside the enclosure, the north west wall has the equinox along the wall to the opening, the solstice and 52° are to the central wall ends and the tree corners. The main dividing wall has the eastern section on the 52° with A and B the two entrances. The other curved wall section is for the lifecycle and the solstice alignments are between the two ends, with entrance C on the equinox for the passing on of knowledge. The northern main wall from the angled corner is on the equinox, which is now 20° out of alignment which dates the ruin to about the same age as the Circular Ruins.

From the south corner the equinox is to the short wall, the 52° and solstice are to the entrance A, B, and from the end of this wall the equinox is along the wall to the entrance and north west of the short single wall, the 52° is to entrance B.

From the south west corner wall join, the equinox is to the entrance C, the solstice and 52° are to the two entrances on the curved central wall.

The Inner patterned wall gives the 72°, 52° and the solstice, which are for the lifecycle and the close of life. Entrance C is on the equinox, the solstice is to the north west end of the main enclosure, the 52° is to the north entrance of the equinox wall.

Blackadder Ruin No 1 is a half kilometre east of Umtali river near Harare. The three loopholes 1,2,3, are on the line of the 52° and represent the beginning, middle and end, loophole 6 is on the line of the equinox, the solstice is to the west boulder and the 52° is to the east boulder. Loopholes 7,8,9,10,11, are on the line of the 52°, the corner walling between 9 and 10 gives the equinox to the west and the 30° to the east, the 52° is to the boulder to the north of the corner. The north east walling is on the line of the equinox and initiation. The distance across the enclosure is 42 metres (30,7,5,) and 72 metres for the lifespan.

Unfortunately true north is only approximately 30° out of alignment so 30+13=43x66=2838 or 838 BC.

Legend Ruin of Inyanga Downs is just south of Troutbeck Dam. Enclosure 1 has the main entrance for the geometrical alignments, the equinox is from the north west wall end and south west wall, the second equinox is to the south west wall end. From the central point formed by the equinox, the solstice is taken to the north west wall shaping and the 52° is taken along the south east entrance walling.

Area X. The entrance to this area has the equinox level with the boulder and the south side of the main entrance wall. The north equinox is to the east end of the main entrance to No 1 Enclosure; the solstice is to the indent on the north side of the wall, north of the entrance; the 52° is to the east of the entrance wall.

In Enclosure 2 the equinox is taken from the north loophole 'drain' and across from the west loophole 'drain' to the second Covered Entrance, the solstice is to the boulder east of the north equinox line of the main enclosure wall indent and the 52° is to the boulder west of the equinox line.

Area Y has the solstice along the south west wall, the equinox is to 'Y's north east entrance, the 52° is to the boulder north of the entrance.

Area Z has the equinox across the entrance wall ends, the solstice is between the entrance wall ends and the 52° is to the entrance wall north west of the entrance.

Enclosure 3. The Covered Entrance gives the geometrical alignments, the equinox is north and south along the north wall of the entrance, the solstice is across the entrance wall ends and the 52° is to the covered section of the enclosure.

The circle of stones has the equinox across the main entrance of the enclosure and north to the ends of the curved wall, the 52° is to the indents between the curved join and the main wall, the solstice is to the wall indents just north of the main entrance. The line of stones represents the Sphinx and Zoser and the total gives the age of initiation 12,5,7, and the ten stones are for Zoser.

The Legend Ruin is now 27° out of alignment 27+13=40x66=2640 or 640 BC.

BAVENDA

The BaVenda tribe have a cave called Makapansagat which is probably the one used for obtained stone for the building of the ruin. There is a family which hands down from generation to generation the responsibility for looking after the cave and its contents, an assortment of symbols of various design and material. It is possible that these symbols are kept in special positions to give the equinox, solstice and 52° as well as the science of the universe, just as they would do if they were placed at the ruin. There are drums at the cave which are for special occasions such as initiation.

The BaVenda people have their own area in the Northern Transvaal. The river Matale forms Lake Fundudzi which has fish and crocodiles which are never caught. A python is reputed to live at the lake (representing the serpent which encircles the earth for the lifecycle).

The BaVenda had a special ceremony where a young girl used to be tied by alternate hand and foot with one eye covered. Then she was taken into the middle of the lake and drowned (The Glorious Koran XXVI v 49; LXXXI v 31) (The overthrowing x 8 - 9). This may have connections with the fertility cycle, as explained In the Zimbabwe section of the soapstones. The ceremony was probably held at the time of the equinox, but has been replaced, at Government request, by a black bull and is probably held at the time of the summer solstice.

There is a river Apies near Hammanskraal between Pretoria and Warmbath. The Nyl river flows near Nylstroom and joins the Limpopo (crocodile) river. The rains bring the river down in flood as the Nile in Egypt. The Apies river may be named after Apis the bull of Egypt. Apis is a very special bull, he must show a white eagle mark on his black back, a white square on the forehead and a lump under his tongue for a tortoise. He is treated with great reverence until he reaches the age of 25 when he is drowned. Whether the death is natural or not there is a period of mourning.

The BaVenda claim that they left the kingdom of Monomotopa (Meroe Ethiopia) in the 17th and 18th century, which may explain the inclusion of Apis in the tribal customs and coincides with the introduction of Islam in Egypt.

The gold objects found at Mapugubwe, Limpopo Valley, were designed for the science of the universe and culture of the people who used them. Wood was used because it is heat resistant, light to carry and easy to work. The gold leaf would preserve the wood and prevent it drying out or being eaten by termites and make it easy to recognise as something of importance and value.

The beaten sheet gold rhinoceros had the equinox from the chin to the ear and the solstice to the horn and face join. The angle of the horn is for the 52° and the rise and fall of man through life. The tail gives the equinox and from the tail to the hip gives the angle of the solstice and 52°. The front leg gives another set for the equinox, solstice and 52°.

The bowl of beaten gold has the geometrical alignments and the lifecycle. The sheathing for the 'sceptre' has the equinox and solstice with the staff knob and pattern for the 52°. The knob represents Ra, the spiral Zoser and the Sphinx. The knob and staff together represent the heart and feather of justice and the gold is for royalty and knowledge.

The gold circular shaped beads and tacks are all for the equinox, solstice and 52°, Ra, Zoser and the Sphinx. The wound wire being for the lifecycle and 52° and a measured length.

BIBLIOGRAPHY

The Historical Monuments Commission of Rhodesia
The Museums of Salisbury, Bulawayo, Umtali, Zimbabwe Ruins and Inyanga
Prehistoric Rock Art of the Federation of Rhodesia and Nyasaland
Rock Art of Central Africa - Elizabeth Goodall, C.K.Cooke, FSA, J.D.Clark. OBE, PhD, FSA Edited by Roger Summers.
Rock Art of Southern Africa - C.K.Cooke.
Rock Art of South Africa - A.R.Willcox.
Guide to the Zimbabwe Ruins Compiled by Neville Jones OBE:F.R.A.I.
A Guide to Khami Ruins - K.S.Radcliffe-Robinson F.R.A.I.
A Guide to the Antiquities of Inyanga - P.S.Garlake.
A Guide to the Khami, Naletale and Dhlo Dhlo Ruins and other Antiquities near Bulawayo C.K.Cooke.
The Ruined Cities of Mashonaland - J.Theodore Bent F.R.A.I.;F.R.G.S.
Zimbabwe Rhodesia's Ancient Greatness - A.J.Bruwer
The Prehistory of Southern Africa - J.Desmond Clark.
Excavations at Harleigh Farm near Rusape, Rhodesia 1958-62 P.A.Robins and Anthony Whitty (Fauna by Fagan)
Analytical Concordance of the Holy Bible - Robert Young LLB
The Holy Bible (King James)
The Torah The five books of Moses, A new Translation of The Holy Scriptures according to the Masoretic text.
Scriptures of the Dead Sea Sect, Translated by Theodor H.Gaster.
What the Jews Believe - Rabbi Philip S.Bernstein
A Guide to Jewish Knowledge - Rev Dr Chaim Pearl MA.PhD and The Rev Reuben - S.Brookes
The Bible as History - Werrner Keller Translated from German

William Niel MA, BD, PhD
Israel, Britain - The Great Pyramid by Adam Rutherford FRGS, FCRA, AMInstT
Ancient Egypt by Macdonald Junior Reference Library
The Great Pyramid Decoded - Peter Lemesurier
Secrets of the Great Pyramid - Peter Tompkins
The Pyramids of Egypt - I.E.S. Edwards
Tutankhamen - C Desroches Noblecourt
Archaeology of Palestine - WF Albright
Prehistoric Britain - Barbara Green & Allen Sorrell
Prehistoric England - Grahame Clark
The Ancient Sun Kingdoms of the Americas - Victor Wolfgang von Hagen
Aku Aku - Thor Heyerdahl
The Bull of Minos - Leonard Cottrell
The Harmless People - Elizabeth Marchall Thomas
The Kalahari and its Lost City - AJ Clement
Mythology of Greece and Rome with Eastern and Norse Legends - Thomas Bulfinch
African Mythology - Geoffrey Parrinder
North American Mythology - Cottie Burland
Life World Library Mexico - William Weber Johnson
Life World Library Greece - Alexander Elliott
Life World Library China - Loren Fessler
Life World Library Japan - Edward Seidensticker
South African Tourist Corporation
Land of Magic Waters - John Richard (The Motorist AA SA Nov 1968)
Life, The World of Great Religions/Hinduism
The Meaning of the Glorious Koran and Explanatory Translation by Mohammed Marmaduke Pickthall

Roberts Birds of South Africa revised by McLachlan and Liversidge, illustrated by Lighton Perry & Hopper
Handbook of the Roman Wall - J Collingwood Bruce XII edition revised by Sir Ian Richmond
Northumberland National Park edited by John Philipson MA, FSA
Portrait of Northumberland - Nancy Ridley
A Kingdom by the Sea - Betty James
Hadrian's Wall - AR Birley MA DPhil
Trees and Shrubs of the Kruger National Park - LEW Codd
South Africa Flowers for the Garden - Sima Eliovson
Rocks and Minerals - HS Zim PhD & PR Shaffer PhD, illustrated by R Perlman
Anthony Whittley ARIB; AD Didl, MA(SR) Plans
Old Africa Rediscovered - Basil Davidson
The Grand Rebel - Dennis Kincaid
Bhagavad Gita - Text and Commentary By Sri, Swami Sivananda
The Priests of Ancient Egypt - Serge Sauneron
Mammals of the KRUGER and other National Parks by R.J. Labuschagne and N.J. Van Der Merwe
How did they live - author unknown
Hebrew Amulets - T.Schrire
Story of the Bible World - Nelson Beecher Keyes
The Origin of Races - Carleton S.Coom.
The Childrens Encyclopaedia - Arthur Mee.

INDEX

'A' nhunga single, denga double 24, 99, 189
Ables Cave Cockscomb Mountains Cape Province 181
Ables Cave Drakensberg 173, 181
Abingdon neolithic pottery 74
Acropolis 203
Afnet 130, 131
African musical instruments 94
Alfred King 61, 69, 70
Altar from Chesterholm 76
Altar Kirkandrews 77
Altar of Mithras, Rudchester (Newcastle) 76
Amazon race 85
Amadzimba Cave Matopo Hills 155
Andover Wodehouse District Cape Province 182
Ankh Crux Ruin 235
Animals un/clean 105
Apache Navojo Papago 83
Apse 214
Arlington Road, Hatfield, Harare 104, 140
Arthur King 62
Atlantis, Thera, Santorini 83
Australian Aborigines 87
Avebury 65
Aylesford Bucket 72
Ayrshire Farm Lusaka 190
Aztecs of Teotihuacan 81

Ba suns shadow, duck's foot 195, 218

Bambata Cave Matopos National Park 154
Baptism 50, 108
Barmitzvah, Matmitzvah 50
Baobab - adansonia digitata can live for 1000 years 137
Barrow Hill near Wepener O.F.S. 177
Basuto - Le sotoland 92
Battle Cave Giants Castle Game Reserve Drakensberg 182
Ba Venda artefacts 292
Bay of Pisco Engravings 81
Beast 15
Beehive - chipfuko 267
Beersheba Farm Griqualand East 173
Belas Knap 67
Bell mediaeval Woodhorn 80
Beth Musami 136
Birdlip Bronze mirror 74
Blue fifty science of the universe 22
Black close of life
Bohwe Cave Matopos Hills 153
Bottisham beaker 72
Bonn Farm Macheke 135
Bontebok - damaliscus pygargus 170
Brandberg 143, 170
Bosworth Farm Klerksdorp 192, 193, 194, 196
Buck - antelope does not shed its horns 122
Buddha Siddhata Gautma 45, 91
Bumbuzi Rock Shelter Wankie Area 185
Bushman's Point Robert McIlwaine National Park 132, 137
Byblos 82, 86

Cabbage Tree - cussonia spicata 113
Caegrwle wooden bowl 72
Caftan 178, 180
Cairnsmore Ranch Umvukwe Range 129
Caledon Poort Fouriesberg O.F.S. 181
Camel 231
Candlestick 77
Candelaba 48, 52
Canute King 61
Cape Raven - corvulture albicollis 212
Capstone diagrams 213
Caroline Farm Robert McIlwaine National Park 122, 129
Carved shepherds's stick 79
Cerne Abbas Giant of Dorset Helith of Hercules 69
Chando solstice 42
Changamwibwe Kasama Zambia 165
Chanukah 48, 52
Cherewa Cave Mtoko 146
Chesterholm 76
Chickimin Brock 74
Chifubwa Stream Rock Shelter Solwezi 188, 171
Chikupu Cave Masembura 120, 128, 139, 141
Chipfuko - beehive 267
Chirimo - equinox 99
Chituro - torso 97
Chinamora Reserve Makumbe Cave 124, 126
Chinese porcelain 230
Chlorite schist green 199
Chorongo 268
Christian artefacts 56
Christianity Northumberland 79

Christophers Northumberland 79
Christophers Kraal North of Makumbe 125
Circumcision 52, 101
Coloured beads and soil 273
Confuciusus 45
Copper wire 273, 267
Cork tree - commiphora glandulosa 112, 133
Cremation 74
Crocodile markers 198, 200, 210, 277, 284
Croesus 45
Cross Anka Crux Ruin 166, 235
Cross Celtic diagram
Cross Iron 224
Cross Maltese 194, 235
Cross St Andrews 189, 225, 261
Crown of Glory 54

Daga mud plaster 100
Damra 93
Danebury near Stockbridge, Hampshire 68
Darius 45
Denga 'A' double frame 99
Dengeni Cave Zaka 127, 130, 145, 188
Devil's Arrow, Boroughbridge 69
Dhlo Dhlo rock painting 247
Diana's vow painting 247
Dolerite sphere 236, 272
Domboshawa Cave 120, 146
Doorn Hoek Krugersdorp District 192
Doornkloof Krukersdorp District, Transvaal 192

Dove - streptopelia semitorquata 212
Dragon Hill Uffington Castle 69
Drakensberg Natal 184
Driekopseiland near Kimberley 195
Druids 61
Drum language 94
Dumah 93

Earthenware Cone 237
Earthenware egg shape 244
Earthenware figure 244
Earthenware turtle 242
Easter Islands 86
Ebony - ebenaceae 136
Ebusingata Drakensberg Natal 182
Eierdorp Kopjes 111
Eland Cave Drakensberg Natal 177
Ely Grunty Fen gold torc of Tara 73
Enkeldoorn Mangene Reserve 127
Epworth Mission Farm 138
Equinox - chirimo
Equinox 222, 223
Euphorbiaceae - euphorbia - latex 113
Excalibur 62
Exfoliation of Rock 112, 216, 239, 262
Ezelzacht near Oudtshoorn Cape Province 179

Faience beads 64
False/fools gold pyrite 281

Feather weight 32
Fifty - blue
Fifty - two - life cycle
Figurine 222, 244, 245
Five - Zoser
Fisherville Farm Nyahuvu Farm Headlands 142
Flail 127, 147
Flame lily - gloriosa superba
Food laws 105
Fourty - green 2, 204
Free's Plot Hatfield 124, 133
Friend or foe 116
Frikkie Friars se Kliphuins, Boskloof Clanwilliams Cape 171

Gambarimwa Cave Mtoko 129
Gambles Cave Duhwe Hill Makaha 132
Game board 220
Game farmers 105
Game Pass, Kamberg, Drakensberg 180
Gemsbok Oryx Gazella Kinderdam Vryburg 194
Gestoplefontein near Ottosdal Transvaal 194
Giants Castle Game Reserve Natal 176, 178
Glen-Norah Farm 129, 139
Gnomond half moon 267
Gold pellets 273
Gold Tarc, Grunty Fen near Ely 73
Golden Rule 20, 22
Gol Gumaz 40
Gomokurira Chinamore Reserve 136
Gomokurira Hill 131

Gong 223
Goyo - quern and moisture gauge 95
Goromonzi 157
Grass burning 102
Greek culture 59, 243, 76
Greek Pillars of Hercules 83
Green fourty 20
Green chlorite schist 199
Grumspound Moreton, Hampstead 66
Groot Moot, Krugersdorp District 192
Gypsies Yetholm 78

Hadrian's Wall Northumberland/Cumberland 76
Hairstyles 91
Hari - marker 96, 115, 205
Harnessed - inspan of oxen 172
Harmony 177
Harrow Hills 69
Hauleville's Quoit, Stanton Dew in Somerset 68
Hebrew numerical values 47
Helith or Hercules, Cerne Abbas Giant Dorset 69
Herero 93, 172
Hill Ruin 235
Hindu ethics and colours 43
Horites 3
Housesteads Museum Deities 78
Howick Estate Concession 137
Howickvale Farm Umvukwes 121
Hystaspis 45

Ibo Nigeria 93
Ice Age Stone - Uncletin Newbiggin by the Sea 80
Ikanti Mountain near Sani Pass 180
Ilala Palm - hyphaene crinta 113
Imbwe earth cement marker 98
Incas artefacts 81, 82
Indigo sixty 22
Ingorima Reserve 188
Inoro, Makwe Cave 125
Inanga Rock engravings 188, 191
Irish artefacts 61
Iron God of War 100
Iron Helmet Thames 73
Iron Three footed candlestick Dudchester 77
Iron Wood - euphorbia 216
Isotja Cave Matopos Hills 149, 150
Issau Mussi - Jesus 56
Ivory disk pendent 239
Ivory lions 237, 240
Ivory cylinder 240
Ivory figure 234

Jet necklace 73

Ka descend death 117
Kaffirboom - erythrina caffra 113
Kalahari 109
Kamberg area Sandras Shelter, Drakensberg 177
Kasama Northern Province Zambia, Changamwibwe 160

Kasenga 190
Kenegha Poort, Griqualand East 175
Kerchief 131, 32
Khami artefacts 239
Kharet 53
Khunfu 20
Kinderdam Vryberg District Cape Province 196
King Alfred 62, 69 70
King Arthur 61
King Canute 61
Kirkandrews Altar 77
Kisanzi Farm Darwendale 122
Klein Aasvogelkop, Bouxville O.F.S. 176
Klipfontein Near Kimberley 194
Knobkerrie 101
Knysna Lion shoulder blade painting 184
Kopje - hill (Zimbabwe often a granite rock)
Kranses, Kamberg area Drakensberg 180
Kublai Khan 86, 230
Kukoma Kefete Zambia 169
Kuruman River Northern Cape Province 196
Kwartelfontein near Smithfield O.F.S. 174
Kyle 157

Labyrinth 84, 143, 188
Ladle Hill 67
La Rochelle, Clarens O.F.S. 175
Language of the drums 94
Le sotoland - Basutoland 92
Lions Head Msana Reserve 124, 125

Lions Shoulder blade painting Knysna 184
Lions ivory 237, 240
Longman of Wilminton East Sussex 70
Loophole - equinox optic alignments 'drain hole'
Lorraine near Clanwilliam Cape 181

Ma assent birth 117
Macheke 134, 136
Madzangara Mtoko 138
Maiden Castle Iron Age Hut 66, 67
Majenje Cave Matabeleland 158
Makabusi Farm Harare 130
Makhetas Basutoland 180, 183
Makumbe Cave 121, 137
Makwe Cave Inoro 124
Man Symbol 284
Manemba cave Mtoko 123
Mangweni Drakensberg near Underberg 172
Maoris New Zealand 87
Mapfwa earth construction 268
Mapugubwe artefacts 292
Marongoa Hill Darwendale 128
Marimba - xylophone 94
Martinshoek near Rhodes Cape Province 180
Mashonganyika Farm Goromonzi 121
Maund Ruins 214
Mayas 81
Mbangombe village Chadiza area Fort Jameson District 167
Mbira African piano 94
Mbiva hari vase 267

Meads Griqualand East Cape Province 183
Mediaeval bells Woodhorn Northumberland 80
Meg - spherical stone 96
Megillah - scroll or roll 48
Melsetter area 185
Menorah 48
Merkhet 97
Mermaid 79
Mhiva Ba Vase 267
Mikalongwe Hill or Mwalawolemba Shelter Southern Province Malawi 168
Milecastle 77
Mithraeum 77
Mimosa Farm Harare 133
Mirror Bronze 74
Mithras Altar, Rudchester Newcastle 76
Mitstraim 3
Mitzrain 3
Moel Siabod Bronze buckler 72
Moisture quern - goyo stone
Monolith First Ruin 232
Monkeytail - vellozia retinervis 112
Mossamedes Angola 195
Mpongweni Mountains Underberg Natal 172, 174, 182, 183
Mpunzi Mountains Dedza District Central Malawi 167
Mshaya Mvura Cave Mtoko 140
Mr-directional line 117
Mrewa Cave 126, 131, 135, 140
Mrra-God 101
Mtetengwe River near Beit Bridge Zimbabwe 185, 190
Mtoko 157

Mucheka Area Mrewa 140, 142, 137
Muchezi Cave Gwanda District 153
Mud plaster - daga 100
Mukombe - oblong wall 98
Multi-Cone Ruin 234
Munwa Stream Luapula Valley near Johnstone Falls Kashiba 189
Muromo Farm Umtali Area 143, 188
Musical instruments 93
Mutrro - shadow ducksfoot 97, 268
Mwanambavi Hill Mzimba District Malawi (vermilion) 168
Mwalawolemba Shelter or Milalongwe Hill Malawi 168
Mwela Rock near Kasama Zambia 160
Mwera Rock Kasama 166

Nachitalo Hill Western Province District 163
Nachitalo Cave 160, 164
Nachitalo Ndoga District 164
Nachikufu near Mpika Northern Province Zambia 161, 164
Nanke (see Majenje cave Matabeleland) 158
Natal National Park Mont-aux-Sources 179
Nazarite 53
Nbangombe Chadiza Area Fort Jameson District 167
Ndedema Gorge Drakensberg Natal 177
Ndabele 92
Ndobe Hill Mazoe 127
Needles and pins 241
Neolithic pottery, Peterborough and Abington 74
Newbiggin by the Sea - Ice Age Stone 80
New Zealand 87
Nhungo 'A' single frame 99

Nigeria Ibo 93
N'Kosisana Stream Drakensberg Natal 173
North Brabant Waterberg North West Transvaal 182
Northumberland Christianity 79
Northumbrian pipes 79
Nsalu Cave Serenje District Central Province Zambia 162
Nswatugi Cave Matopos National Park 148
Nyahakwe Museum artefacts 267, 268, 269
Nyahuvu Farm Headlands (Fisherville Farm) 141
Nympsfield Megalithic Tomb Cotswold 66

Oatlands Farm 139
Obilisk optic marker cone
Okovongo Modes Kry 92
Old Transvaal Museum Pretoria 193
Orange twenty 22
Orange Springs - O.F.S. 172
O.F.S. - Orange Free State
Owl - burbonidae family otus scops 141
One unit
Oryx gazella - gemsbok, Kinderdam Vryburg 193

Pahl Tanzania 168
Paint for Rock Art 112
Pakati - hollow 97
Passage Ruin 232
Pecked 193
Pepper tree - kirkia wilmsii mountain seringa 142
Peterborough neolithic pottery 74

Phillips Ruins 210
Pima Indians 84
Pins and needles 241
Pioneer Painting South West Cape 172
Pisac near Urumbamba Gorge 81
Precipice Ruin 233
Pretoria, Old Transvaal Museum 193
Prospect Farm Harare 128
Pulpit Rock Mwela Rock Kasama 166
Pyrite - fools gold 281
Posselt Ruin 210
Protea - Proteaceae

Quartz 214, 234
Quern - goyo grinding and moisture measure 95, 191
Qumran Caves 53

Ra God apex 110, 117
Rainbow colours and values 22
Rakodze Farm Marandellas 128, 132
Redan Transvaal 196
Red ten youth 22
Red Indians artefacts 82, 85
Rickshaw and owners 91
Rillaton gold beaker 72
Rhino - black pointed lip, white square lip 147
Robe colours 54
Robert McIlwaine National Park 121, 122, 123
Rock Art surface 111

Rock Art engravings 114
Rock Art paint dyes 112
Rocklands Farm Fort Jameson 160
Rockydrift near Nelspruit East Transvaal 182
Rodedede Mtoko 125
Roman numerals 60
Rose Cottage Cave, Ladybrand O.F.S. 181
Rose Hill Gilsland or Rockliffe sculptured fragments 77
Ruchera Cave Mtoko 126, 127, 133, 139
Rudchester Altar of Mithras 76, 77
Rudchester iron candlestick 77
Ruin vegetation 113
Rumwanda Rock Shelter Ndanga Fort Victoria 130
Runanga Domboshawa 137

Saffron Walden Farm 135
Sahara Jebil Ubi Darfur 90
Samfya Lake Bangweulu grooves Zambia 189
Scapular painting 184
Schematic painting Nachikufu Northern Province Zambia 164
Schist chlorite green 199
Seringa - kirkia wilemsii - peppertree - mountain seringa 112, 135
Seven - Zoser Sphinx
Seven Stages of Man 20, 199
Seventy - violet 22
Seventytwo life span
Shetland Islands - Broch at Clickmin 74
Shiviji 40
Sibafo Shelter near Sibafu Hill Matopo Hills 156
Silozwane Cave Matapos National Park 150

Sixty - indigo 22
Snail Down Tidworth 67
Soapstone 211
Soil colours 273
Solstice 12
Sontorini, Atlantis, Thera 4
Somerby Farm 122
Sphinx Golden Rule 16, 20, 110, 97
Spirostachys Africanus - tambootie tree 112
Springfontein Farm Figtree, Bulalima-Mangwe District 154
Stone table 277
Stonehenge 63, 211, 266
Stanton Dew in Somerset Hauleville's Quoit 68
Stanwix - Stone Tomb 77
Sun-Zuva 101
Sunga Road Shelter Spoor Engravings Wankie 189
Surtic Farm Mazoe 138
Swazi 92
Sweitzer Reneke District SW Transvaal 193
Sword dance 78

Table stone 277
Tambootie tree - spirostachys africanus 112
Tanganyika language 92
Tasili Plateau painting 89
Ten - red youth quaternary 22
Thames near Battersea enamelled bronze shield 73
Thames iron helmet 73
Thera, Atlantis, Sontorini 4, 59, 83, 108
Thethevy Dolmen 66

Theydon Mashonaland 128
Thirty yellow mature
Three - beginning middle and end
Torah 53
Torso chituro 97
Tortoise 17, 110, 200, 206, 261, 268, 283, 284, 285
Totem poles 87
Trade routes 55, 45, 231
Trekboer Kraal 197
Trio 31
Trundle Goodwood, neolithic iron age 66
Tsodillo Hills Botswana 111, 159
Tsoelike River Basutoland 175
Tuli 158
Tullie House Museum Carlisle 78
Twenty - orange 22
Twenty four - initiation
Tynindini Herschel District 178

Uffington Hill and Dragon Hill 69
Umtali artefacts 284
Uncletin ice age stone Newbiggin by the Sea 80
Unit - one
Unfinished Pyramid at Zawiyet - Aryan 32
Uysberg Ladyhand O.F.S. 175

Varna cast 42
Vase mhiro ba (mbiva hari) 267
Vegetation 113

Veldt grass land (burning) 101
Ventersburg Farm near Harare 134
Vlei Ruin 234
Vryburg District Cape Province 193
Vermilion painting Mwanambvi Hill Mzimba District Northern Province Malawi 168
Violet seventy 22

Waltondale Farm Marandallas 123, 143
Washing stones 285
Weapons metal 241
Wedget 272
White Horse Dorchester 69
White Horse Uffington Castle 69
White Lady Brandenberg Mountains Tsisab Gorge South West Africa 170
White zero 22
White Rhino Shelter Matopos Hills 147
Wilmington East Sussex Long Man 70
Willow Grove, Wodehouse District Cape Province 176
Witch doctors 102
Woodbury near Salisbury iron age 66
Wooden bowl Caergwle 72
Woodhorn mediaeval bells square belfry 80
Worozi 90
Wormwood comet 1
Wrights Shelter Kamberg Area Drakensberg Natal 178

Xhosa 92

Yetholm gypsies 78
Yeti 46
Ye Zessif or Yus Asaf - Jesus 56
Yellow thirty culture 22

'Z' 33, 216
Zawi Hill Fort Jameson District East Province 160
Zawizet El-Aryan Unfinished Pyramid 32, 33
Zero white void
Zimbabwe 29, 74, 66, 85, 90, 110, 115, 117, 24
Zimbabwe artefacts 218, 191
Zimbabwe Soapstone Bird 211
Zimbo Hill near Merwe Mission Petauke District, Eastern Province Zambia 166
Zingalume Village Chadiza Area Fort Jameson Eastern District 167
Zion African 101
Ziva to know everything 110
Zodikite Essene 53, 54, 116
Zoekoe Valley Great Karoo Hillton Bushman 197
Zoetviel 197
Zombepata Cave Sipolilo Area 134
Zoroaster 45, 116
Zoser Science Golden Rule 20, 110
Zulu 84, 116
Zuva Sun 101
Zwimba Reserve 124, 133